The Cross of Matter

Real Life Astrology: Book Two

Sara Shipman

ISBN: 9798353329886

Website:

https://starcrazypie.com

Published by Starcrazy Press. Oxford. UK

Other books in this series:

Planets, Signs & Houses

The Planets in Signs

The Planets in Houses

Planets & Aspects

Contents

Introduction

About This Book

As I was writing the first book in this series, ***Planets, Signs & Houses***, I realised that the angles in astrology did not fit into the subject matter of that book. **The Ascendant (AC), Descendant (DC), Midheaven (MC) and Nadir (IC)** are important and influential points in your natal chart and deserve a book to themselves. So, I held on to that thought, and I've written a book that I hope will answer some of the questions you may have about the angles in your birth chart. Many of you will already be familiar with the Ascendant and the Midheaven. However, the corresponding points in your natal chart - the Descendant and the Nadir - are often overlooked. Yet, all of the angular points in your birth chart are equally important. They anchor you to reality and represent the most important things in your life - your family, your partner, your career and, most of all, your own self-image.

Each one of the angles - your cardinal points - tells a story within your own life story. The image you project of who you are (AC) your primary relationships (DC), your family background (IC) and your worldly achievements (MC) - all of them frame the narrative of your life. How they do so is revealed by the signs in which they fall, the connections they make to each other and the connections they make to the planets in your natal chart. Anyone who ever wrote a story knows how important it is to get the framework right so, in this book, my focus is on giving you the information you need to understand your 'tales within a tale' and frame (or even re-frame) your own personal narrative.

The **Cross of Matter** is the key to unlocking the secrets within your natal chart - largely because it underpins the framework that holds your life story together. Understand that and you'll begin to appreciate just how important the cardinal points are when it comes to 'holding things together' - in all senses of those words. In the first chapter of this book, I explore how the horizon and meridian lines combine to create the Cross of Matter and how those simple lines lay the foundation for the construction of your entire natal chart. This chapter builds on the detail I set out at the beginning of the first book in the series, ***Planets, Signs & Houses,*** so I hope you'll find it a useful addition to the material I used in that book.

In the second chapter, the fun begins as we take a tour of all the Ascendant-Descendant pairs of signs - one of them will, of course, be your own 'Axis of Awareness'. You'll discover what the Ascendant and Descendant mean in astrological terms, and you'll find everything you need to know about your own rising and descending signs. We then move on to examine the principles that underpin the Midheaven-Nadir axis, also known as the 'Axis of Experience'. In chapter three, you'll find all you need to know about those placements in your own natal chart.

Everyone who ever read - and enjoyed - a good story knows that some of the best bits are those that reveal the underlying connections between the main storyline and a whole range of sub-plots. Your life story is no different; it's like a good detective story where you follow the hidden clues to discover what's really going on. So, when we look at the AC-DC axis and IC-MC axis, it makes sense to look at the planets that are in close aspect to the angles. They are part of your story and will have a significant influence on how the cardinal points are expressed in your birth chart. Planets become more powerful when they make a close contact with a natal chart angle - particularly when they are conjunct an angle. I've concentrated my attention on the conjunction and opposition aspects because when a planet is conjunct one angle (for example the Ascendant) it is automatically opposite the opposing angle (the Descendant in this example). However, planets conjunct the Ascendant or Descendant are not always square your Midheaven/Nadir points, so I'll be leaving the other major aspects to the cardinal points to my forthcoming aspects book, ***Real Life Astrology: Planets & Aspects***.

Finally, I want to draw everything together by looking at how we build the narrative of our lives. Unsurprisingly, the threads of that narrative are attached to the angles of your birth chart. All of the things you will have read bring you to that point; the complex of interwoven strands that connect the AC-DC horizon and the IC-MC prime meridian run deep - in all senses. The final chapter looks at one more layer of interpretation - how sign rulerships affect the ways your cardinal points are expressed. Rulerships are a large and complex topic - and this is not a book about them - but they have a significant role in showing us how our personal narrative is built - and where that story has the most resonance in our lives. So, in this chapter, we look at how the angle rulers - and the Ascendant ruler in particular - affect the ways in which our personal stories are experienced and understood. I've used examples from my own birth chart (and personal narrative) as examples of how everything in your chart - and in astrology - is connected. As ever, all good tales have a beginning, a middle and an end, so let's start at the very beginning - the moment of your birth.

Chapter One

The Angles in Your Natal Chart

We're going to go back in time, to the moment before your birth. This is astrology, and there's a little bit of magic thrown in, so we can do this. Are you ready? Picture this. There you are, in spirit, hovering in the universe, waiting to be channelled into a new human being. As your mother gives birth, the Sun rises in the east (because the Sun is always rising in the east somewhere on this Earth) and you find yourself not only taking your first breath but (if we think of this with our astrological head on) you are also placed at the centre of your own natal chart at the moment of your birth.

Look around you, but this time I want you to focus on the houses in your natal chart. They are radiating away from you like spokes on a wheel. You look over to where the Sun has just risen. That marks the cusp of the first house - your Ascendant (AC). You begin to feel the heat of the midday sun above you. You may feel exposed, as if everyone can see you. That marks the cusp of your tenth house - the Midheaven (MC) the highest and most visible point of your natal chart. Above you, you can see the great blue bowl of the heavens (the weather is always good in astrology) and you watch the Sun traverse the sky to set at the western point, directly opposite the place it rose at the moment of your birth. That's the cusp of your seventh house, the Descendant (DC). Suddenly it's dark. The temperature falls and it's almost impossible to see. At midnight, when you're most in need of comfort and security (they are essential if you're going to survive the night) you make it to the cusp of the fourth house, the Nadir or 'Imum Coeli' (IC), the lowest - and most private - part of your natal chart.

What I hope you will get from this visualisation is the sense of the angles representing distinct shifts in consciousness as you move around your natal chart. I'll explain that in more detail in a moment, but before I do that, I need to get you to do one more visualisation exercise. If you're familiar with the opening chapter of ***Planets, Signs & Houses***, you may recall I asked you to imagine your chart as a complete entity - planets, signs, houses and all - and I called this 'The Circle of Life'. This time I want you to visualise two lines drawn across your natal chart, from the Ascendant to the Descendant, and from the Midheaven to the Nadir. The 'Circle of Life' is now bisected by the 'Cross of Matter'

The Cross of Matter

The Circle of Life you encountered earlier has now been cut into pieces, like a pie or a cake. But before you decide to eat, let's consider what the Cross of Matter represents because it is, after all, what this book is about. The simple explanation is this. The Cross of Matter connects the points in your natal chart where life gets unavoidably real. More important than that, the lines connecting those points keep us attached to the underlying forces that shape our lives.

Never forget, that as you stand at the centre of your natal chart, you stand at the centre of the Cross of Matter. Its lines cross at the intersection of everything in your life - after all, it's your own natal chart that you're living in. It may be your life, but what are the underlying forces that shape your life? What makes things real? My answer to both of those questions is this. What we understand as 'reality' is an interplay between our experiences of life and our perceptions about those experiences. Those two lines - experience and perception - co-exist in our consciousness. We may think of one as 'objective' and the other as 'subjective', but whatever labels they are given, they need to reach some form of agreement in our psyche to enable us to function.

It's at this point that it becomes helpful to understand the symbolic nature of the two lines that form the Cross of Matter, as well as their basic function in your natal chart. It's their functional aspect I'm going to deal with first - and I'm going to begin with the line that connects the Ascendant and Descendent. This line cuts your natal chart in two from the point of sunrise to the point of sunset. Essentially, it divides the chart into a symbolic representation of day and night. So, what happens during those hours? That's not hard to answer that question as you know as well as I do, that during the day, things are lit up; they're obvious, they can be seen. During daylight hours everything is a known quantity because you can see what you're dealing with. This **'Axis of Awareness'** is the line that separates the objective reality of the brightly lit **southern hemisphere (houses 7-12)** of your natal chart from the darkness of the **northern hemisphere (houses 1-6)**.

The northern hemisphere is a very different place. For a moment, I want you to recall your own impressions of the night. I'm sure you would agree with me that, in the darkness, even the most familiar things can seem strange. Your perceptions change. You cannot see clearly, if at all. You use your intuition or memories to avoid losing yourself in the shadows. In astrological terms, the northern hemisphere is the place to be if you want to keep things hidden. Reality becomes subjective when viewed from below the horizon.

What of the line that connects midday and midnight, the Midheaven and Nadir? The **'Axis of Experience'** (also known as the Meridian or Prime Vertical) crosses your natal chart from north to south and bisects the chart into two more hemispheres - east and west. However, as each hemisphere contains both day and night, how are we supposed to negotiate our way around them? The answer to that lies in the nature of the sunlight available to you in each hemisphere. The **eastern hemisphere (houses 10-3)** may contain both day and night, but it's the place where the Sun rises. The symbolism of the rising sun is a powerful one because of what the Sun represents in your natal chart. The Sun is your power source and when it rises, everything is possible. Your potential and capacity to direct your own life and consciously exercise your will is strong in the eastern hemisphere of the natal chart.

Does that mean the the **western hemisphere (houses 4-9)**, where the Sun goes down, gets a raw deal? The answer is no, and once more, we need to look at the symbolism of the setting sun to discover what this hemisphere represents at a fundamental level. As the Sun sets, it has accrued the wisdom and experience of the day. This makes the western hemisphere a reactive place.

There is a greater capacity to respond to life's eventualities in this hemisphere. It is the place where events seem fated. There is the implication that those with an emphasis on this hemisphere in their natal charts are at the mercy of events. This isn't necessarily so; it's simply that as the light fades, there may be a recognition that all things come to pass and it is time for reflection and acceptance, rather than revolution.

Hemispheres & Quadrants

The **Cross of Matter** divides your natal chart, and the resulting sectors provide the 'base layer' on which everything else is overlaid. You already know that the natal chart houses are derived from the Ascendant point, and, in quadrant house systems, the cusps of the angular houses align with the points of the Ascendant (AC), Nadir (IC), Descendant (DC) and Midheaven (MC). When the planets are added to your chart, they are not only distributed between the houses in your chart, but those houses are also positioned over the underlying sectors that have been created by the Cross of Matter - the hemispheres and quadrants. So, when I begin to analyse a natal chart, one of the first things I do is look at where the planets are distributed in the hemispheres and quadrants. Why do I do that? The answer is that this 'base layer' tells me about your orientation in life. Let me explain what I mean by that. Orientation is how you get your bearings. It's how you familiarise yourself with life. It's how you align yourself with the world and, when you know a person's orientation, you begin to understand where their basic inclinations in life are coming from. Your orientation shows that your life has a certain 'shape' or form. You may even think of your life as having a certain 'flavour' or that it points you in a certain direction. All of that is fine, however, I prefer to use the term 'orientation' and this is why.

I want to take you back to your natal chart and ask you, once more, to visualise the Cross of Matter. The four cardinal points (AC, IC, DC and MC) are like the points of the compass and, when we start to look at them in detail, that image makes sense, as we refer to the angles in directional terms, as well as using the time-based descriptions you read earlier. Of course, the two things are connected. The Sun rises in the east, sets in the west, is due south at midday and at midnight, we know the Sun is the opposite to due south - in other words we are looking north. So, I'm going to ask you to think of the points of your Cross of Matter in the following way. Align them with the compass points so that **AC=east, IC=north, DC=west and MC=south**. It may seem like a small point, but when you're navigating your way around the hemispheres (and your life) you may discover that it's a little visualisation technique that comes in useful. It's good to know which way you're facing.

The Hemispheres

Your fundamental orientation is found in the most heavily tenanted sectors of your natal chart, so it's important to know what each of the chart sectors represents. Building on what we discussed earlier, the **northern hemisphere (houses 1-6)** is a reflective and self-contained place. If you have an emphasis on this hemisphere, you're likely to be a more private person, feel things more personally, be more subjective than objective and your orientation will be towards those parts of your life that support your natural inclinations. You will also be a product of your 'past' and, by that, I mean your core identity will derive from where you come from rather than where you are headed.

In contrast, the **southern hemisphere (houses 7-12)** is a public space. Your orientation is more outward looking, and your alignment is with social and collective concerns rather than personal or private ones. You derive your identity from your engagement with the world and you are objective in your outlook. The southern hemisphere is a place where social identity is important to you and your natural inclination is to fully develop that aspect of your life.

If we turn to the hemispheres created by the 'Axis of Experience' (the line drawn between the IC and MC), the **eastern hemisphere (houses 10-3)** is where we find self-motivation. We grow our personal power in this hemisphere because it is a place of initiative, optimism, positivity, openness and freedom. An emphasis here shows your inclination is to be active and self-directing and your orientation is to live life and grow as an individual by asserting your own will. Your experiences will be self-made, and you prefer to cater to your own needs rather than those of other people.

The **western hemisphere (houses 4-9)** is, of course, a very different place. If I characterise it as a place where you are inclined to be 'considerate', I hope I'm not going to offend those of you with an eastern hemisphere orientation; it's just that the western hemisphere is where the needs of others are often put first. There is a receptivity to collective engagement - and that may be with people or ideas. The orientation in the western hemisphere is, therefore, one of resolution. To become involved and engage with life as a reactive process is the inclination here.

So how does that work in real life? As a real-life example, let's look at the chart of a real person - and it's my own. I have most of my personal planets in the northern hemisphere. Am I a subjective, private individual? I would say yes - I even write and practice under my working, professional name rather than my given name - and I'm going to confess to being a home-bird. I even work from home. I like people, but even my best friends would not describe me as a social animal. My background has 'made' me and I feel secure in who I am. I have never had any inclination to become other than that what I am in this respect. No matter the stage of my life, or what I have achieved, that shape of my life has been constant. And I'm fine with that.

Now, if I turn to the eastern and western hemispheres, all my planets fall in the west. So how does that work for me? If you're reading this book, then you can tell (I hope) that I'm a person who engages with ideas. I have often had to be adaptable in my life, working around the responsibilities and practicalities of looking after other people. Sometimes, as a western hemisphere person, it can seem that no matter what you do, you tend to accommodate the needs of others as a matter of course. Compromise seems to be a very western hemisphere word.

The Quadrants

This brings us back to the Cross of Matter. It will be obvious to you all that the cross also divides your natal chart into four quadrants. They also form an important part of the 'base layer' of your chart as they underpin the life experiences represented by the houses that overlay them. In this way, they emphasise the component parts of what astrologers refer to as your journey through life. They describe the root orientation towards self and identity, creative self-expression, relationships and social and cultural inclusion - depending, of course, upon where the emphasis lies in your chart. They show where the main areas of focus will be throughout your life and the meanings associated with the most tenanted quadrant will dominate.

So, to flesh that out, the **first quadrant (houses 1-3)** is concerned with your identity and becoming established as an independent individual. You will be focused on your own needs throughout your life and this is likely to include being recognised as unique or self-made in some way.

The **second quadrant (houses 4-6)** focuses on the development of your skills and capabilities. Becoming proficient, creative and productive will be a focus throughout your life and your identity will be informed by the way you build your present life on the base of the past - your pre-existing foundations.

The **third quadrant (houses 7-9)** focuses your attention on relationships. Co-operation and collaboration will feature strongly throughout your life, as you will have a need to relate to others in all that you do. The focus here is one of mutuality and reciprocity.

Finally, the **fourth quadrant (houses 10-12)** is where we find individuals whose focus is on social integration and participation. The fourth quadrant is focused on establishing a recognisable place in society and on maximising your personal ambitions and success in the public arena. There is also a focus on creating social cohesion and a sense of belonging in a societal sense.

So, let's continue with looking at how this works in the real world - and once more I'm going to use my own chart as an example. So far, we know that I have a northern and western hemispheric emphasis, so which quadrant dominates my focus? Almost all my planets fall in the second quadrant. This makes me a person whose lifelong concerns reflect the productive nature of this sector - and I wouldn't disagree with that. I am a creative person, not necessarily in the 'great artist' sense of the word, but I am creative in accordance with the word's original meaning which is 'to bring something new or original into the world'. To have original ideas and the ability to follow them through is something you find in the second quadrant. In my experience, having a good project to engage with is essential for me - whether it's a writing project or something else that involves producing something from the germ of an idea.

The examples above are my 'base layer' and it may be an interesting exercise for many of you to work out your own orientation in that way. There's a further point I want to make. You can't change your orientation or natural inclinations, or your dominant focus. They are the basis of who you are. However, each of us approaches our own orientation differently. The reason for this is, of course, that we are unique. The universe only made one of you. So, The Cross of Matter, tying together those critical points in our natal chart, enables us to be firmly anchored in the way our life is oriented, but how we perceive or respond to that alignment is another thing entirely. It's an individual response.

This is where the signs on the angles come into play. We approach our individual life orientation in accordance with the qualities of the signs at the end of each axis. For example, a person whose angles are in the mutable signs will express their orientation in a different way to a person with them in cardinal or fixed signs. And, of course, you may (and usually will have) angles in different types of signs. You may also have an emphasis on a particular element, or your angular points may include all the elements. In my own example, I have one axis in mutable signs and the other in fixed signs, with the elemental focus on fire and air. You will have your own combination but, whatever the combination of modes or elements may be, we all have this in common. The signs on the angles provide us with a particular frame of reference. We express our personal orientation in accordance with that frame of reference and integrate ourselves into the world accordingly. That is why the angles are so important in your natal chart.

The Cardinal Points

Regardless of the zodiac signs in which they fall, the angles of your natal chart are are known as cardinal points because they align with the cusps of the 'cardinal houses', (houses 1, 4, 7 and 10). Those houses represent the parts of your life that are the most real and the most important to you. After all, what is more important to you than your identity, family, relationships and place in the world? As I mentioned earlier, the base layer of hemispheres and quadrants is overlaid by the natal chart houses and, if your chart has been drawn using a quadrant system of houses, those houses are held in place by the cardinal points. Whether you think of the angles as reference points, anchor points, corner posts, staging posts or touchstones, they hold your life in place because they show how you identify with - and integrate with - the real world. The concepts of **'orientation'**

and 'integration' are the key terms to become familiar with when you are getting to know the angles of your natal chart. To illustrate this point, I'm going to return to the image I asked you to visualise earlier in this chapter.

There you are, once more, standing at the centre of your birth chart. You can see the houses arranged over your base layer, and how they 'snap' to the cardinal points, with the cusp of the first house aligned with the Ascendant (AC), the fourth house cusp to the Nadir (IC), the seventh house cusp to the Descendant (DC) and the tenth house cusp to the Midheaven (MC). Of course, you already know this as I mentioned it earlier. However, there are a couple of basic questions still to be addressed. First, what do each of the cardinal posts represent individually and second, how do the cardinal points relate to each other? To answer those questions, I'm going to 'begin at the beginning' and look at the points that lie at each end of the horizontal axis, the **'Axis of Awareness' (the AC-DC line)** and I'm going to start with **the Ascendant**.

The Ascendant

We know the Ascendant represents the moment of your birth - but it's so much more than that. It may mark the beginning of your life journey, but it also informs all your beginnings. It's where - and how - you start things. In his book, ***The Astrological Houses*** (CRCS Publications, Sebastopol, CA) the renowned astrology, Dane Rudhyar, also described this eastern end of the 'Axis of Awareness' as the origin of 'selfhood'. Selfhood is a great concept for the Ascendant point because it's where you establish yourself as an individual. You become aware of the importance of your own individuality - and that's what you 'give out' into the world. Everything from your name to your appearance proclaims, 'I am' and your basic orientation - your approach to life - is informed by the sign on the Ascendant, your rising sign.

It's often called your 'mask' as it's the part of you that is most visible - in fact your Ascending sign is often far more evident than your Sun sign, especially when you're young. Its function in your life is an important one; the qualities of your Ascendant are used to develop and express your solar nature. You express who you are using your outer personality - and it's your ascending sign that influences the type of personality you develop. Do remember, however, that personality and character are two different things. Your Sun sign always determines your basic character. As an individual you channel the qualities of the Sun through your Ascendant - it's often regarded as the lens through which you see the world.

The Descendant

The world is filled with other people. You can't be a loner all your life, so at the other end of the 'Axis of Awareness' lies what Dane Rudhyar termed 'relatedness' - the point at which you have to acknowledge the existence of other people. The Descendant point marks our integration into our social world. We learn to do this through our relationships with people who begin as strangers to us, as they belong outside of the networks we regard as family. We need external relationships to integrate ourselves into the world and it's through those relationships that we become 'socialised'. Human beings are social animals, but we only become so by engaging with our 'other'.

We discern that the 'other' has qualities that enable us to become more than we could be on our own; that may be internally (at an emotional level) or externally in the material world. In fact, it's usually both of those things. We also project our own latent or 'as yet undiscovered' qualities onto the 'others' in our lives. This may be because we have problems acknowledging certain traits, or integrating certain aspects of ourselves, into our psyche. In this way, the 'Axis of Awareness', the horizon that crosses from east to west, is marked by 'selfhood and otherness'. It is our awareness - or consciousness - of our own, unique self, and how we relate to others, that enables us to exteriorise or incarnate our sense of being. It's a duality that exists in all of us and the signs on each end of the 'Axis of Awareness' indicate how we develop that consciousness.

The Nadir

The vertical axis (or meridian), the **'Axis of Experience'**, runs from the **Nadir (IC)** to the **Midheaven (MC)** and it marks our integration into life in a much more concrete and experiential sense. The Nadir lies at the bottom of your chart (as you view it on a printed sheet of paper) and that's the 'north point' or cusp of the fourth house. Whichever way you choose to view it, it represents your foundation. Traditionally the fourth house is associated with foundations in a historical or familial sense, but the Nadir is more focused than that. To become effective in life, we need to feel secure and have a sense of where we're coming from. That means being centred (or grounded) in a psychological sense, because that gives you a firm base on which you can construct your own life. The sign on the Nadir shows you how this is best achieved.

We associate the fourth house in general with your home, family and domestic life, as well as your ancestry, homeland and sense of belonging, but the Nadir represents the impulse to take root as a separate entity. You may be a product of your heritage, but you are also a distinct individual who needs your own base. We all come from somewhere, but we also need a secure base on which we can build on a fruitful and productive life. If we cling to the past, it inhibits us from embracing the future; if we forget who we are, we fail to develop the sense of direction that we need to find our place in the world.

The Midheaven

At the other end of the vertical axis, the Midheaven is where you find your place in the world. You are defined by your place in your community - and this is where the Midheaven's association with career and status originates. However, how do you define career and status? In ***Planets, Signs & Houses***, I wrote that the tenth house was the place where we were identified by a social role - and sometimes that is our 'work face'. That role may be career related (such as doctor or business executive or any 'label' that enables you to say "I'm a whatever") or it may relate to a social status that is defined by your community's traditions and laws, such as being married, divorced or retired. Having a 'status' in life does not automatically mean that you're a billionaire or powerful politician; we all have a status in this world regardless of how humble or powerful we are.

When you think of the Midheaven in that sense, the thing that stands out is how it symbolises the point where you fit into society. You've moved on from creating your personal identity; you've moved away from the family unit to create your own base and you've become socialised by engaging with personal relationships that remind you that you are part of a larger world. The Midheaven, in this context, represents the culmination of a particular life cycle - it's where you are headed - and you may have several of those cycles during your time on this earth.

*****

This takes me back to something I said earlier, about the angles in your natal chart being like staging posts on your life's journey. If you think of them in that way, the cardinal points mark your progress along the pathway of 'individuation' - the journey you make towards becoming a self-aware, unique person with a particular place in society. The signs in which the angles are located hint at how this journey unfolds - but they also hint at how difficult (or easy) your journey may be. It's tempting to think of the Cross of Matter as being a 'perfect' cross - all the lines intersect at right angles to make a grand square. Of course, for most of us that's not going to be so. The Cross of Matter is more often 'the cross we have to bear', as the relationship between the ends of each axis may be problematic.

Many of you will find that the points of your Cross of Matter aren't in aspect to each other because they're not in orb or, if they are in aspect, that aspect may not be a perfect square aspect. In some cases, they could be in trine/sextile relationships because where and when you were born determines where the horizontal and vertical horizons are placed on your natal chart. Those of you who were born in more northerly latitudes will have an imbalance in the size of your quadrants and the houses that overlay them. Similarly, the time of day you emerged into the world will also determine exactly how the angles relate to each other.

So, when you begin to read your natal chart, it's important to note how your angles are connected. Are the points on the 'Axis of Awareness' in aspect to those on the 'Axis of Experience'? Do they share an element (fire, earth, air or water) or mode of expression (cardinal, fixed or mutable) or is there a disconnect somewhere? Those connections - or lack of them - are important pointers to how your orientation to life manifests - and to the degree of comfort you experience with that. As you progress to the next two chapters and explore your own points in their signs, you may want to think about. how those two horizons are connected in your own birth chart.

Chapter Two

The Axis of Awareness

What are the key concepts we need to focus on when we're looking at the 'Axis of Awareness', the AC-DC line? Here are a few ideas: the integration of self and relationship; the qualities you own and the qualities you project; what you give out and what you attract; being an individual and becoming part of a whole; defining your autonomy and collaborating with others. All those binary pairs describe the key attributes of the 'Axis of Awareness' and they are first, how you become yourself (let's call it 'being' yourself) and second, how that self becomes socialised by joining with other people in a relational sense. This may involve having a relationship with one other person (in a personal relationship) or entering partnerships with groups of people in a business or professional sense. So, in the descriptions you're about to read, I want to make an explicit connection between the concepts I've just listed above and how they manifest in real life.

However, to become even more connected with ourselves, we need to drill a little deeper into the concepts outlined in the previous paragraph (and in the previous chapter) to really get to the essence of how the 'Axis of Awareness' manifests. If we dig into the AC end of the line, we can see that it's concerned with your own self-awareness, but that raises a couple of questions. How do you become self-aware? And how exactly do you define 'self'? If you look at the qualities of your ascending sign, it will certainly describe your outer personality - the 'mask' we encountered earlier - but to develop self-awareness means that you need to understand how and why that mask was created. It may not have involved paper, crayons, string and glue, but your mask will be made of the things you do; your behaviour and activities enable you to express your inner character - your 'self' - in a particular way. You approach life in the style of your mask, and you begin things in accordance with the characteristic expression of your ascending sign. Your inner substance is informed by the qualities of your sun sign, but your style is expressed in accordance with the sign of your Ascendant.

Those same principles apply to the DC end of the axis. The Descendant represents the point where we become aware of 'the other' and, as you'll recall from the previous chapter, it describes what we seek in our primary relationships. However, the descending sign acts not only as the signifier to the type of partner you are attracted to, it also serves as a guide to the nature of the relationship itself. The things we look for in a partner are often those things that are unaddressed in our own psyche; we project the things we find hard to own, which is why the descending sign often gives us a literal description of our 'other half'. To become socialised - and learn how to relate to others - we often need to own those qualities rather than project them. Your primary relationship is the vehicle that will enable you to incorporate your descending sign traits into your own life.

There's an important point that I want to make before you rush to check out the characteristics of your own rising and descending signs. These things come in pairs. You can't pay more attention to one end of the horizon than you do to the other end. If you're going to integrate and orient yourself successfully, then you need both ends of the axis to be in equilibrium. When you read about the pairs of signs that form your 'Axis of Awareness', it's important to recognise that one end of the axis provides the context for the other end. The connection between them cannot be broken. So, how can you ensure that you integrate the signs on your Ascendant-Descendant axis rather than be pulled apart by them? When you have signs in opposition, it's possible to be pulled one way and another repeatedly. The tension between the two ends of the axis will cause you some discomfort, but there is nothing like discomfort to raise your awareness!

Finding the middle way and becoming aware that the signs at each end of the 'Axis of Awareness' are not simply opposed, but that they are complementary too, is the challenge you face. When you attempt to integrate yourself with another person something new is created - the relationship itself. The relationship is the point where you find your point of integration with your 'other', but you need to ensure that you don't lose yourself in the process. Maintaining that balance is the key to successful integration - and the key to creating a successful relationship between you and your other.

So, before you begin to explore the angles in their signs, I want to remind you that the signs show *how* our energies are expressed. So, under each heading you'll see that there's a line or two that I hope you'll find a useful pointer towards the ways in which the energies of each pair of signs may be an observable reality in your life. The signs on each end of the 'Axis of Awareness' are often experienced in the most literal ways - as you will see when you read the descriptions below.

Aries AC - Libra DC

The rebel needs a cause; assertion is much more effective when it's done on behalf of others who are not as courageous as you.

Aries Ascendant

With Aries as the ascending sign in your natal chart, the sign's influence is visible. No one will ever be in any doubt about the 'me first' nature of your Ascendant. I'll begin with a first impression; when you were born, the Universe decided that here was a person who needed to meet the world 'head-on' from that day forward. So, the first impression of someone with Aries rising is usually of a person with tremendous energy. You may be viewed as someone who is a 'force of nature' as you are up-front, decisive, assertive, bold and unafraid of anything. You tend to be dismissive of those who disagree with you; you are a born fighter, and you are likely to have a willful steak a mile wide. You are also likely to be enthusiastic, engaging and genuinely friendly. However, it takes more than a lively and strong personality to define who you are.

How do you define who you are when you have an Aries Ascendant? What is it about this sign that enables you to effectively project who you are into the world? Of all the signs, Aries is the one most oriented towards 'projection', because it's such an outgoing, extraverted and expressive energy. However, it's an energy that needs a focus because it can become self-defeating if not channeled with a sense of purpose. With an

Aries Ascendant you need to own that energy and the potentials it has, as you are unlikely to be able to handle frustration of any kind if that energy is misdirected.

So, you define yourself by how you use that energy. It needs to be outwardly expressed - often physically so - and the ranks of those with this ascending sign will be filled with those who excel at sport - or at least have a great enthusiasm for it. You may fight for a good cause (or your country) or you may direct your passionate approach towards any activity that enables you to safely express the assertive - and sometimes aggressive - facets of your outer personality in ways that are socially acceptable. Remember, when it comes to integration, you need to project who you are in a manner that won't scare the horses.

However, while your energies may be expressed in a physical sense (and this is a physically energetic Ascendant), the ways in which you use that Aries energy are not limited to physical expression alone. Aries on the Ascendant gives you the ability to strike out on your own. You are likely to be independent to a marked degree, but it's often a qualified kind of independence. You are not a natural loner - you are far too outwardly gregarious for that - so your independence is more likely to manifest in, for example, starting a business or heading up a team, task force or department where you can be the person in charge, thus retaining a satisfactory level of autonomy as that is your natural orientation. Aries on the Ascendant gives you leadership abilities - but that Libra Descendant means you always need a team to lead.

Being the leader of the pack is a key part of how you integrate and express who you are. For you, the challenge is often finding the balance between self-assertion and being able to compromise enough to keep people on-side. When you're not getting your own way, you can be abrupt or 'brusque', especially if you feel that other people - or their actions - are having a negative impact on the way you would like to be seen. A strong self-image is important to you. Aries is an egotistical energy, and you are unusually sensitive to anything that impacts on how you are going to be perceived; that can result in a flare-up of the famous Aries temper, often with even more spectacular pyrotechnics than you get with some Aries Sun subjects.

Not that you will appear to give a damn about that. You will have made your point. And that's what counts. You approach life with all the impulsive and unrestrained passions of someone who is eager to make their mark on the world. You show initiative. You get things done. You never procrastinate. And that fearless and engaging personality will open many doors for you if you use it well. You are keenly aware that you can use the force of your personality to make exactly the impression you want to make.

However, there is no guile own 'hidden agenda' underpinning your actions. You are blunt and honest, and you will happily articulate the uncomfortable truths that other people would prefer not to hear. Your approach to life is direct. You sell yourself well. Challenges do not faze you, but you may tend to rush into action without thinking ahead. All the same, you're the kind of person who is good to have around in a difficult situation. So, what defines you? Energy. Initiative. Child-like enthusiasm. The thrill of the chase. Bravery. Leadership. Will-power. A sense of direction. And, almost always, a great sense of fun. You know how to play the game.

Libra Descendant

Aries Ascendant's outer personality may appear overpowering at times, but it would be wrong to think of your Libra Descendant as some kind of 'weak spot' in your make-up. The Descendant is a cardinal point and Libra is a cardinal sign whose purpose is to remind you that life is not all about you. And being reminded of this will have been an important lesson you learned early in your 'me-centred' Aries world. There is a point in our lives where we become aware of the existence of others, of people outside of our immediate, familial environment.

Socialisation is an important part of being human and your socialisation will have had Libra overtones. At an early age, you will have discovered that your passions and enthusiasms were much more fun if you shared them with other people. And it may not have been an easy lesson to learn, as an Aries Ascendant means you will always tend to put yourself first. Learning to co-operate is the primary lesson to be learned when you have Libra as your descending sign.

Fortunately, Libra here also indicates you are a social animal, so in order to integrate yourself into the 'team' that you so desperately want to join, you seek out those who have the 'Libra-type' qualities that you feel you lack. Libra is renowned as the peacemaker of the Zodiac, with a natural orientation that is socially skilled and collaborative in nature. With Libra on the Descendant, you possess all those skills, but you need to engage with the process of socialisation for them to become fully developed. That process is played out in the arena of personal relationships. You will have learned that if you come on 'too strong' or act like 'the boss' - typically Aries-type traits - then people walk away from you. It may be tough to learn that relationships don't work like that.

Fortunately, you are a romantic at heart. The Aries-Libra combination on your 'Axis of Awareness' is the duo that gave the world the knight in shining armour and the princess who braves an encounter with the dragon but gets her prince in the end. Deep down, that assertive Aries outer personality is balanced by a softer, adaptable, considerate side of you that prizes active, harmonious relationships. You like to be active, doing things together - and the emphasis there is on 'together'. It may not always be a fairy-tale, but it works for you.

So, how do you find your ideal partner? One function of the Descendant in your natal chart is that is offers you a space where you can project the things you find hard to own about yourself. When your Aries persona is so assertive and 'Mars-like', you may find it hard to own your softer, 'Venusian' qualities. They become idealised and embodied in your image of 'the other' and, with a Libra Descendant, your ideal other will usually have to be aesthetically appealing. Good looks in a partner will be important to you - regardless of gender. As you may recall, that fairy-tale prince (or princess) is always handsome or beautiful - and not just in your eyes but in the eyes of the world.

You're going to be attracted to those who embody some version of your Libra ideal - good looking, physically attractive, well presented, charming, sociable polite and refined. You may feel that they have a civilising influence on you, perhaps they rub off those sharp corners or offer gentle restraint when you're being headstrong. And they are likely to be more relaxed than you. And it works both ways as your partner may be attracted to you because you embody their projected Mars-type qualities. You're funny, vivacious, spirited, friendly and outgoing. What's not to like? With the right person you make a driven and fiercely loyal partner.

In the real world, those with whom you have one-on-one relationships will carry a Libra signature somewhere in their natal chart - and that's as true for business or professional relationships as it is for personal and romantic ones. Libra may be their Sun sign - or a sign that is prominent in their primal triad. Venus may be their ruling planet or in close conjunction to an angle or the Sun or Moon. Their chart may have a prominent, heavily tenanted seventh house, as that would show a tendency for relationships to play a major part in their life. Of course, you're unlikely to be familiar with your partner's chart (especially on a first date or business meeting…) but you'll likely discover what they do for a living.

The Libra signature may appear in their career choices or personal interests, so look for jobs connected to money and business management (Libra is money and business oriented) or design of all kinds (think of everything from a hairdresser to an architect) or the arts in general. The Libra influence also extends to jobs that involve negotiating or have anything to do with relationships (such as PR or Human Resource Management) or managing 'teams' of any kind. You may even be in a business partnership that has a 'Libra signature'. Whatever the nature of the relationship, it will always provide the balance (very Libra) to your forthright (Aries) personality - and bring balance into your life in a very real sense.

Taurus AC - Scorpio DC

It's good to have pride in your achievements; it's even better to share those achievements with others.

TAURUS ASCENDANT

I have always had the feeling that if you asked someone with Taurus rising how they defined their sense of self, the answer would be a long time coming. That would tell me most of what I needed to know. So, for those of you who are expecting to read a few more words in this section, I'll elaborate on that. Taurus on the Ascendant gives you a steady, earthy, grounded personality that is not given to either (a) flights of fancy or (b) inner ruminations. No matter what your sun sign is - even if it's one of the flakier ones - Taurus rising gives the impression of stability and life lived firmly in the present. That is the first impression you make. One of solidity, stability - yet often physically attractive too.

Taurus on the Ascendant gives you an appearance that is often sensual and alluring in some way, be that handsome, beautiful, elegant or simply well-presented in a traditional manner. You know how to make the best of yourself, as Taurus is a Venus-ruled sign. You're also stubborn, set in your ways and materially oriented. So, if you were to define yourself, I would suggest starting by looking at what you think you are worth. Taurus is the sign associated with value and 'values' (in all senses of the word) and there will be many Taurus rising subjects who define themselves by what they own.

This emphasis on the material side of life often leads to an involvement in the world of business, property and finance. Taurus rising isn't necessarily born into this world, but you enter it because your orientation is tilted towards material security. The ability to be realistic about your prospects coupled with a traditional approach to life, means you are unlikely to take unnecessary risks - unless other factors in your natal chart determine otherwise. Even then, you try to arrange your life so that it contains as few shocks or surprises as possible. That may turn you into a creature of habit, as you prefer to follow a well-worn path rather than striking out in an unknown direction.

However, what if the unexpected happens? Fortunately, you are usually able to take such eventualities in your stride. You're a difficult person to wrong-foot because you appear to be so well held together - but how accurate an assessment is that? When Taurus is your rising sign, your mask is unlikely to reveal any sign of the emotional responses that may be burning under a surface that remains calm in almost all situations. You are not without emotional reflexes, but someone must push you long and hard before they get that Taurus-style 'bullish', bellowing response.

So far, I've made you out to be a grasping, unemotional social conservative who is also shrewd and drives a hard bargain. That much may be true, but it's far from the complete picture of Taurus on the Ascendant. Sure, your instinct is to monetise and hold on to what you have, but it's also in your nature to conserve in the best sense. You often find the best expression of your outer personality in this way. Taurus is one of the nurturing signs and it's not unusual for those with a Taurus Ascendant to approach life in that spirit. Growing and tending to the things that you value are the key concepts here - and that may be evidenced in a literal manner; you may identify with the natural world through pursuits such as gardening or caring for the environment and you may care for animals, your family or prioritise satisfying your own physical needs.

Taurus rising likes to be comfortable, so one of the first things you do - in all circumstances - is arrange your environment so you are comfortably situated within it. This enables you to project yourself with much more solidity and genuine warmth than would otherwise be the case. There is always a personal, comforting and feminine touch when you have the Ascendant placed in this sign and it counters the somewhat functional and materialistic associations that would otherwise prevail.

So, what defines those of you with the Ascendant in this sign? Down to earth practicality coupled with a strong desire nature that finds satisfaction in all things Venus-related as you would expect with Taurus. Personal satisfaction is found in an appreciation of beauty and value - and preferably a combination of both. Appearances matter, so Taurus rising people will leave you in no doubt about how much they value themselves. They may appear unemotional, but they are invested in what they have - and that's the impression they want to make on the world. With Taurus here, you are calm, capable and dependable and will always do things at your own, unhurried pace - even if your sun sign is in one of the more 'rushed' signs.

Taurus on the Ascendant will lend a great deal of grounded 'earthiness' to a natal chart that that would otherwise lack a sense of anchorage; it also gives staying power and bullish determination to your personality. It makes you stubborn and determined to see things through. Taurus rising does not give in easily - if at all. If something is worthwhile, then you will move heaven and earth for it, but if you feel that something isn't worth your time and effort? It won't get you out of bed in the morning, that's for sure.

Scorpio Descendant

And speaking of bed… When you have a Taurus Ascendant, 'over-sexed' Scorpio is found on the Descendant. Is that blessing or a curse? Let's drill down into the Scorpio depths to find out. Intense, prone to jealousy, suspicious, vengeful, controlling, manipulative and vindictive are some of the less than kind things that have been said about Scorpio. What would attract stable, sensible Taurus to go within a country mile of, let alone partner up with, someone with a drop of Scorpio blood in their veins? Of course, the answer to that is that it goes way back to the socialisation process that you, with Taurus on your Ascendant, experienced in your early years.

There you were playing with your building blocks. You had just finished building a beautiful house when this Scorpio-type kid came over and knocked it down. I can imagine how that felt. The towering rage you felt at such willful destruction. The release of primeval emotions that shocked you to the core. Something may have stirred in your soul as you watched your nemesis savouring the power, he or she had over you. Yet, fresh from that Scorpio induced rubble, you picked up your blocks and re-built your house and made it better than it was before.

That's a hypothetical scenario, but what it demonstrates is the reality of having Scorpio on the Descendant. To build something worthwhile - a personal relationship or a business relationship -

you need to feel that intensity and passion. Depth of feeling is something you often find difficult to access, yet it's through the medium of personal relationships that you discover it's okay to express how you feel about things. However, you may prefer to import that function into your life by projecting it onto someone who can handle the transformational trauma that you would prefer to ignore.

Scorpio on the Descendant enables you to become socialised by recognising that sometimes you need to be blasted out of your rut. Although you may not (at first) enjoy shaking the dust out of your hair, joining with other people gives you the opportunity to bring about transformational and constructive creative change in your life. There's an implicit recognition, with a Scorpio Descendant, that coming together with your 'other' enables that process to take place, but - importantly - this process can only develop if it's built on trust. Trust is the most important building block of all.

When you have a Scorpio Descendant, trust is your keystone. You need to know that whatever you build isn't going to be kicked over by anyone, anytime soon. Preferably forever. So, you look for a partner who knows, intuitively, how important the relationship is to you. You need permanence. Trust. Fidelity. Emotional security. These are huge issues when you have Scorpio here, largely because you know how easily such things can be broken. However, acknowledging that can be a big issue for Taurus rising. You cannot admit it to yourself, but you have a great fear of losing 'ownership' of anything - and anyone - so your Scorpio Descendant projects that not only by seeking those traits in your 'other half', but by seeking to exercise control over those relationships too.

You need to connect at a deep emotional level, but without those emotions being used in a power-play against you. This instinctive and intense awareness of how fragile human relationships can be, combined with your ascending sign's need for ownership, can make you overly possessive in relationships. It's a classic Scorpio trait - and it's a destructive one if it becomes the dominant factor. Trying to maintain that balance and learning to understand your deeper relationship needs - rather than projecting them - will be the challenge you need to meet.

You're going to need a strong partner who enhances your personal power because they are intuitively aware of your relationship needs - emotional, sexual and material - without any of those matters being a subject of debate. Trust is also as important to your partner as it is to you. That person may literally be a Sun Scorpio, or they may have Scorpio emphasised in their primal triad. They may have a prominent Pluto (conjunct an angle, for example) or a heavily tenanted eighth house. Those are the astrological markers; your partner will be someone who carries those Scorpio-type traits, or they may be someone who triggers those Scorpio-type relationship responses in you.

Whichever relationship scenario ensues (and it could be both across a wide range of one-to-one relationships) there will be a combination of attributes in play that are characteristic of your relating style. Dependability mixed with private passions. Duty with unwavering commitment. Strong yet vulnerable. Stubborn, but you know the value of compromise. This is a powerful combination of signs to have on your 'Axis of Awareness'. The thing is it doesn't take an astrologer to tell you that. You've known it forever.

Gemini AC - Sagittarius DC

I find myself though knowledge but,
unless I develop a deeper understanding
of the how and where to apply it, I will
remain unfulfilled in splendid isolation.

GEMINI ASCENDANT

How do you pin down Gemini rising? With this sign on the Ascendant, it's too easy to go for the trite responses such as 'the butterfly of the zodiac' or make the hackneyed claim that Gemini is shallow and gossipy. At worst, the traits 'inconsistent' or 'easily distracted' spring to mind. That also may appear unkind, but with Gemini here that may be the appearance that you project as the Ascendant is the most visible clue to the person you are. It may be more accurate to state that the first impression you make often reflects the versatility that is a mark of this sign. Flexibility and duality are the mechanisms you use to express your sense of who you are.

So, it's perfectly possible to see Gemini rising in the chatty salesperson, the bookish - yet scattered - academic or the busy parent who holds down two jobs but manages to find time for weekly book club and never misses checking the children's homework. Gemini rising manifests in a multitude of ways at the surface level and it's easy to assume that 'the surface' is all there is to those with the Ascendant on this sign. But is that so? Gemini rising people seem to know a little about so many things - but thinking that is all there is to them is a trap for the unwary.

Developing self-awareness when you have a Gemini Ascendant is essentially an information thing. You are what you know. Or at least, that's what you want the world to see. Gemini is an intellectual sign, but it's often considered to be an intellect fed on tidbits of information that serve some fleeting purpose and are then discarded like yesterday's news. That does Gemini rising a disservice. It's a quick, clever sign and the minds of those who are born with it make connections at speed. The deft of tongue and thought may be found in the ranks of those with this Ascendant, but that does not mean Gemini influenced people are incapable of learning a great deal about a subject if it interests them. And that's often the crux of the matter; 'if it interests them'.

When your attention is caught by a great number of things, it may seem churlish to narrow your options. That mental energy often translates itself into a kind of physical energy too, but like its intellectual equivalent, it can seem inconsistent. Physically, you're often dexterous and have a nervous energy that may even keep you awake at night. Gemini Ascendant was designed for the sprint (preferably the relay) not the marathon and is happiest when the race is sidetracked down numerous interesting diversions.

I suspect most Gemini Ascendant people are happy to define themselves by their interests in words, books and connections and communications of all kinds - because how else are they supposed to discover who they are? Regardless of your Sun sign, you approach life with the desire to know more and you aim to construct your own narrative - or version - of your life. Like the other 'dual' signs. Pisces and Libra, you're aware of alternative opinions and arguments. You understand concepts and ideas that may conflict with each other - yet that does not make you conflicted. This makes you one of the most tolerant of all personalities. However, your real strength is in communication. If there is a defining attribute that can be ascribed to Gemini on the Ascendant, it's the ability to give a coherent and articulate form to ideas. What goes in must come out, and this makes you a great conduit for learning, teaching and conveying information - even if it's done on an informal basis.

One of the issues you have is that, as an air sign, Gemini is relatively unemotional. Integrating yourself with the rest of the world isn't something that you can do by feeling your way. Asserting your identity must be done on the mental plane. You cannot connect with yourself in any other way. The seed must be planted in your mind; for you, everything begins with an idea. Even the most complex of feelings need to be understood and expressed at an intellectual level and, as a result, this may make you appear impersonal to those who function best on a feeling or emotional plane.

Perhaps the best expression of a Gemini Ascendant is not found in the overcrowded, eclectic and disorderly bookshelves of your mind (though they are undoubtedly entertaining) but in your ability to make the connections between the variable and potentially dislocated parts of your own personality. Use your inherent ability to 'join the dots' at an inner level, so you can project yourself as an integrated whole rather than by attempting to be, as the saying goes, 'all things to all men'.

SAGITTARIUS DESCENDANT

Gemini on the Ascendant gives an outgoing personality, and one that's curious about life and the world around them. As the world is populated by other people, it's natural to assume that Gemini's need to contact and connect extends to the other members of the human race. You don't get to hear the latest gossip unless you engage - and Gemini likes nothing more than being kept in the loop. That makes it easy for you to initiate relationships; you will have discovered that your fiery Sagittarius Descendant is more than useful to you in this respect.

Sagittarius is good natured, funny, adventurous and sometimes prone to excess, so when you learned to socialise, fun and good times may have been the things you were most drawn to. It may have been difficult for you to know where to draw the line between love and friendship or, in later life, professional and personal relationships. You may have been attracted to those who took a lighthearted and less serious approach to life, and no doubt they were attracted to you - an amusing socially oriented individual, skimming across the surface of life without ever falling into the cold and murky waters below.

Sagittarius is intellectually stimulating; in your one-to-one relationships, that is important to you, as you need someone with whom you can debate and exchange ideas. All of this is as natural to Sagittarius as it is to Gemini and a communicative relationship is a mark of having this particular 'Axis of Awareness'. So, what's the problem? Problems may occur when those you relate to want more from you than you are willing - or able - to give. As I mentioned earlier, Gemini is not an emotional sign - you need space to breathe. When you are in a relationship you appreciate the sense of freedom that a Sagittarius Descendant gives you. Sagittarius is reluctant to be tied down and, if you apply this to relationships, there are clearly going to be a few issues here. Let's call it the 'freedom - closeness dilemma'. The Descendant requires commitment, and that can be a real issue when you have Gemini-Sagittarius on this axis; any hint of an emotional demand from your partner may trigger the escape mechanism.

In real life, it often works like this. Sagittarius-type partners attract you - and it's mutual. There's often a great meeting of minds, it's fun, it's easygoing, it's undemanding and you're having a good time - until the day you're not. One of you becomes bored with the relationship. Or one of you may want something deeper, like an emotional commitment. That's difficult, because resolving the 'freedom-closeness' dilemma is not easy when you're so used to functioning at the surface level. The mutable nature of both signs also may not be doing you a favour.

Now, a proviso. If your overall character is such that you can live with this scenario (maybe you have a mutable, airy, or fiery, freedom-loving Sun or Moon for example) then this may be less of an issue for you. If, however, you have a fundamental character that needs something rather more supportive and solid, this could be a painful experience - especially as it's likely to become a repetitive pattern in your relating life. So, how do you resolve this? You need to acknowledge that you may have been projecting your own reluctance to commit onto your partner, so you attract those who are not going to provide you with the kind of relationship that you need. Don't blame them - or yourself. Such misunderstandings occur. However, the biggest misunderstanding may be that of you not understanding your own relationship needs.

The Gemini-Sagittarius axis may be all the things I've previously described, but there is one way to resolve the 'freedom-closeness' dilemma and that's by recognising that it's not so binary after all. Rather than seeking out Sagittarius-type people as partners - and projecting your own need for freedom and adventure onto them - the relationship itself needs to embody the best of that spirited sign. The relationship (as an entity) needs to make space for you as an individual. It needs to be a place where you can follow your own interests and be regarded as an equal by your partner - intellectually and otherwise. Those are your relationship essentials.

Of course, this must be achieved without compromising on the emotional ties and commitments you may have made. Sound impossible? Think of it this way. The things that keep you interested (and interesting) are the things you both bring to the party. Maintaining your interests - together and apart - and thereby creating a space where you can develop a deeper understanding of each other is, perhaps, the key to resolving the challenge facing those of you with a Sagittarius Descendant. It may take some time to get there - but the journey will have been enlightening.

Cancer AC - Capricorn DC

I find myself by nurturing and making things whole, but I need others to make my world secure.

Cancer Ascendant

Of all the ascending signs, Cancer is the most sensitive. With your Ascendant in this sign, self-awareness is closely allied to self-defence. And no wonder. Yours is the ascending sign that gives out so much emotionally and, as a result, is prone to feeling defenceless against the tempests and storms of life. You are a creature of the senses and when you sense danger, you scuttle back under the nearest rock. That is classic Cancer, and when it's on the Ascendant, it acts as a barrier between you and the rest of the world. Those of you with Cancer on the Ascendant present with a tough and seemingly impenetrable outer shell and that can make you hard to get to know.

Those people who seem sensitive, defensive and easy to offend? They have all the traits of Cancer rising. You are naturally guarded and, while you are not as naturally suspicious as your Scorpio rising cousins, you have similar trust issues. Your natural orientation is geared towards protecting your own interests and the interests of those you love. That may primarily be the interests of your family (and you are likely to be family-oriented, even if your definition of 'family' is non-traditional) or it may be the defence of friends and close associates you trust enough to 'have your back'; in return you will certainly have theirs as you are notable for your displays of quiet loyalty.

So far, I've made you sound like the hermit crab of the astrological world - and that's a little unfair. You approach life from a cautious angle because you sense danger more readily than most people do. If something's not right, you tune into it and respond accordingly. You have a gift for reading the room that is an asset you can use across a whole spectrum of life experiences. The natural 'feel' that you possess for both people and situations enables you to tune into the underlying reasons why people feel and behave in certain ways. You have a natural and sympathy with those who are less fortunate than you and, as a result, there are many people with this ascending sign who will be found in the healing professions.

Your nurturing instincts have a broad application, and with this Ascendant, you will find your personality a natural fit with the creative arts and any imaginative form of expression. You may have an interest in history or historical artefacts (you may be a great collector) or in 'cultivation' in all its forms. You may mentor young people, for example, or cultivate a vegetable garden. It's all part of a personality that puts emotional security first, so you prefer to engage in activities that help you to do that. Creating a safe space is important to you.

At this point, grab yourself a coffee because I think we need to talk about food and drink. One of the ways you integrate yourself into the world is by sharing meals. Food is important to you in an emotional sense; It's so much more than fuel for the body. For some of you it may become a form of emotional support, and this may lead to some of you having a complex relationship with food and drink - especially if you become emotionally stressed or hurt in any way. Your sensitivity can also result in moodiness, regardless of your Sun or Moon sign.

One issue you have is that you may have porous boundaries. That's not uncommon with the water signs, and you may experience times in your life when you feel emotionally unsettled because you've absorbed negative feelings from those around you. That core vulnerability is the kind of thing that may make you withdraw. Unfortunately, withdrawal won't resolve the issue, because feelings (like many other things) are something you cling onto. Some Cancer rising people may give the appearance of having a 'clingy' persona, as they hold onto people and situations that would be best left to slip away. Another thing you cling onto is money. Your need for security extends to your finances too; many with this ascending sign are shrewd investors, so you may feel comfortable in the world of finance or real estate. Comfort comes in many forms.

So how would you define yourself? Caring, gentle - yet surprisingly tough. You're often a tenacious and determined person. Cancer on the Ascendant produces a person who knows exactly what they want. You will do whatever is necessary to achieve your aims - though not in an outwardly aggressive manner. As a cardinal sign there is considerable drive to your personality though it may be expressed privately or in an understated way. This is a hard-working ascending sign, as the visibly nervous energy associated with Cancer rising needs a productive outlet.

Many with this Ascendant will be notably maternal, regardless of gender or parental status. However, that natural kindness may lead to the development of personality types that seem to be archetypal expressions of this ascending sign. Your caring nature may lead you to 'smother' those you are close to by becoming too controlling, as you seek to make yourself indispensable to them.

You may also become a 'people pleaser', as you try to hold onto the people you have 'collected'. This may lead to you being unable to reinforce the boundaries that are essential to your wellbeing. It's a trust issue - but remember that, when your trust is abused, you were given powerful claws for a reason.

Capricorn Descendant

Cancer finds its complement in Capricorn, the sign on the Descendant. If we think of Cancer as the feeling sign, Capricorn is the antithesis of that. The Descendant is where we become aware of 'the other' and, as you know how defensive a Cancer Ascendant can be, it's no surprise that control played a large part in your socialisation process. We often think of Cancer rising as 'shy' because that's the appearance you give out, but in order to feel comfortable in relationships, you ensure that your trust is given only to those who demonstrate the high degree of loyalty that you demand from a relationship. For you, loyalty equals security, and with Capricorn descending, loyalty is the ultimate prize in a relationship. You will often seek to control the relationship to ensure that loyalty is given to you.

That may sound a little manipulative, but your primary concern is one of ensuring that you get what you need from your relationships. Leave emotional manipulation to the Scorpio types; with Capricorn here, relational core values are demonstrated in a practical fashion. So, you drive relationships forward by demonstrating how responsible and reliable you are. You are supportive but have high standards and expectations of your partner in return. And when you partner up - in any context - it's a serious and committed endeavour. Cancer ascending's need for security is found in the stable and long-term relationships that are a hallmark of Capricorn descending. This is not a descending sign populated with those who are fickle and prone to 'buyer's remorse'.

Capricorn here implies a degree of patience in making your relationship choices and that reflects the guarded approach that dominates both ends of your 'Axis of Awareness'. Capricorn takes a mature and pragmatic approach to all kinds of relationships - and it's likely that you learned this at an early age. As a child you may have been equally pernickety about choosing a 'best friend'. Childhood best friends are the relational 'trial runs' that prepare us for relating in our adult life. In your early years, you may have sensed that a bad choice would cause you deep emotional hurt; it was not a risk that you were prepared to take. So, you learned the valuable lesson of choosing well - and you may even have chosen the most sensible and least threatening kid to buddy up with. In other words, your Cancer rising intuition and Capricorn relating style attracted you to a Capricorn-type. With a Cancer - Capricorn axis you may still be friends today.

You will be attracted to Capricorn types - and they will be attracted to you. Partners may have this sign emphasised in their natal chart, or there may be a strong Saturn or tenth house emphasis. The Capricorn signature may also manifest in other ways; this is a sign associated with serious, hard-working people, so your partner's career or approach to life may reflect the qualities of this sign. Capricorn's characteristics include ambition and being reliable, respectable and responsible. It's an awesome collection of traits. When you have Cancer-Capricorn at each end of your 'Axis of Awareness', you don't trust to luck when it comes to relationships; you are prepared to work hard at them to make them work. When security - both emotional and financial -

are your primary considerations, it seems a logical approach to take.

However, there is another side to this. Capricorn is associated with being solitary and, on the Descendant, it may indicate a preference for solitude or remaining single. This may occur because your standards are so high that, when to comes to choosing a partner, that no-one ever makes the grade. Having high standards is not a problem - in fact it's an admirable thing - but, given the defensive and cool nature of the Cancer-Capricorn axis, it's not unusual for those with this Descendant to partner up later in life - in romantic situations that is. For business relationships, however, it's an excellent combination; business and professional partnerships may even be the preferred route to social integration.

The characteristics of the descending sign are often projected onto the partner, rather than being a characteristic of the relationship itself. That's not just a facet of this AC-DC combination by the way. The best expression of any sign on the Descendant is that the relationship itself should embody the best traits of the sign in question. In practice it may be difficult to achieve this because, often, we find it difficult to own the characteristics of our descending sign.

By way of an example, let's consider the following. Cancer is a cardinal sign, but (unlike Aries or Capricorn) it's one that may find it hard to overtly own its assertiveness. When a Capricorn-type partner is seen as the 'strong one' in the relationship, that satisfies the requirements of this descending sign. However, what a Capricorn Descendant is asking you to do, is to develop your own strengths within the relationship and that may include you being the strong and supportive one in the relationship. The relationship itself may also be integral to the way in which you are able to realise your own ambitions as it may provide you with a supportive and secure framework for your own personal development. The message here? Own your inner Capricorn - though it may take a firm, steady and committed relationship to help you to do just that.

Leo AC - Aquarius DC

The grand gesture, the spellbinding performance, the creative spirit; they mean nothing unless you truly connect with the audience.

Leo Ascendant

Whenever I've written about Leo, I've always said that it's the performative sign above all others. There is some stiff competition for that position in the fire sign tribe, but for sheer drama and overall presentation skills, Leo takes first place. With this sign on the Ascendant, no matter what your Sun sign, you will be noticed. In fact, you will make it your business to be noticed. It's a cliche to say that a Leo Ascendant gives you a warm and sunny personality; some of you may have that, but what tends to be the most noticeable thing about you is your awareness of how your personality has such a powerful impact on other people.

Leo ascending has great charisma and some of you may be prone to dramatising your appearance - either behaviourally or with a certain sense of personal style. Your orientation is towards dramatic self-expression and being centre-stage - and I mean that in the broadest sense. You may not be a professional actor (though I wouldn't rule it out for some of you), but there is often a theatricality about this sign as your outer personality is used to 'perform' who you are. Unfortunately, there can also be a tendency to perform by 'acting out' or 'acting up' and that's rather more problematical - as we shall see.

One of the issues that may affect you because of the need to exteriorise 'Leo', is the loss of that sense of who you are on the inside. It's easy to live life through your outer personality, but you would be better served by using it as a vehicle to express your inner self. Let me explain. When you approach life as if it's a branch of the entertainment industry, it's guaranteed that you'll be the centre of attention. Leo ascending loves attention - and you radiate such charm and good humour that it's impossible not to notice and admire you. So, you need to ask yourself, what's the purpose of this approach to life? Is it to satisfy your own ego by drawing attention to yourself? Or is it to express yourself with a positive, radiant persona that enables you to develop a sense of pride in who you are?

Leo is a proud sign, but this sign on the Ascendant can result in pride becoming an issue. True pride is not arrogant, nor does it result in overweening self-regard or entitlement. You are not above the concerns and mundane issues that affect us all, nor are you superior to the people you surround yourself with. As a Leo rising, you need to develop a sense of pride in who you are and what you do - but it needs to be done with humility. In this life, you will need to mop floors just like everyone else.

There is no doubt that some with this Ascendant will act like the proverbial 'little princes' or 'princesses. When your natal chart ruler is the Sun, it's inevitable that sometimes you will act as if the world revolves around you. When this ascending sign goes wrong, the more self-centred traits are usually the ones in full view. Leo rising can be temperamental and thin-skinned. You may be overly concerned with challenges to your status, whether those challenges are real or imagined. Leo ascending, your task is to approach life with a creative and positive spirit, not an appearance of long-suffering martyrdom. If your overly entitled attitude means that you sometimes cause offence, the fault may not lie with those being offended.

Fortunately, the great gift that comes with this ascending sign is the ability to approach life with a generous spirit. You are a deeply loyal and considerate person and, when Leo on the Ascendant is working at its best, you approach life in an exuberant, joyous, manner. Leo is a fixed sign, so you present yourself in a way that infers you are confident, reliable fun-loving and stable - regardless of your sun sign. You also enjoy your creature comforts; a good night's sleep is as important to you as the social whirl that precedes it.

So, how do you define yourself? The Ascendant's role is to enable your solar traits to shine. Self-confidence is often a measure of how well we're doing on that front and, for many of you with Leo here, confidence seems to come easily. Yet, you may also appear egocentric - always a risk in a chart ruled by the Sun. In public, you may prefer to use humour, self-deprecation and humility to take the edge of this. In private, you are likely to regard yourself as outgoing, creative, confident, sociable - and a person who can play hard and work hard.

Where work is concerned, however, you tend to do only what interests you. More importantly your work needs to reflect who (or want) you want to be - and preferably enjoyable. You have such a relaxed attitude that you may appear lazy at times - and that's not helped by your reluctance to get your hands dirty. You're not lazy by the way; it's simply that you like work to be fun, so making the distinction between work and leisure may be difficult for you at times. It's all part of the drama and colour that you surround yourself with. Where the production called 'My Life' is concerned, you will always take the starring role.

Aquarius Descendant

If Leo is the light and playful, you may be tempted to think that Aquarius, its opposite, is somehow a bit of a weird loner. You would be entirely wrong to think that. In this pairing of signs on the 'Axis of Awareness', 'light' is balanced by 'enlightenment' and enlightenment means using reason and insight to increase your understanding of how the world works. That sounds like a noble aspiration - and it is - so why does Aquarius have such a reputation for being off-beat, a bit cranky and independently minded to the point of being contrary?

Later in this book, you'll read a few words about sign rulerships. I'm not going to pre-empt that here, but it's no accident that the planet Uranus - the 'modern' ruler of Aquarius - was discovered during the 'Age of Enlightenment'. It was a period in history that witnessed the French and American Revolutions, and it also marked the birth of modern science. All received wisdom and known 'facts' were challenged. Ask yourself this. Is this what you really want to attract into your life? If you have a Leo - Aquarius 'Axis of Awareness', the answer to that question is "Yes".

Of course, having Aquarius descending does not mean that you're destined to date mad scientists or political extremists. One manifestation may be that you may partner up with those who have scientific or technological inclinations. They may also be involved in social or societal issues. Aquarius is an intellectual sign, so you may look for significant amounts of intelligence in your partner. At the very least, you may admire those with a certain independence of spirit. As with all descending signs, those you partner up with may have a literal Aquarius signature. The sign may feature prominently in their birth chart, they may have a heavily tenanted eleventh house or Uranus may be prominent in their natal chart.

As I've also mentioned in this chapter, the Descendant may provide you with a working description of your partner, but it may also describe your own relationship needs. That dynamic is something to be borne in mind as we drill down into the deeper meanings associated with this descending sign. Let's recall a few of the points that were raised in connection with the Leo ascendant. Leo needs to shine. You present a warm, proud and dignified exterior. Some of you may even have a need to appear superior in some way; certainly, you have little problem with being the centre of attention. How does this end of the 'Axis of Awareness' affect your awareness of 'the other' in your life? When discussing the descendent end of the 'Axis of Awareness', we can't overlook the importance of projection. There will be things about yourself that you may find difficult to own, and one of those things may be your own need for attention - and how it impacts on other people.

This leads to a certain paradox when it comes to your relating style. You need a partner who matches your own high standards, but you but you don't necessarily want them to compete with you for the same space. So, they need to be different from you. They may be accomplished or notable in their own way because this reflects well on you by augmenting your own self-image. You may simply need a partner to be 'different' from the 'norm' in some way - and 'difference' is the Aquarius descendant super-power bar none. So, initially, you may pair up with people you appear to have little in common with. If that sounds far-fetched, then consider this.

What you are projecting onto your partner is your own need for your relationship space to be special in some way. When you're as sociable as Leo ascending, it can be easy to lose yourself in your own self-image - especially when you perform it so well. You love an audience, but you need to be reminded of what it's like to really be yourself - and that comes to you, ironically, through your relationships. So, choosing those who stand apart or those who have an enhanced sense of independence - and often a marked need for their own space - enables you to develop your own sense of autonomy and a more secure sense of self. You no longer depend on the admiration of others when you know that being true to yourself is all that you need to be.

Of course, this also means that the descending sign may not be an easy place for you to occupy. You naturally seek an audience, so it may seem painful for you to realise that the person who appears to be the most attractive to you may be the one who will pay you the least attention. Or so it may seem initially. What they are doing is giving you the space to develop your own sense of identity - but within the safe context of a relationship. It's an important lesson and it's one that epitomises the key role of the Descendent - to enable you to integrate your sense of who you are with your need to relate to other people.

However, Aquarius on the Descendant pushes this a step further. As any professional actor knows, every performance requires you 'to act in concert with others. To do this effectively, there is no room for a 'Prima Donna'. Therefore, the basis of a good relationship, when you have this descending sign, is equality. You meet in this relational space as equals, nothing else. It's a mark of Aquarius here that relationships need to be based on friendship more than anything else. This is the place where your partner will be your best friend - and that will apply regardless of the type of partnership you have. That is the Aquarian ideal.

Virgo AC - Pisces DC

I know there must be mid-point somewhere between hyper-criticism and blind devotion. I need you to help me find it.

Virgo Ascendant

Someone has to say this, so I will. Virgo is one of the sensible signs of the zodiac. As an earth sign, you wouldn't expect anything else. It's also Mercury ruled so there's a degree of nervous tension that isn't present with its earthy cousins, Taurus and Capricorn. When you present with a Virgo exterior - which is what your Ascendant does - that underlying 'twitchiness' is there for all to see. However - unlike your more agitated Mercury-ruled Gemini counterparts - that nervousness is directed inwards, so that those with a Virgo Ascendant may appear to be uncertain of themselves at times. This may express as self-doubt, a self-deprecating attitude or the kind of cautious approach to life that almost invites disappointment.

However, this is an Ascendant that has considerable strengths. You have a marked ability to consider things carefully. You develop your self-awareness by refining your life choices until you are satisfied you have made the right decision - and even then, you may feel tempted to re-examine your chosen path from time to time. The Virgin associated with this sign is often pictured separating the wheat from the chaff - and that's a highly appropriate image for you, as it summarises, in visual form, your approach to all things.

I'll get straight to the point by asking you a direct question. Is this how you define yourself? Are you the zodiac's perpetual organiser? You are likely to regard yourself as the person whose eye for detail is rarely (if ever) out of focus. One of the words that is often used to describe Virgo is 'refined' and it's almost certain you will present yourself as a person with a refined and discerning personality. As I mentioned earlier, you choose things carefully - everything from your words to your food and clothes undergoes a rigorous selection process - but it would be a mistake to think that this is an attempt to conform to someone else's ideas of who you should be. The opposite is true.

You have a very clear idea about how you need to present yourself. The process of refinement that is such a part of who you are, has a specific object in mind - and that's to carefully craft an image that works for you. It's less of a uniform and more of a bespoke suit, created with the kind of attention to detail you would expect in order to ensure a perfect fit. Far from being buttoned up and constrained, the Ascendant in Virgo provides you with a pragmatic and practical starting point for all that you do. The realism we expect to find in this, the most intellectual of the Earth signs, defines your first point of contact with the world around you. And it's shown by the way in which you engage with the activities that you feel best define who you are.

So how do you engage? At the most literal level, there will be many of you whose interest is captured by any of the things that have 'Virgo' written on the instruction manual. However, the things that capture your gaze are not necessarily Virgo-themed. It's how you engage with them that matters. Some people associate Virgo with mundane activities, but it really doesn't matter if your 'thing' is housework or skydiving; there will be a diligent, methodical, tidy and organised approach to all that you do. That's because you believe that everything has a place - and it's an approach that manifests in your life at both an inner and outer level. You understand how things work and you have a strong aversion to chaos. You also benefit from channeling your mercurial energy in a productive manner.

There is an inevitable comparison to be made between Gemini and Virgo; like Gemini, Virgo is filled with intellectual curiosity but it's a curiosity that is less scattered. You know what is worth your attention - and what is not. You're also patient and that enables you to tackle projects and tasks that require both mental application and/or manual dexterity. In fact, this is an ascending sign that gives you a 'hands-on' approach in all that you do. Your inner nature is expressed with an emphasis on practical creativity. Things have purpose or are done for a reason. It's how you integrate who you are with the demands of the world around you.

So, disciplined, patient, organised and tidy. I suspect without having those things in place you would find it hard to function. There is a danger, however, that you can become too sensitive and critical of anything that does not accord with your natural sense of order. This is the ascending sign of the micro-manager, the hypochondriac and the fault finder. A talent for constructive criticism (in the positive sense) can easily become hyper-critical and harsh. That serious-minded yet engaging personality can all too often become overlaid with negativity. Perhaps you need to remember that Virgo is also one of the nurturing signs - and that begins by taking care of yourself.

You develop self-awareness by becoming flexible in nature thus allowing yourself to respond to the world rather than by trying to control it. Remember, the Ascendant is concerned with you - and you alone - so put aside those defensive measures and allow yourself to stand tall on your own merits. Your only challenge with a Virgo Ascendant is to be your 'best self'. Again, that's an easy thing to say, but for Virgo rising subjects it's more meaningful than it is for many people. You know that it's only by presenting yourself in that way, that your world becomes a better place.

PISCES DESCENDANT

Remember what I said about Virgo and chaos? Meet the Descendant in Pisces. The very thing that Virgo rising cannot bear, now appears to be the object of its affections. There are some opposites that stand out, and Pisces-Virgo (in whatever order) is one of them. The signs on the 'Axis of Awareness' are far more outwardly visible than your Sun or Moon sign and when you look at this pair, you may find yourself wondering whether something has gone wrong with the basic geometry, as they seem more antithetical than many of the other sign pairs.

But let's look a little closer. Astrology doesn't work like that. It's never one sided and if you attempt to make it that way, it will come at you from the opposite direction - and for you with your Virgo ascendant, that means via your partner. So, given that you may be feeling nervous at this point, I'm going to deal with your worst fears first. And I'm going to do it by pointing out something that should be obvious to most people. You can't control anyone but yourself - even though I know that you're going to try to do exactly that.

And that's why you love - and feel inclined to partner up with - those who have a touch of Pisces in their life. Or even more than a touch. They need fixing - and you are just the person to do it. When you went through the process of socialisation, I suspect you encountered a few people who disturbed you at a deep level. They may have seemed fragile or sensitive, or they may have seemed unable to get to grips with the practicalities of everyday life. It's the kind of encounter that brings out the organiser in you. "Don't worry, I'll do it", you hear yourself say, as you tidy up their toy box, their room - and ultimately their life. And, for all your efforts, what do you get in return?

All relationships are a two-way street and the reciprocity you seek, with Pisces descending, is that your partner gives you the key to unlock a magical world of fantasy and imagination. When your first response to everything is so grounded and practical, it may take another, more vulnerable or less worldly human being to remind you that it takes all kinds of people - and all kinds of experiences - to make the world go round. It also takes a Pisces-type partner to remind you that not everything can be fixed. Sometimes you simply must accept life as it is - broken bits and all.

To accept flaws in people or situations is a big ask when your natural orientation is inclined towards refinement and improvement. You do detail, but your partner may tell you that, in the grand scheme of things, such things don't really matter. And deep down, you know that too. It's the one thing that you find so hard to admit to yourself. The sky won't fall in if the bookshelf isn't arranged to the Dewey decimal system, or with the spines in 'colour-wheel order' - or whatever your current system happens to be. According to your Pisces partner, having something out of place doesn't matter because it allows to to open yourself up to the unexpected event or the serendipitous meeting.

It enables you to find time for relaxation and reflection. Such apparent indulgences (in your eyes) are often the first casualties when you live life according to your wall-planner. However, you need to remember this; spontaneity cannot be scheduled. So, when that person with a lot of Pisces in their chart, a packed twelfth house or Neptune in all the right places, asks you to drop everything and go with the flow? Do it. You know you want to. Stop projecting that empathetic, tender and gentle part of yourself onto your partner and begin to own your compassion. A good way to do that is to start being kind to yourself.

With the Descendant in Pisces, your relationships need to be influenced by this sign; in fact, that's always the best outcome, as projection may lead to frustration and disappointment with your partner. Some of you may - inevitably - feel disillusioned if you feel that the relationship is one-sided or that your feelings and needs are being ignored. You may feel a sense of 'martyrdom' if you feel that you're continually having to look after your partner in some way. Your partner may, in some instances, be helpless (or hopeless - you decide) but this may be because you have enabled them to be so. In some instances, however, your partner may have a genuine affliction or disorder.

Such feelings and experiences, incidentally, are also examples of Pisces descending in action. The universe works in mysterious ways. To experience the best of this sign, the relationship itself needs to embrace the tender, loving deep emotional bonds that connect you both. You need the relationship to be a creative and inspiring place to be. It needs to be a quiet nurturing space that enables you both to let go of the noise and nuisance that we accumulate all too easily in our lives. Let go of that baggage and immerse yourself in a loving, secure partnership. It's what the universe is telling you to do - and you would do well to listen.

Libra AC - Aries DC

It's through collaboration and co-operation with other people, that I learn who I am.

LIBRA ASCENDANT

I have always assumed that those of you who were born with the Ascendant in Libra are truly blessed. To have a natural inclination towards relationships, coupled with a great sense of style, probably puts Libra rising close to the top of the wish list of all the souls waiting to be born. Of course, I'm joking there. You can no more pick your birth time and ascending sign than you can hold water in your hand, but there is something about those with the Ascendant in this sign that is immediately cordial and congenial, and that is why it is such an attractive mask to wear.

When we begin to develop our sense of who we are, the Ascendant's role is a vital one. The things we associate with your ascending sign are the things that enable you to develop your sense of self. The Ascendant is the conduit you use to develop those key solar traits of confidence and competence. With Libra here, the road to individuation is paved with charm, grace, diplomacy and an in-built sense of fairness. However, unlike a Libra Sun, those qualities are not who you are on the inside, they are simply the means to an end - and that end is to create the outer persona that enables you to best express and develop your sense of who you are, and to project that image to the rest of the world.

So, let's start at the beginning. With a Libra Ascendant, you will have learned that appearances matter. I've always held the view that our basic looks are due to our genetic inheritance, but what we do with that raw material is very much associated with the Ascendant. For Libra rising, self-awareness is closely allied to self-image in a much more tangible way than it is for many signs. You attach great importance in how you present yourself aesthetically; it's not a question of adopting a particular look or slavishly following fashion. Being confident about the way you appear enables you to grow in confidence about other things too.

Once you've mastered your sense of style, it becomes a self-referencing metaphor for how you approach life in general. And, if you think about it, that makes perfect sense. The Ascendant is where you define yourself, so for you it's about personal style, your aesthetic sensibility and your cultural and artistic interests. However, it's not all about good looks; the way you carry yourself physically and the way you interact with others (always in a polite and considerate fashion) are important displays of who you are too. All these things show the world how you want to be perceived. However, are you presenting an accurate image of yourself?

Your Ascendant is the mask you wear. At its best, it will enable your inner self to shine. Unfortunately, there is a danger that the mask becomes a pretence - albeit a beautifully manicured one. With Libra here, appearances may come to matter more than they should, as you may confuse who you are with how you look. Like Gemini and Pisces, Libra is one of the 'dual' signs. However, unlike those signs, the sign of the scales is not comprised of two separate bodies: the balance tips one way or the other over a central fulcrum. The object is to be balanced, but it's easy for the scales to fall heavily one way or the other. As you develop your self-awareness, you will recognise the importance of maintaining your balance.

Sometimes, that's not as easy as it sounds. Although you seek to achieve harmony, you may develop an outer personality that tips from side to side. You're able to see two sides to every argument, but you're also acutely aware that if you choose a side, your choice will present you in a particular way. So, you need to evaluate which position is going to be best for you - and that's not easy. Valuing one thing - or one person - more than another is difficult when your natural orientation is to see equal merit in all things. Yet, there is a proviso in this statement. Everything (or everyone) you engage with needs to pass through your personal 'quality control' in the first place. So, you may find it easy to draw up a shortlist - but making the final choice is often a tough call. Decisions do not come easy.

As we approach the point where we're going to discuss your descending sign, I'm sure you can see where we're headed. The 'see-saw' personality can make you present yourself as a people pleaser because you hate to disagree with anyone. Conciliatory to a fault, you may fall into the trap of presenting a harmonious front when behind the scenes, things are far from perfect. You may be so keen not to cause offence that you give credence to other people's beliefs or values rather than develop your own and this may prevent you from expressing who you really are.

The risk is that you become like a 'Fabergé Egg' (the jewel encrusted decorative eggs beloved of the old Tsars of Russia), which means that you may be beautiful on the outside - but with nothing within. So, the challenge with this ascending sign, may be to keep the focus on yourself at a deeper level. Beauty is more than skin deep, so if you don't want to be regarded as shallow or vain, you need to develop a meaningful relationship with yourself. You need to love yourself for who you are, before you can even begin to love anyone else.

Aries Descendant

It won't have escaped your notice that with Libra-Aries on the 'Axis of Awareness' (in that order), that there is an inversion of the natural order of the universe. Just as you must accommodate the sign of relationships at the point where you need to define yourself, you have the sign of 'self' at the point where you need to engage with relationships. It's a paradox that you're going to have to work with all your life, so let's start here.

First, you are naturally outgoing and friendly with a warm outer personality. Your ascendant sign presents you as gentle, accommodating and refined, yet you have a fiercely determined base layer. That base layer will have come into its own as you began to develop relationships. And that's a blessing, as you will have soon discovered a need for some core resilience. You may have been unprepared for the rough, aggressive and self-serving attitudes you encountered in some of the people you met. It may have been a shock to your system, but it was a shock you needed to deal with - and fast. Fortunately, you learned quickly.

With Aries on the Descendant, you're able to hold your own - or at least that's the theory. What may have happened, however, is that you projected this more heroic or tougher part of your nature onto someone else. Assertive single-mindedness is hard to own when you regard yourself as a well-balanced, cultured, socially aware individual. It seems alien to you. Yet, part of you wants to be exactly that, so you import that part of you into your life through your relationships. Of course, you don't want to hook up with a monster - that's also not your style - but you're happy to look on your partner as your 'hero' figure, someone who will fight the corner for both of you, so that you don't have to.

Regardless of your gender or sexual orientation, the partner you seek will often be assertive half of the duo. This doesn't mean that you're a pushover; it simply means that your partner is the one who carries an Aries signature. They may be an Aries Sun or have Aries prominent in their birth chart or have Mars or the first house flagged up for all to see. They may also have an Aries-type profession or be sporty and physically active. Even a fast car (preferably red) carries the Aries imprint.

It's no surprise that many of us are drawn to those who embody the qualities of the sign on the Descendant - even if we find hard to live with, or acknowledge, those qualities in ourselves. With an Aries Descendant there is the risk that the hero turns out to be the monster you hoped to avoid. However, in a more ideal relationship - and you are big on creating the ideal - the heroic qualities you seek will embodied in the relationship itself, rather than your other half. Your partner will carry an Aries signature (in your eyes as least), but it's more likely that you will sense the potential that the relationship has for bringing something new and pro-active into your life.

Aries is one of the signs associated with new beginnings and creating something passionate and exciting. That is, perhaps, a part of you that goes unacknowledged rather more than you would care to admit. The relationship itself may have those qualities and, through your relationship, you may discover that you and your partner can become more adventurous and take a few risks. You may assert your identity as a duo. You may even re-discover the simple child-like pleasures of being yourself, unfiltered and unmediated, as nature intended. If it pleases the two of you to buy that red sports car? Go right ahead. You don't have to please the rest of the world all your life - but you may have to (re)learn to please yourself before you can present your authentic self to the one you love.

Authenticity is something that may be an issue with this particular 'Axis of Awareness'. Having a Libra Ascendant can lead to a surfeit of 'style over substance', as I mentioned earlier, but when you are in a relationship, authenticity is an essential factor in keeping things - and the two of you - together. However, if image is everything to you, you may struggle to access the person who lies beneath. With Aries on the Descendant, the assertive and aggressive potentials contained in that sign may be used to protect your own self-image against any incursions by your partner. In other words, the monster in the relationship may be closer to home than you think.

In your drive to maintain harmony and balance, you may attack those you perceive to be a threat to the image you wish to present - and that threat could be your partner. The qualities that attracted you may come to repel you, so you become the one who is short-tempered, demanding and selfish at times. You have owned your Aries attributes - just not in a good way. The key to resolving this is our old friend, authenticity. Aries descending may indicate that you need to take the lead sometimes or learn to stand up for yourself within your relationships. However, it's far better to do that from a position of self-awareness than from behind a thin skin.

Scorpio AC - Taurus DC

Use your power well; self-aggrandisement at the expense of others does not equal personal fulfilment. It's an abuse of power and that's a different thing entirely.

SCORPIO ASCENDANT

When you have a Scorpio Ascendant, it doesn't take you long to realise you hold a remarkable amount of power in your hands. If the Ascendant shows how you go about owning your own power, Scorpio here not only enables you to work out where that power is coming from, it also gives you the instinctive knowledge that enables you to use it to its best effect. However, what you do with that power is your decision - and yours alone. One thing I want to say at the outset - just as a reminder - is that, deep down inside, you are not a Scorpio (unless you have a Scorpio Sun, in which case you are a Scorpio through and through). It's important to remember the difference between those two positions - especially with this sign.

With the Ascendant, you present in Scorpio-style. This means that, whatever your sun sign, there will be a powerful, charismatic intensity about you that may repel as many people as it attracts. It's often said about those with the Ascendant in this sign that they have a dark, brooding presence about them, as if they carry the burden of secrets too terrible to be told. There may be some of you with this ascending sign who traverse the earth like the eternally damned, but guess what? Most of you present as regular, happy, funny, everyday souls - albeit with a penchant for the dark side of life.

So, as we have established that you are not the spawn of the devil, what makes a Scorpio Ascendant so distinctive? If I can think of one signature feature, then it's this. You can re-create yourself in your own chosen image. Scorpio is the sign of transformation, and over the course of your life, your self-image may be one that undergoes deep and lasting change. One reason for this is a deep desire to connect with your inner self in the most authentic way that you can. You don't do superficial, so the image you present to the world is an uncompromising portrait of how you see yourself on the inside. Likes, dislikes, passions and obsessions - they're all up there, in black and white. There are no shades of grey.

There is an intense focus to you; you can be brutally honest with yourself and that means you are able to discard those parts of yourself (at both an inner and outer level) that you feel are not in tune with who you want to be. It's a mark of this ascending sign that you can cast off your 'dead skin' and emerge fresh and new from situations that, for many people, would seem terminal - which in your experience means stifling, dull and generally unrewarding.

So, in the real world, what does that mean? If the circumstances of your life are holding you back, you'll leave them behind. People, places, friends or enemies, habits, jobs - or even your own appearance. If they're not doing it for you then you will move on without a backward glance. However, this is not the flightiness you would associate with a sign like Gemini, or the restlessness of neighbouring Sagittarius. This outer behaviour is often a quest for truth - and survival. Most likely your life is not in mortal danger, but you are likely to feel that your spirit is under threat - and that's an issue for you because it's your deep inner essence that you need to express, not the superficial outer layers.

This gives you a personality that is refreshingly honest. You may be blunt, and you may appear to be extreme or abrasive in the eyes of some people, but you are also genuine and kind to those you feel need your support. Again, it's binary with you. You will not hesitate to tell people what you think of them (or indeed any other subject) however, you are as likely to praise someone (or something) as you are to condemn them. All in all, this makes you a person that people tend to admire - even if they are wary of you at times. You are often fiercely independent, and you hate criticism - largely because you need to be the person who is in control of your life. You know what you want and, frankly, you don't need anyone else telling you what they think you should want. If you want an opinion - you'll ask for it.

So, Scorpio rising, how do you define yourself? There is clearly that 'don't mess with me' attitude, together with a strong personality that makes you fearless in your approach to life. You may not be a direct as Aries (the other Mars sign) because you are far more subtle and nuanced than that. You approach life with a deep and abiding passion, as if you know instinctively that once the moment is lost then it has gone forever. For that reason, every second counts. You hate to waste your time - or have it wasted by someone else. In fact, you hate waste in any form. This can be seen in some of the things that are big issues in your life; you may be passionate about re-cycling and not wasting the earth's resources - or your own.

You may even have an interest in 'repairing' things - or even 'repairing' people. Such things come naturally to you because you can see to the heart of any matter. You don't forget injuries - or acts of kindness. In fact, you don't forget many things at all. So, if I were to supply you with what I think is a reasonable answer to the question at the head of the previous paragraph, I think it would be as follows: Scorpio rising, you define yourself by your experience of the past and your ability to rise above it. Whatever you have survived in this life (or any previous lives for that matter) those experiences have made you what you are today. Tomorrow, however, may be another thing entirely.

Taurus Descendant

With your Ascendant in Scorpio, the Descendant falls in reliable, grounded Taurus. And that may be a blessing for an ascendant sign that can sometimes feel insecure - even if outer appearances suggest otherwise. Scorpio rising can be plagued by emotional storms - and all that rain needs somewhere to go. Having stability, certainty and a firm base on which to anchor your life makes the difference between being secure in who you are - or being tortured by your own feelings of vulnerability.

So, here's the paradox with this combination that I want to deal with up-front; with the descendant in Taurus, it's hard for you to own the fact that you need a steady hand on the tiller - and that seems odd for what appears to be, at face value, an 'Axis of Awareness' comprising two tough and enduring signs. Yet the Descendant in Taurus indicates that security, anchorage and consistency are sought through relationships. It's as if those of you with the Ascendant in Scorpio can't trust yourselves to recognise objective reality when you see it, because you know how emotionally subjective you can be. The issue is, however, can you trust someone else to do it for you?

Your early experiences of relationships may suggest otherwise. If you have been unlucky, you may have encountered partners who have been unwilling (or unable) to meet your emotional demands and uncompromising manner. You soon realise (hopefully) that for other people to like you, you need to attract those who will take the occasional melt-down (yours, that is) in their stride, and who are robust enough to weather the storms of criticism that may come their way. So, you are drawn to Taurus-types - as they are drawn to you. Why? They seem tough when you feel vulnerable; they also appear unlikely to ever surprise you - and that is something you covet. You need a rock to cling to.

Both Taurus and Scorpio are fixed signs, and they share a need for a certain solidity in their lives. So, with Taurus on the Descendant you are drawn to those who seem unfazed by the vicissitudes of life. Secretly, you yearn to be as resilient as they seem to be, to prove that your outer toughness is not all show. However, without a calming, reliable and trustworthy partner, you find it difficult to access the personal resolve that is necessary to achieve that. So, it's often projected onto that Taurus Sun person you keep hooking up with, or the person with the well-tenanted second house or with an earthy Venus somewhere in their astrological make-up.

This is the type of partner who provides a container for your sometimes dark and volatile view of yourself - and it's a view that you do your best to hide. You may regard your partner as the one who can liberate you from the torture of mistrust and suspicion that can so often undermine your relationships with the wider world, but the only person who can do that is you - with a little help from your partner. It's through your relationships that you eventually learn to trust, not just your partner, but yourself.

Trust in that dependable Taurus transforms your life from one of being on constant alert for betrayal, to one of pragmatic acceptance and emotional resilience. You feel secure and grounded in the present moment and those feelings develop because you can reciprocate feelings of loyalty and commitment to the person who has given them to you. Taurus on the Descendant enables you to relax into your relationships rather more than your Scorpio Ascendant would suggest. You learn to appreciate the warmth of human interaction, the value of intimacy and the pleasure of taking life as it comes. What could be better than that?

Taurus is a possessive sign, and it's this quality that enables you to integrate both ends of your 'Axis of Awareness', as Scorpio is also a possessive sign. However, the tensions between material (physical) and emotional possession can only be resolved by approaching your relationships with total honesty. You can only possess that which is freely given, so the relationship itself becomes the vehicle through which your Taurus Descendent functions at the highest level. The relationship itself is the entity that is steady, secure, supportive, productive and realistic. It's valued by you, and your partner, because of the calm and creative space it provides in your lives.

No matter what happens in the world around you, your relationship gives you a strong and steady place to retreat to when the going gets tough. You value your relationship because you recognise what it gives you - and you are happy to take ownership of this beautiful space that the two of you have created. For those of you with a Scorpio-Taurus 'Axis of Awareness', your relationship is the most valuable possession you will ever own. Guard it well.

Sagittarius AC - Gemini DC

It's one thing to search for the truth; it's another thing to admit you can't find it. It takes humility to share that discovery.

Sagittarius Ascendant

I can hear those of you with a Sagittarius Ascendant attempting to define yourselves. A voice pipes up. "I'm a person who always sees the big picture". And indeed, you do. However, the Ascendant needs to be focused on you - and you alone - and that's a tough call for an ascending sign that has a broad focus and a philosophical nature. Those qualities radiate from this fiery ascending sign, and they inform your entire approach to life - and your construct of who you really are. I have an image of a Sagittarius Ascendant that I assume was taken from a great height. There are always a few additional objects crowding into the frame, as if Sagittarius rising cannot bear to be parted from the lofty, expansive, inclusive world that inevitably grabs their attention from the day they were born.

If you have this ascending sign, I suspect you may define yourself as the eternal wanderer, or the great adventurer. Nothing in your life predisposes you to being content with the way things are, so you need to look at things from your own lofty perspective. So, you approach life with a deeply personal desire to know more, be more or go further than you thought was possible. And when you have arrived at your destination, you usually find it's a waypoint or brief rising place that leads you in the direction of even more pastures new.

As it's so easy for you to amass interests of all kinds, you may attempt to define yourself by the things that you do. With this ascending sign, you're almost certain to travel. It's as if the world you came into is too small for you. Travelling is, however, merely one outlet for an ascending sign that seeks to expand everything it contacts. When that's as up-front and personal as it is with you, it means that your own 'personal anchorage' needs to be expressed on a grand scale. You connect with yourself best when you seek to broaden your horizons.

You may make that connection when you purchase an airline ticket; it may come from academic study and stretching the boundaries of your mind, or you may expand your world view with new cultural experiences in order to deepen your understanding of the human condition. Inevitably, Sagittarius on the Ascendant will result in a persona that pushes the boundaries because you ask questions. I doubt there is anyone with this ascending sign who does not use the word 'why' more than most. It's indicative of a mental and intellectual restlessness that is often reflected in physical restlessness too. You find it difficult to be in one place for too long - and you need to be outside more than most. Your world needs to be open, not confined.

Whatever your sun sign may be, its core characteristics are viewed through an expansive lens. This gives you a 'broad brush' approach to life. The details will be filled in later - or whenever. The faith that you have in the generosity of the universe cannot be restricted to any conventional understanding of what faith means. Your abiding faith (outside of any religious affiliation - or none) is simply this: you have faith in what the future holds. This gives you the appearance of being one of the world's eternal optimists - and you do present a cheerful front. As personalities go, yours is one of the most open and approachable of rising signs.

On the surface you are cheerful, funny and engaging. You're also interesting, clever and appear to know a great deal - you may even have a degree of expertise in a particular field, such is your ability to study. By the way, that sizeable fount of knowledge could be about your favourite sports team; not every Sagittarius rising is an intellectual powerhouse, though many of you are exactly that. You're engaging and often thought provoking, though you may sometimes be provocative. You don't do small mindedness in any form and will be surprisingly blunt and dismissive of those who commit this most heinous of crimes.

There is one more thing that is notable about you. It concerns the truth. If there is a defining characteristic you are ready to recognise in yourself, then it may be this. Like George Washington, you cannot tell a lie, so you would, perhaps, best define yourself as a seeker of truth - in whatever shape or form that truth may be. Truth, however, is often relative, so those of you with Sagittarius on the Ascendant will often proclaim the truth to be that which simply aligns with your world view - whatever that world view may be. This can make those with a Sagittarius Ascendant act as the sign of the preacher personified - and that may be interpreted in all the ways that you think it could possibly mean.

It is also the Ascendant of those who 'lay down the law' - and that has many potential possibilities for interpretation too. However, there is one thing that is certain; the best attribute of the Ascendant in Sagittarius is your extraordinary positivity. This is an ascending sign that gives you remarkable self-belief, and even those of you who have this Ascendant in combination with one of the 'quieter' sun signs will have a core belief that there is nothing beyond your capabilities. Of course, whether that is true may be another matter. Even if that is the case, it's unlikely to hold you back. You know that you're more than capable of learning as you go. To you, life is all the education you need.

Gemini Descendant

With your Descendant placed in Gemini, there is a literal interpretation of this placement that describes your relationship needs perfectly. You need a mental connection. That's Gemini. However, if that was all there is to it, this section would be the shortest one in this book. So, I want to give you a basic reminder of what the Descendant is about. If the Ascendant is where we contact who we are as an individual, the Descendant is where we touch base with the world outside of ourselves through our relationships - our one-to-one relationships in particular.

It's through relating with another person (and that's not simply in a romantic context) that we either project the qualities we find difficult to own, or the relationship itself carries those qualities, or we learn to recognise and assimilate our 'othered' qualities through our relationship(s) with another person. That's the educational bit - and it applies to all of us regardless of the signs at each end of the 'Axis of Awareness'. However, with the Descendant in Gemini, it's the concept of 'one other person' that may be the issue.

Gemini doesn't do things in singles. The sign of the twins specialises in multiples and that can result in a few problems at the point where relationships become real. Reconciling the commitment to a one-to-one relationship that is required of the Descendant with a sign that expresses in multiples is often difficult for those with the 'Axis of Awareness' in Sagittarius-Gemini. The all too real awareness that life contains a variety of relationship options - in perpetuity - often makes it difficult to settle into a steady relationship or be 'reliable' in relationships. Even those who appear to resolve this conundrum seem to find that the challenge of maintaining a relationship gets to them after a while.

Is it boredom? Is it a feeling of being trapped or confined? Whatever the reasons may be, at a personal and individual level, feelings of restriction are likely to be a factor in the way in which those with a Gemini Descendant relate to their partners - and when we drill down into what's happening under the surface we can appreciate why. Gemini is the sign associated with breathing - and in your relationships you need space to breathe. A partner who is demanding or wants to stick to you like glue can seem suffocating, so you are naturally drawn to those who seem as light on their feet as you would like to be.

There is often an element of projection in personal relationships and, although a Gemini-type partner may provide you with mental stimulation, great conversations and the freedom and flexibility that are so important to you, the question you need to ask yourself is this; what are you projecting onto your partner and the relationship itself? With Gemini here, you're constantly reminded - often by the partner that you are/were so attracted to - that there are a lot of things that fall outside of the world view that you have so carefully cultivated over the years. Yes, you appear to be flexible and open minded about many things, but you treasure being able to cultivate wisdom and understanding based on experience. That means developing a sense of perspective. But how do you do that?

The simple answer is that you need to acquire information and experience in order to have your world view, your opinions and your knowledge challenged. And it's that challenge that enables you to deepen your understanding of the world. This is what a Gemini-type partner can do for you - and you may find that difficult, as it also challenges your own version of 'the truth' (and Sagittarius Ascendant is big on truth) rather more than you would like. Gemini's curiosity, that habit of asking the awkward question, the ability to make connections and breadth (rather than depth) of knowledge spurs you on to know more.

For a Gemini Descendant to work well, you need to get over any tendency to regard a Gemini-type partner as shallow. You also need to get over your own tendency to be the unreliable, hectoring, inconsistent, careless or excessive one in relationships. It's easy to claim that you're bored or stifled or need a greater sense of adventure or excitement, but it's much harder to acknowledge that maybe you don't know what it is that you're looking for in the first place. That's the danger with Gemini here; to overcome that, it's the relationship itself that needs to encompass the best attributes of this sign. When this happens, it's the relationship that gives you the space to breathe.

A Gemini oriented relationship enables you to be communicative in the best sense. Many relationships founder because the partners don't talk, or they don't understand where the other is coming from. With the Descendant in Gemini, there can be a continual verbal affirmation that the world is a better and more interesting place with the two of you in it together. The concept of twin souls is strong with the Descendant in this sign - however, you are more likely to see your partner as being your complement, rather than a carbon copy of yourself. And that, more than anything, is the best way to engage with the duality of the Descendant in Gemini. You are more effective together than apart - simply because life makes more sense that way.

Capricorn AC - Cancer DC

There is nothing wrong with ambition but, when it's pursued to the exclusion of all else, you may discover that it's lonely a the top.

Capricorn Ascendant

There are so many things we associate with the sign of Capricorn, but fun and laughter are not usually the first things that come to mind. That's a shame, as those with the Ascendant in Capricorn are not only as cheerful (or otherwise) as the rest of us, but they're also often the ones who are most motivated to achieve - or simply get things done. If the thing that needs to be done is to move a mountain, then those of you with the Ascendant in this sign will not think twice about putting your shoulder to the hill. Similarly, if the task ahead is to let your hair down and have a good time, then Capricorn here will ensure that you do exactly that - and will move heaven and earth to ensure that it's the best good time that you ever had - while ensuring that things don't get out of hand.

However, it's a mistake to assume that because a Capricorn Ascendant is hard working, thorough, disciplined and ambitious, that they are no more than robots in human guise. Approaching life in this way doesn't make you any less prone to the wants, needs, desires, emotions or feelings that assail the whole of humankind, but it does give you a head-start when it comes to being in control of the more self-destructive or unstable elements of that thing that passes for human nature.

There is no doubt that you present a controlled image. Often, you will appear to be the reliable one, the person who has calculated the odds of every action and carried out your own risk analysis before anyone else has even worked out the time of day. It's an impressive superpower as these things go, but it does raise as many questions as it answers, the most fundamental one being, why do you do that? I'm sure that even you would find that question difficult to answer, largely because you tend to define yourself by the very qualities that I'm asking you to put under the microscope.

I'll put it this way. When you are defined - in your own eyes - by your tangible sense of duty, responsibility, capability and moral authority, it's difficult to appreciate that there is a need to ask such a question at all. With a Capricorn Ascendant, the response is likely to be a shrug of the shoulders and a reply along the lines of, "that's simply how it is". There is no need for any kind of abstract analysis or introspective soul searching. Your approach is firmly down to earth and rooted. If you were to define yourself, I'm sure that reality - and the quality of being realistic about all things - would win the day.

It's your innate realism that enables you to assess how you can best make an impression on the world - and be effective in doing so. You are never going to over-estimate your own abilities or present yourself as something that you are not, and that's because there are a few things in play here that I'm sure you are already aware of. First, you have a fundamental honesty regarding your own capabilities. You know what you can do and what you can't do. You also know what you need to do to ensure that you get to where you want to be in life - and you will have planned your personal mission carefully and within the bounds of what is realistic for you to achieve.

This brings me onto my second point. Your realistic attitude owes itself, in many respects, to an abundance of caution as much as it does to a sense of doing things to the best of your ability. And here is where I'm going to stray into territory that may be less comfortable for you because it implies that there is a degree of self-doubt that underpins the self-image that appears to be so resolute. One of the drivers of your realistic approach to life is an awareness of the downsides that exist to trap those who are less careful than you. You may not spend your entire life looking over your shoulder, but you know that someone is watching everything that you do - even if that 'spy' is simply your own conscience.

This may result in you behaving with caution and consideration, and with a well-developed awareness of what is the right thing to do. This affects everything that you do because, with the Ascendant in Capricorn, there's a moral imperative that comes into play. No, you're not always perfect and sometimes your behaviour will be as bad (well, bad-ish), although you don't expect that to occur too often. Self-discipline is pronounced in those with this ascending sign, because you create a personal image that acts as a touchstone; your self-image is based on a set of rules that not only gives you clear guidelines about how to live your life, but those rules also tend to accord with how society thinks you should run your life too.

So, you will tend to act in a conventional manner (even your transgressions will be conventional), you tend to dress in a conventional manner and your focus in all areas of your life follows a pathway that is traditional, tried and tested. So, does this make you as predictable as the sign of Capricorn is reputed to be? The answer is probably yes, but in your judgement (and you usually make a good call) that is no bad thing. The world needs those who are both consistent and ambitious, and who seek personal validation through following the right path. Leave the distractions and blind alleys for someone else to pursue; your path is the one that leads straight to your own promised land.

CANCER DESCENDANT

Here is where we encounter the flip side of the Capricorn rising coin. That sure-footed, controlled and reliable persona needs to have a complement somewhere and it finds it in the most sensitive and emotional sign of the zodiac. With Cancer on the Descendant there are issues of emotional projection in play - whether you realise it or not. At an early age, you may have realised that here is a part of yourself that is hard for you to own - and that's the emotionally sensitive and vulnerable side. I can hear you muttering that no such part of you exists. Well, here's the big news. It does; it's alive and kicking and it may be sitting on the other end of the couch from you.

I am, of course, talking about your partner - and I'm also talking about the way in which your partner reflects your emotional self. With the Descendant in Cancer that's a lot of emotion piled up at the other end of the living room. So, there's a question that I want to put to you. Why is it so difficult for you to own your feelings? As you sit there to think about this, I have no doubt that the person opposite you will asking you if everything is okay and will, perhaps, offer to make you a warm drink as they act out the comforting routine that's so hard for you to initiate for yourself.

The dynamic that I have just described is one that you may be familiar with, as it's been a factor in your relationships since time began. You're a tough and independent person whose concerns are more aligned with getting on in life. Smelling the coffee is for wimps and you certainly don't want to be one of those. Then, one day, you discover it's lonely at the top. The wimps of this world seem to be having a much better time of it than you - and this is largely because they're in touch with their feelings. With a Cancer Descendant, you may have that tough Capricorn Ascendant self-image, but when it comes to becoming socialised, you have an instinctive awareness that something may be missing in your life - even if you're not quite certain what that 'something' is.

That 'something' is the smell of the coffee, or the roses, or simply the time it takes to feel the wind in your hair and realise that the world around you may be more important than your working day. You don't have to have a full schedule. Give yourself some space - and that is the lesson that usually comes to you through your relationships. You encounter someone who embodies the things you find so hard to embrace and, through your relationship with that person, you gain some insight into the mysterious world of feelings and emotions. You may even learn how to take care of your own needs - as well as those of someone else.

Of course, it may be easy -and tempting - to allow your partner to do that for you. With Cancer on the Descendant, you may seek a nurturing soul who takes care of your emotional needs. They may even take care of you in the broadest sense, addressing all your nurturing and domestic requirements, so you can focus on the things you prefer to do and the person you prefer to be - the one in charge of operations. Your partner may have the sign of Cancer emphasised in their natal chart or they may have a heavily tenanted fourth house - or any of the other astrological indications that would produce the type of caring person who is in tune with the feeling world that you find so hard to access. Your partner may even be a 'professional' Cancer-type person whose career reflects the sensitive and empathetic nature of this sign. Rest assured; the Cancer imprint will be evident in your partner somewhere.

However, it would be wrong to think that your partner's role is to provide you with a 'get out of jail card' when it comes to the soft and fluffy parts of life that you don't quite get. In fact, if you see your relationship in those terms, it's possible that you will also experience the downside of having the Descendant in Cancer - and that's something that you may find even more difficult to deal with. It can get messy. Be warned.

Mess is not your thing, so I feel it's only fair to point out some of the difficulties you may encounter with the Descendant in Cancer. First, a general point. You're more likely to encounter the downside if you project the qualities of your descending sign onto your partner without engaging with - or admitting that you possess - those qualities yourself. In this case, your Cancer-type 'other half' is likely to also need some emotional reassurance from time to time - and if it's not forthcoming, there could be scenes. Emotional scenes with all the tears, touchiness and moodiness that you love to hate. Of course, it could be you who expresses this kind of defensive, sullen or even sarcastic behaviour towards your partner. Why? Because you feel equally hurt, frustrated and relationally misunderstood.

To overcome this, you need to learn a few emotional lessons from your partner - in the right kind of way. And that, perhaps, is the true purpose of a relationship when you have a Cancer Descendant. You need that emotional investment - and whether that takes the shape of a devoted family and domestic life or any other Cancer-style theme - the key thing is that the relationship itself needs to be a 'Cancer thing' and provide you both with a haven from life's storms. Only then can that deep, instinctive, comfortable bond between you take root and grow.

Aquarius AC - Leo DC

I am nothing without culture and community, but no-one ever formed a community on their own. I need you to make it with me.

Aquarius Ascendant

To be born with the Ascendant in Aquarius is to be born with the fierce determination to live life by your own rules. From your earliest days you are acutely aware that you exist as an individual who is different from those around you. And that suits you well. Unlike many other people, you don't feel any overwhelming desire to fit in, in fact you often feel the opposite. Regardless of your Sun sign and your basic character, you seek to express who you are in your own distinctive way, and you generally approach this objective by demanding the freedom to do exactly that. Freedom is a key component of the Aquarius personality, and with your Ascendant here that is what you will have. The mask you wear will be one that defies the norms and pressures of the society around you and, as a result, it gives you the space to be yourself.

You may be the one in your family who is different in some way - and by that I don't mean to imply that you're the family weirdo; being different can take many forms. Often, being the one who stands out from the crowd means that you simply approach life differently from those around you or you don't conform to the norms of the family or society in which you live. That can be anything from being the clever kid in a non-academic family (Aquarius is one of the intellectual zodiac signs) or being the argumentative one when all around you are passive and easy going. Aquarius on the Ascendant is good at arguments too.

One of the reasons you may be good at standing your ground is that your favourite role, as the person who questions any definition of 'normal', is often regarded as being provocative. And there may be those around you who may (often justifiably) accuse you of having a provocative approach to life. Of course, you are unlikely to see things that way. What those around you call provocation (or 'being difficult') is simply your way of making things happen. You're not a person who is comfortable with the status quo. You have opinions on things and you're not afraid to speak up on matters that you feel need to be brought to the attention of wider society.

Whatever your inner drive or motivation is telling you to do, it's often framed in revolutionary terms. That's not necessarily because you have a perverse desire to upset the world around you simply for the sake of it, but it's because you regard yourself as an idealist who believes that things can be done differently In your opinion, innovation, reform and a more scientific and rational approach is the way to go to improve the lot of all humankind - or at least the parts of it that interest you the most. However, there are issues and concepts that you can be fanatical about, and you will often express your inner self in ways that may appear extreme to more conventional souls.

Yet, for all your reactionary ideals, you are a highly sociable person with an engaging personality to match. You may be quirky (and perhaps erratic at times) but you are fun to be with. An irreverent sense of humour combines with a broad intellect and a left of field take on many subjects - and that makes you an interesting conversationalist, a great debater and a lively addition to any party, group, or cause you align yourself with. I mention 'cause' or 'group' as there is a notable humanitarian side to you. Causes, campaigns and wider social issues attract your attention. You are often acutely aware of what's going on in the world and you like to keep up to date with events.

You need to know what is happening out there - and if you can become a part of it then so much the better. Yet, for all your humanitarian impulses, you often prefer to keep your distance from humanity itself and this can make you can appear unpredictable. Friendly one moment and aloof the next, it is as if there's a part of you that will forever be isolated from the emotional constraints that bind other mortals together. So, here we have our image of the Aquarius Ascendant - and I suspect it's an image that corresponds with how you see yourself. Your orientation is tilted towards the radical end of the spectrum but remember that you're not that way deep inside (unless you have an Aquarius Sun or Moon). It's simply the way that you see yourself - and present yourself to the world.

So, how would you define yourself? Independent probably covers most bases. It's an approach to life that is your touchstone when it comes to how you express your authentic self. And authenticity is important to you. Whatever your basic character and temperament may be, having the Ascendant in Aquarius enables your true self to emerge as a rational and unapologetically frank expression of who you are. However, what often surprises people (and with the Ascendant in Uranus-ruled Aquarius you can be surprising) is how such a forward looking and progressive person can be so fixed in their opinions. For all your revolutionary fervour or clever, abstract, reasoning, you can be as stubborn as a mule.

There's no other way to describe it. When you dig your heels in over an issue - any issue - you're often obstinate to the point of madness. This makes you a much more forceful personality than cerebral Aquarius on the Ascendant is often taken to be. That said, you make up for this unrelenting approach with your genuine sincerity. With the Ascendant in this sign, truth and objectivity underpin your self-awareness and, if you maintain a sense of reason, it's a stance that will enable you to position yourself as a true original.

Leo Descendant

With Aquarius on the Ascendant, the point at which you integrate into society through your personal relationships falls in Leo. Never were two signs so diametrically opposed. Honestly. Cool, aloof Aquarius and warm, sunny Leo. How on earth are you supposed to reconcile both sides of that combination on your 'Axis of Awareness'? Let's wind the clock back to the point at which you became aware that other people (outside of your family network) existed. How you became socialised may have been something like this. For someone who is fiercely independent, yet socially oriented, it may have with some conflicted feelings that you engaged with your first significant other - and that is likely to have been a friend rather than a love interest, as we practice our relating skills on our unsuspecting 'best friends' long before we are let loose on the loves of our life.

Wanting to be involved in a relationship while simultaneously wanting to be recognised as a singular and unique person is a difficult trick to master. At first you may have been confused by those sunny individuals who were able to command attention by the warmth of their personality. They did not have to resort to blowing hot and cold or be 'difficult' to get their own way. Instead, people were drawn to them and basked in their glow. It seemed effortless. And that intrigued you.

With a Leo Descendant, you look for that warmth in a relationship. Leo's emotional ease and, it must be said, their dramatic and theatrical responses to life are something you find hard to access in your own psyche. Leo's natural joy and vitality may initially leave you feeling uncertain, because your instinctive response is to disengage from such 'over-the-top' behaviour. When your self-image is naturally on the cool side, successful integration requires that persona to melt a little. Projecting your own need for attention onto your partner is something that enables you to have those Leo qualities reflected at you.

In a successful relationship, over time, you may learn to accept that they are also part of your own nature - but that's unlikely to stop you from being highly critical of your partner's Leo nature from time to time. It's a cruel fact, that we are attracted to the very things we often find hardest to live with. What needs to be borne in mind is that relating is a learning process and, fortunately, learning is something that interests you. When you criticise your partner's need for attention, or feel overshadowed by their star qualities, or you wish that they would take life a bit more seriously, then it should be telling you more about yourself than it does about your partner.

So, what is it you need to learn? Let's start at the top. Leo is an outgoing expressive sign, known for its confidence and loyalty.

Let's think about those characteristics for a moment and how they fit with you in a relational sense. And let's start with you. You can be cranky, extreme, emotionally distant and, frankly, not the easiest person to live with because you're so self-sufficient and self-contained. You may be sociable in a crowd, but when there's only two of you in the room it can be a different matter. You like things to be done your way. Preferably alone. So, how do you resolve this?

You need someone who is confident and secure enough in their own sense of who they are to be able to stand up to that. You need someone who is emotionally aware and honest enough to tell you how your behaviours and attitudes affect them - and how they affect you. You need someone who is strong enough to counter some of the extreme positions you are prone to indulge in, and who can shine their light on your cool isolation - and someone who can remind you that relationships are a warm and comfortable place to be. And, best of all, they can do this with good humour, playfulness, magnanimity and fierce determination. Meet Leo. The person I have just described and the most loyal and courageous partner you will ever have. And, given your Aquarius persona, they will need to be.

So, about your other half. You are always going to be attracted to those with Leonine traits. They may be a Sun Leo with all of Leo's characteristics as a fundamental part of their nature, or they may have Leo emphasised in their 'Primal Triad', with either a Leo Moon or Ascendant. Either of those placements would lend a distinctly Leo 'feel' to your partner, either emotionally or behaviourally, and a Leo Ascendant would be very visibly Leo on the surface. Even if you believe that your partner is not 'a Leo', the sign may be emphasised in their natal chart in some way.

They may also have an emphasis on the fifth house in their natal chart and the Sun, as the ruler of Leo, will be prominent if it is close to any of the cardinal points - particularly the Ascendant or Midheaven. You may even see Leo manifesting in your loved one's career. However, a more fundamental point is this; it's the relationship itself that needs to reflect the qualities of this sign. The relationship needs to be marked by sincerity, courage, generosity, trust, fidelity and warmth. It needs to provide a space where both of you can express yourselves with unconscious childlike enthusiasm for life You need to enjoy each other's company in an entertaining and joyous way. There's no place for competing egocentricity, vanity, conceit or self-indulgence. If you can live with that, then relating through your Leo Descendant will be your happy place.

Pisces AC - Virgo DC

Alone, I am never afraid of going into the unknown, but with you? I need to know where I stand before I take you on that journey.

PISCES ASCENDANT

How can anyone define Pisces rising? The ultimate shape shifter, ruled by nebulous Neptune; being born with this sign on the Ascendant is to be born with an invisible cloak. Regardless of your sun sign, to be born with Pisces ascending is to be born the ultimate chameleon, as you change your colour to suit whatever circumstances you find yourself in - and whoever you find yourself with. That mutable, flexible and ever-adaptable quality can make it difficult for people to really get to know the person underneath - and it can make it difficult for you to get to know yourself too.

The cloak of invisibility is part of your diffuse, ethereal persona. You slip away from yourself as easily as you slip away from others because there is something about you that yearns to escape from every set of circumstances you find yourself in. I think I need to point out that you don't always physically leave the room; it's often more of an attention thing. You tune out by tuning into a higher consciousness. Some would call it daydreaming and some would call it imagination, but the impression you give out is one of not always being 'quite there', as if you cannot bear to entirely leave your fantasy world.

And why would you want to leave that haven? When you have Pisces as the ascending sign, your dream world is always going to be preferable to reality. In the real world, you find yourself confronted with things you would prefer not to think about, so you tend to go with the flow. It may be a consequence of being indecisive, or being unwilling to upset people, or finding the challenge of setting boundaries far too overwhelming to contemplate. However, going with the flow can mean become a follower and not a leader. You may be easily led - and not always in the right direction. Another issue that you may suffer from (if suffer is the right word) is that you tend to see good in other people - even if it's not warranted. You may want to see what you believe, rather than believe what you see.

That's not always a bad thing, as you are highly sympathetic to those who are having a hard time, and whose plight is all too easily ignored. However, it may make you vulnerable to those who would take advantage of you. You can be easily manipulated, and you find it difficult to believe that others could behave in negative ways towards you. When this happens, you can feel lost and alone, wrapped once more in that invisible cloak. On those occasions, if you were to define yourself, the terms 'victim' or 'lost soul' may seem a natural fit, as you can give out those vibes more easily than most people. You may need to make a conscious effort to avoid making the impression that 'victimhood' is all that there is to you.

Yet is that how you see yourself? I sincerely doubt it. With Pisces rising, those powers of imagination can be put to good use on more occasions than not. You approach things from a different direction to the rest of us; your imaginative capabilities enable you to visualise different outcomes, appreciate subtle connections and understand symbolic meanings and emotional communications. Without your sensitive and intuitive faculties, those subtleties would be lost to us - and that would be to everyone's detriment, including yours. Pisces ascending is often shrewd and more 'tuned-in' than it's given credit for. Like the Pisces fishes, you can swim into much calmer water when the seas get too rough. You sense where the best opportunities are going to be - but you seem to avoid displaying the naked ambition or self-assertion that would be obvious in others. That cloak of invisibility is a useful garment.

In an otherwise stable chart, you may follow the dream and make it real, you may inspire others, or you may be able to knock down the barriers that would otherwise prevent you - and others - from making the most of what life has to offer. You are often able to feel your way through life with remarkable accuracy, and this intuitive approach enables you to land on your feet, perhaps more times than you deserve. One thing you share with Jupiter-ruled Sagittarius is an almost boundless optimism. Except you take it a stage further. You not only have boundless faith that the Universe will provide, but you also live in a state of perpetual hope. And hope is a condition that means you are alert to the possibility that your dreams will come true. In fact, you never expect it to be otherwise. Even when life lets you down, a guardian angel always appears.

This may seem lucky but, as the old saying goes, we make our own luck. Those who have a positive outlook - and the ability to let go and move on - tend to be the luckiest people out there. Pisces rising falls into that category. You can make the best of any situation - and you are often thankful for what you have, as things could always be a lot worse. You begin from a state of compassion, both for yourself and others; that is usually where the journey begins for you - and compassion tempts you out into the real world. Whatever your inner motivations are, allowing them to be expressed in a manner that transcends personal desire is always a good thing for you. You have a personality that is remarkably selfless and deeply caring.

The desire to save something - people, animals, the world, your soul - is what interests you most because it allows you to merge with an entity that's greater than yourself. For some of you with this ascending sign, that will translate into a giving, selfless persona whose efforts are directed towards a universal good. You escape from 'grim' reality through devotion to something that enables you to transcend your personal, individual limitations. That must be the best option with this Ascendant. The downside may be an addiction to other forms of escapism or self-delusion that are much more detrimental to your soul.

Virgo Descendant

So, Pisces rising, what happens when you make it out into the world and realise that other people are not quite as wonderful as you would like them to be? Once you have wiped the fog from your rose-tinted spectacles, you soon realise that you're going to need someone to help you navigate through life's more ordinary waters. Unless you have someone, who can act as your pilot, you may find the social seas are a dangerous and unnerving place. You need a rock to cling to - and that's where Virgo, the person at the helm of the rescue launch, becomes your lifeguard *par excellence*. Unlike you, they seem to have the ability to work out who is worth your time and effort - and who is not.

Okay, they may also have the annoying habit of pointing out when (and why) you're being totally unrealistic about things, but the upside is that they are completely reliable. They may correct you, but they also contain you and, like all other water signs, you need the earth to give form to your life. The question is, at what point does a fertile and productive relationship become 'mud and flood'? As I mentioned earlier, some opposites seem to form a neat complement to each other, and others seem so far opposed it's hard to imagine them inhabiting the same planet. Of course, each opposition has the potential for both - it's up to you to work on the best relationship potential there is.

With a Virgo Descendent, the thing you seek is that sense of containment. You don't want to be bothered by the mundane realities of life. As a dreamer, you don't tend to do detail - certainly not the sort of detail that exists outside of your imagination. However, what you do find easy to do is project your fantasies onto another human being. You can conjure up the image of a perfect partner as easily as you can wave that magic wand and given your abundant charm and chameleon-like ability to present yourself as 'all things to all people', you usually have no problem in making that ideal a reality. So far so good. However, in all relationships, the initial magic soon wears thin. Successful relationships rely on the good old-fashioned (and not very exciting) nuts and bolts of daily life.

Togetherness involves organisation and planning in one form or another; for all the time spent on romance and adventure, there is an equal amount of time that needs to be spent on washing the dishes. The 'Axis of Awareness' exists to remind us that life is about balance - and that's something you may struggle with as it's a reminder that reality needs to be dealt with. When you have Virgo on the Descendant, the universe has given you a clue how to achieve that balance and deal with reality. Of course, it may turn out that Virgo is the person who will deal with reality so that you don't have to. And it is surprising how many people with a Virgo Descendant are happy to subscribe to that and your Virgo-type partner may be equally happy with this arrangement.

Your partner may literally be a Virgo, or the sign may feature prominently in their primal triad (they may have it as their moon or ascending sign) or they may have a heavily tenanted sixth house. However the Virgo-type partner manifests, part of your attraction to them is that they can be relied on to pay the bills, organise the groceries and put out the rubbish for collection - thus leaving you free to concentrate on the things you prefer to do (shopping, spending someone else's money, enjoying life and generally being glamorous) or, if you're the other kind of Pisces rising, you may go down the hopeless, 'please rescue me' victim-playing route. And that applies to all sorts of people who may otherwise seem as capable as anyone - if they're doing what they want to do, rather than what they need to do.

Either way, this will only work if your partner is willing to carry the burden of responsibility. And that's what this is about. Responsibility. It's a big word, an even bigger concept, and it's the thing you find most difficult to own. At the risk of enraging all of you with a Pisces-Virgo 'Axis of Awareness', I would suggest that responsibility is something you need to become acquainted with sooner rather than later. Fortunately, your Virgo mate is not only ideally placed to help you address this issue, but they are also likely to be keen to teach you the lesson. One way or another. Make sure it happens in a good way.

Of course, it's far better to engage with this learning process from a position of willingness, but - as you know - it may be tempting for you to blank out or try to slip away from the prospect. In fact, that's probably your default position. In that situation, when your partner is trying to impress on you the importance of budgetary restraint or personal organisation, you may resort to your default position and accuse them of being a stick in the 'mud' I mentioned earlier. There may even be floods of tears, as your responses are likely to be emotional. Stop for a moment and consider this. Every relationship serves a purpose. Just as your partner brings containment and stability to your life, you bring a little light and magic to theirs. It's a two-way street - and that gives you both the opportunity to meet in the middle.

Through your relationships, you learn when you need to be grounded, without losing that wonderful ability you must bring some sparkle - and a great deal of empathy - into the life of your significant other. You are also at your best when you're offering support and, potentially, offering a secure emotional container for someone who may otherwise have felt emotionally 'buttoned up' or difficult to engage. What others may see as a weakness is your greatest strength. The best relationship will allow you to realise your strengths and offer them, selflessly, to your partner. Rest assured; they will do the same for you.

Chapter Three

The Axis of Experience

More than anything, the 'Axis of Experience' represents the journey from where you begin to where you are going - indeed, it's often said that the Midheaven marks the place where you have arrived, particularly if you look at it from a career-based point of view. Of course, astrology works at a much deeper and symbolic level than that and the vertical axis ('the prime vertical' as it's also known) marks the passage from your origins to the fulfilment of your destiny - whatever that individual destiny may be. That sounds like a big ask for a simple line drawn across your natal chart, so I'll break it down so that it doesn't seem like such a big deal. The Nadir (IC) end of the axis is where you feel on solid ground - so much so that you take it for granted - even of you discover that the earth is moving beneath you.

And what about the Midheaven (MC) end of the axis? In her excellent book, ***Incarnation: The Four Angles and Moon's Nodes*** (7th Edition, Starwalker Press, London) Melanie Reinhart describes the Midheaven as symbolising not only what we offer to the world, but also what the world asks of us. It's the place where things come to fruition. So, themes like achievement, authority, vocation, destiny and our attitudes towards a whole range of things we associate with the Midheaven - like duty, responsibility and so on - are dependent on how successful (or otherwise) we were at establishing a secure foundation at the base of the chart. It's a view that I wholeheartedly agree with.

We often associate the Nadir (IC) with the general principles of the fourth house in astrology - the home and homeland, family, the past, memories, history and so on. However, the Nadir goes much deeper than that. It makes the vital connection between your past - where you came from in all senses - and the need for you to build on that foundation in your own, unique way. The sign of the Nadir describes how you can approach that issue and ensure you provide yourself with the best possible start in life - even if you feel your birth or familial circumstances were less than favourable. We all carry a history - it's up to us to re-frame the narrative to suit our present and future needs.

So, let's look up to the Midheaven. When we are secure in our sense of where we are coming from, then we will be confident that we will be able to do what is asked of us. One of the things I find useful to focus on when discussing the meridian is the word, 'experience'. It's there for a reason. The signs at either end of the axis often indicate the kinds of formative experiences we have at the Nadir as well as the kinds of public roles we will be asked to play in order to fulfil the destiny that the Universe had in mind for us. As with the signs on the 'Axis of Awareness' you read about earlier, signs on the vertically aligned axis are also highly visible and may be literal in their manifestation. With that in mind, let's look at the 'Axis of Experience' by the signs it occupies in your natal chart.

Aries IC - Libra MC

Focus your enthusiasm and get involved;
sometimes you need to knock heads
together to reach an agreement.

Aries Nadir

Aries on the Nadir indicates that you have an assertive - and potentially aggressive - base to your personal life, which makes it unlikely that yours was the most peaceful family in town. Your family background will resonate to all things that have an Aries signature - and that's not just the things you associate with your immediate birth family. Aries will extend deep into the past; it's where you come from and what you were born into. So, how does it manifest? Let's begin with the things you know best - your own experiences as you grew up with this sign. So, what was it like? As with the dynamics of every sign there are a wide range of experiences to choose from - but they all fit the Aries pattern.

Not all of you will have been born into a literal war zone, but there are many of you will recall your early years as a confection of disagreements, arguments and, sadly, violence. Again, that may not be the experience of most of you. Aries may have given some of you a family background that was associated with military service or a family tradition of dangerous occupations, such as working for the fire service or any career or profession that involves knives or blades. Courage, risk and a 'can do' attitude is part of the Aries mix. One or the other of your parents may have been a solar Aries or carried an Aries signature, with the Moon or Ascendant in that sign, or perhaps one of them had a heavily tenanted first house, or Mars prominent in their natal chart.

Some your earliest memories may go back to family gatherings where you were told stories by your parents or elder relatives - and those tales may have impressed on your the bravery of previous generations of your family; the grandfather who won a military medal, the uncle who saved a dog from drowning, the grandmother who played football better than most men, the aunt who became a motor mechanic (at a time when most women didn't even wear trousers) or the cousin who came to nothing because he spent his life fighting and chasing after lost causes. Every family has a story - and your family legends will have an Aries flavour. Our sense of where we belong is often formed by those memories; the place you belong - or at least the place you came from - has Aries (and all that implies) at its core.

We tend to think of other parts of your birth chart when it comes to inheritance (The eighth house for example) and in a material sense that may be true - but the Nadir represents your roots and your roots have taken hold in the most assertive, fiery and volatile of all the zodiac signs. You will have experienced this through your parents, your childhood, your home life and even wider familial relationships going across, forwards and backwards though the generations. There will be Aries-type heritage issues and an Aries-type domestic environment, as you move forwards to establish your own base. The question for you, will be how much of the past do you take with you?

Before you answer that question, you may need to recall, a simple fact. We all carry our past with us. Quite simply, it's not that easy to shed - in fact it's impossible to do so. The main issue you must face, is whether you find your past burdensome - or not. If your natal chart is so inclined, you may have felt comfortable in that dynamic, volatile, macho, active, sporty, driven or competitive family environment. It may have enabled your natural enthusiasm and passion to drive you forwards in life. However, if your natural inclination tends towards something 'softer' and emotionally supportive, then you may have found your early years less comfortable than you would have liked them to be.

Does this mean that Aries on the Nadir in your natal chart was somehow an astrological error (that doesn't happen), or that it's your own cross to bear? You will carry it with you for sure - but you will also have developed a great deal of resilience and the willful independence that enabled you to strike out on your own with confidence. Even now, you may not realise that (1) the qualities of this sign are available to you and will help you to stabilise your life because (2) they form the foundation of your own emotional base. The qualities of the Nadir's sign are often buried deeply in our subconscious, and they can take some time to be unearthed.

So, if you're having problems touching base with your Aries Nadir in a constructive manner, what can you do to bring its buried treasure to light? The Nadir is about being secure and grounded. That may seem anathema to those who have Aries influencing this cardinal point - but there are many ways in which being centred happens. For those of you with Aries here, being stable means being active in whatever way life grabs your attention. It means pursuing something; a hobby, a sport, a passion for whatever you have a passion for. It means pro-actively taking care of your life - you are not one of life's bystanders. It means that your own interests take first place when you are deciding the best way to push ahead in life.

That doesn't mean you need to be insensitive to the needs of those around you. Being firm and resolute in what you want to do, while maintaining friendly and selfless relationships with those you share your life with, is the best way to develop your reputation as an effective leader - or as the head of the family. You need to enthuse your family (however 'family' is defined in your life), gain their respect and take them with you on the journey. You know you've found your comfort zone when you feel as though you have a space that enables you to be passionate about the things that matter to you. You need a space to be yourself without restraint and you need to acknowledgement that life is not just one big adventure - it's a whole series of smaller ones too. That pioneering spirit, where you greet each day as the starting block for a whole series of new possibilities, is essential to your physical and emotional wellbeing.

Libra Midheaven

With Libra on the Midheaven, where are you headed? Your Aries base will have made it clear that you can be an effective and driven operator, so it's possible that you will be launched towards the Libra Midheaven like a guided missile. You are eager to take on the world and that could have disastrous consequences if the world doesn't recognise you for the supreme being that you undoubtedly are. However, the Aries Nadir will have taught you - one way or another - that life isn't all about you getting your own way. If you haven't learned that lesson by the time you approach the top of your chart, you could be in for a rude awakening.

Libra may be regarded as one of the gentle signs - but it's no pushover. And it's there to remind you that in public and in the workplace, when it comes to achieving your ambitions, you are going to need to be part of a team. That is how your world is going to work. Fortunately, with Libra here, you know how important it is to get people onside. Libra at the top of your natal chart inclines you towards that aim. You will have arrived at that point with more confidence than most people have. Whether it's born of a certain naive arrogance, or a genuine enthusiasm for getting things done, the result is the same. The concept of failure is something alien to you, and this enables you to reach out and engage with confidence. You haven't fought to get to the top for nothing and you can relate with ease, to those in the same position.

That easygoing 'work-face' is characteristic of Libra here. When you are confident in your ability - in whatever career you pursue - it makes your job a pleasure. You radiate calm confidence and that enables you to cultivate good relationships with those who are important to you in the context of getting the job done. Getting people onside and getting them to pull with you - rather than against you - is made easier with the Midheaven in Libra. When an agreed aim, strategy or direction is essential to making progress in a business or professional context, you are the person who not only identifies the best way to move forward (it's that Aries base working well for you there), but you also have the useful skill of being able to assemble an effective team whom you direct towards that stated objective.

You know who (or what) works best in any given position; matching a person to a task or understanding that some people work better together than others, comes easily to you. You are likely to have natural management and professional relating skills. As you know how to get the best from people without losing sight of the overall objective that you're aiming to achieve. It's a balance that many people would find difficult, but balance is where Libra scores well; with the Midheaven in this sign, a balanced, rational, firm (yet friendly) approach is something you will be recognised for. In fact, it will often be the key to your worldly success.

So, you're a cool people manager who knows how to get the job done. It's a skillset you deploy in all kinds of situations - not just in the work arena - and you would find it hard to achieve that without having that tough, robust and resilient core, courtesy of the Nadir in Aries. Libra and Aries are both ambitious, cardinal signs and when they occupy the 'Axis of Experience', experience tell us that the ambitious and driven qualities of both signs form the basis of your life path. However, I have a question to ask. What is it that you're trying to to achieve? To begin to answer that, once again we must look back to that Aries Nadir, the place that you came from.

Let's begin with the premise that Aries at your base may be conflicted. Being conflicted or coming from a place of actual conflict (in any form), means that peace matters to you. You will have worked out at an early age that your world is a better place without fighting and discord. So, whatever you do in this world - and whatever you become - your ambition is to achieve it without strife playing a starring role. You've had enough of that dynamic, yet the fierce determination that saw you through that stage in your life also gave you the fiercely competitive streak that enabled you to get to where you wanted to be. A lot of people do not appreciate how competitive Libra energy can be, as it's expressed quietly and with such charm.

Your aim will have been to create a collaborative and harmonious environment in which to thrive and prosper. That will have been your overriding concern. In the real world, that approach takes you to career choices where those qualities are expressed in material form - either through the relationships that you create or through your impact on the physical world around you. People management, team building, reaching out to work collaboratively with other groups or organisations, establishing business, professional collaborations or joint ventures, resolving disputes, seeking justice and fairness - all of these are examples of how that Libra Midheaven works in practice. It's what underpins your career and relational choices and your public commitments.

However, Libra here can also be expressed in another way. Your approach to creating a harmonious world may be aesthetic in nature. You need your environment to appear harmonious and that may lead you to have an interest in style, design or the arts - both personally and professionally. Of course, even for Libra, it's not a binary choice. There may be a fusion of both ways of expressing Libra here; professional interests may involve artistic or stylistic collaboration. Alternatively, your workface or public image may be particularly stylish or well regarded. However, it manifests, you'll present a harmonious appearance - in public at least. Your private life, however, may still be conflicted, hyperactive or independent. You will always have to deal with Aries in that realm.

Taurus IC - Scorpio MC

Your roots go deep and that gives you an unwavering sense of purpose. Power is never achieved through vacillation.

Taurus Nadir

Taurus is one of the nurturing signs. It's earthy, stable and grounded. And it's exactly the kind of sign you would want to see at the base of your natal chart. You could be forgiven for wearing a smile of self-satisfaction when you have the Nadir in this sign - and understandably so. It's a placement that points towards a background that may have instilled you with a set of solid, traditional values, a respect for hard work and an understanding that money does not grow on trees. You may also have developed an appreciation of the the aesthetic side of life and the importance of being productive. All of this sounds as if it would have given you a stable and secure start to life - and for many of you with Taurus here, that may have been so.

Although Taurus is a sign associated with money and resources, its presence on the Nadir is not necessarily an indicator that you came from a wealthy background; the opposite may be true. Taurus shows a concern with the material world - and a lack of resources can prompt those concerns more readily than anything else. You may have learned to be resourceful because you were challenged by scarcity; you may have been taught that waste (in all its forms) was unacceptable and that the only person you could rely on - was you. Taurus may be a nurturing sign - but taking care of things will start at home when you have Taurus here.

The result of this - regardless of how wealthy (or otherwise) your birth family may have been, is that you learned how to manage your resources very carefully indeed. You also appreciate the things you possess, to the extent that your feelings of personal security may be bound up with how much cash you have stashed in your savings account. One of the most negative things you can say about Taurus here is that you can seem tight-fisted. Being mean with money is not, however, a character judgement - it's a statement of how emotionally connected you are to the things you own.

When your emotional base is so materially based, holding on to what you have - whether it's money or other possessions that have either material or emotional value to you (they may or may not be the same thing) is the difference between having a stable life or having the walls knocked down all around you. So, where does this deep need come from, to not only construct a base that is emotionally secure, but is also physically tangible? The answer, paradoxically, may be that your background was not as stable and secure as your Taurus Nadir would have us believe.

The Nadir may reflect the material circumstances of your birth, but it's also about how you respond to those circumstances. In an unstable world - which may manifest in your life for a variety of reasons - you may respond to changes or unsettling events by holding on to what you have. If all around you is uncertain, the only thing you can be certain of is your own ability to manage your life circumstances and provide for your physical needs. Food, warmth and shelter - and the means to pay for them

- become the bedrock of your life plan. That is where you come from. When you secure the essentials, everything else is a bonus. And Taurus here really does deal in the essentials.

The things that make you feel grounded are often the products of the earth - and the earth itself. Pity the Taurus Nadir person who does not have access to forests, green hills or a plot of land in which to grow flowers, vegetables or herbs. Even a pot on a city balcony will establish that vital connection to the earth, without which a Taurus Nadir feels lost in space. One pot of leaves is not going to provide for all your material and emotional needs, but that's not the point; it goes deeper than that. That pot of leaves, plot of land or a walk in the park evokes something within you that makes you feel 'at home' - and at peace with yourself. All becomes well with your world when you are in the presence of nature.

Why is that? Quite simply, it enables you to take root - even if those roots are temporary. More than any other sign (apart from Cancer) Taurus on the Nadir needs to belong. It removes the stress, so having a sense of place that you can call your own is important to you. This may manifest in your life as a desire to have your own home from an early age, or it may manifest as a desire to be comfortable in your living environment - and that implies everything from relaxed and congenial living conditions, a focus on physical pleasures like food and drink, having a garden or even a desire to see your home well-appointed and aesthetically pleasing. It may extend to the wider environment too. Taurus here - no matter what your financial status - will strive to meet those needs at all costs.

However, there is another way in which a Taurus Nadir becomes real - and that is through an attachment to tradition. You may have been brought up in a traditional family unit, a strict household or a conservative one - and you may naturally follow in that path as an adult. Taurus is a naturally conservative sign and, though you may not be politically conservative, the impulse 'to conserve' runs through you like a seam of gold. Conservation means being protective; it also means appreciating the lasting, enduring value of material goods and resources, but it also means that you are likely to be a creature of habit. With Taurus here, there is a risk you become overly inflexible; sticking with what you know - including patterns of behaviour - may be the price you pay for that steady, unshakeable base.

SCORPIO MIDHEAVEN

Let's assume you come from a more solid place than most people. My guess is you would like to keep it that way, so with Scorpio here, you not only have that objective, but you also aim to control the world around you to ensure that nothing deflects from that aim. Of course, when you seek to exercise that level of control, you're inviting something - or someone - to challenge that position. With Scorpio on the Midheaven, you are acutely aware of how easily your best laid plans can - in the words of the famous Scottish poet, Robert Burns, "gang aft aglay". For those of you unfamiliar with the Scottish dialect, it simply means that if things can go wrong, then that is what they will do.

Scorpio is always prepared for the worst that can happen - often overly so - because your default position seems to be that you believe the universe is out to get you. So, in order to foil your enemies - and keep the universe guessing - you may prefer to keep your best laid plans to yourself. With Scorpio here, you are often circumspect about your aims and ambitions in life. As the old saying goes, you keep your friends close - and your enemies closer. In the context of a Scorpio Midheaven, that approach makes you appear like one of life's great strategic thinkers - except it's not logical deduction that's at work here. It's your basic survival instinct that's running the show.

If we stop for a moment to think about what the Midheaven represents, we can see that it's about the way in which you are regarded in a social sense. In earlier parts of this book I've described the Midheaven as your 'work-face', a social role that defines your public status, such as a trade or professional 'label'. You may feel a sense of vocation or 'destiny' at this point in your chart. So, how does this work with Scorpio here? Scorpio is an independent sign, but it's also one with a well-developed sense of self-preservation. This means that when a crisis comes to town, the person who is best equipped to deal with it usually has Scorpio on the Midheaven.

The Midheaven is a public facing place, not a private space, but the personal management skills and self-control found at the base of your chart - that Taurus legacy - are usefully transformed into tools that can be used to create the kind of personal authority and expertise that benefits society at large, rather than benefitting you alone. That's not an altruistic position; the underlying motive is the same need for control that dominates your life in the private sphere. Staying cool, calm and collected in the face of 'danger' (however that is defined) is a mark of those who have Scorpio here, and the trade or profession you gravitate towards may reflect that reality.

Dealing with often emotive or difficult situations is a difficult life path to follow, both professionally and personally, and it's one that often results in personal or social transformation - in fact, it may be difficult for you to separate the two when you have Scorpio here. However, that deeply rooted Taurus base enables you to tread that line with as much certainty as anyone can. You are clear with boundaries in that sense, because you know the difference between what is relevant and meaningful and what is merely superficial and a waste of your time. You understand what motivates you - and what motivates other people too - and with Scorpio on the Midheaven that is particularly relevant to both your career choices and experiences.

As a natural psychologist (and some of you may pursue that profession on a professional basis), identifying the underlying patterns and behaviours that dictate how both people and organisations operate is relatively easy for you. You can become a shrewd political operator - in the broadest sense - as you are able to navigate the murky waters of workplace power-plays and intrigues more easily than most people. You may even use your political abilities to further your own ambitions. That may seem an extreme response, but never forget how extreme Scorpio can be; an attraction to power for its own sake is a logical - if problematic - extension of Scorpio here. Manipulating circumstances to further your own ambition is where such behaviour may reach its logical - if less palatable - conclusion.

As suspected, Scorpio brings with it the possibility of extreme responses and, often a moral or ethical dimension to your life path. However, it's also a deeply passionate sign. Of course, passions can be directed in extreme directions too, but with this sign at the apex of your birth chart, the most beneficial use of passion is that which is directed towards developing your sense of purpose - and that sense of purpose may not be revealed until you reach a position of maturity and wisdom. The secretiveness and wariness that is associated with this sign means that you may not trust the world to accept the person you aim to be. You may keep yourself hidden. It sometimes takes time and the ageing process to reveal who you truly are.

We often overlook the fact that the Midheaven represents a point of culmination; it's the high point of our life and, with Scorpio here, that high point may be less concerned with manifesting as an outer power play, and more concerned with developing the inner power to accept and deal with life's existential crises with dignity and grace. No matter what outward public persona, or career, you adopt with Scorpio here, your high point may be the realisation that you have overcome considerable obstacles to get where you are now. Or you may realise that your life path has transformed you into a better person than you ever thought you could be. Either way, a Scorpio Midheaven speaks of a need to embrace your power and authority - what you do with it is your call.

Gemini IC - Sagittarius MC

Your curiosity will make you restless and long to explore, but your place in this world will be determined by how far you allow yourself to travel.

Gemini Nadir

Gemini energy is busy. It's scattered and noisy. It's communicative and mobile. It's information rich, but fragmented. There's a lot to think about when you have Gemini at the Nadir, not least of which is how do those varied and multitudinous expressions of Gemini energy translate into the lived experiences associated with the base of your natal chart? Like the other air signs, Libra and Aquarius, Gemini energy can focus on the abstract rather than the physical, and the mental rather than the emotional aspects of our lives. Yet, the Nadir is where life is private, personal, emotional and raw. We take root here, we are formed here - and, arguably, nothing has a greater impact on our lives, emotionally or psychologically, than the place from which we came.

With Gemini here, that place may feel everything from sociable to superficial; your experiences here may be a varied as the sign itself. So, let's look at some of the possible backstories that you may have. Was yours a family where education was seen as important? Was yours a household where things were always on the move? Did you spend your time split between two family homes, say, if your parents were divorced? Were your parents always so busy that you became independently minded at an early age? Did you struggle to be heard in your early years, so you escaped into the world of books? Only one thing is certain. Your backstory will have Gemini at its heart.

The things that belong in your personal history are the things that make you feel as if you belong to a particular family, place or tribe. With Gemini here, you may be more aware than most of your own history. Family stories may have been handed down to you - though it's possible that you will have prompted their telling with a barrage of the questions that Gemini is famous for. You may have enjoyed hearing those tales from your parents or grandparents - and the reason for this is that you have a deep need to construct that family narrative.

Personal histories are deeply felt; and your history is one that you are likely to be skilled at re-framing and re-telling in your turn. That is how you take root and, though it's a process that accords entirely with Gemini's communicative abilities, it's not necessarily a process that will come easily to you. This may sound paradoxical but let me remind you of something that will always be part of the Gemini experience, its duality. Reclaiming your own story is an important part of building your base, but that process also helps you to deflect from a part of the past that may be more difficult to connect with - the emotional attachments that require you to acknowledge the links between the past and your present. A narrative that enables you to cultivate a sense of personal detachment may be how you deal with the burden of emotional baggage. Gemini likes to travel light.

When it comes to your own space, the things that matter to you are the things that re-create that sense of enquiry and independence you may have fostered as a child. If books are your thing, then you will have shelves packed with them and they will, no doubt, reflect the eclectic interests you have acquired over the years. Emotional attachments (if you can think of them in that sense) are to the things that mean something to you at a mental level. Reading, writing, handicrafts (Gemini, like Virgo, is a dexterous sign), getting out on your cycle to explore the world around you, engaging with friends, neighbours, strangers, technology and media; the 'busy-ness' that marked your early years remains at your core - even if its form of expression is deeply personal to you.

I have a question. All of that 'busy-ness', what is it for? Of all the things that you think or worry about, I can guarantee that your own hyperactivity will not be one of them. Those of you with Gemini at the Nadir will be as varied as grains of sand, but you will all have one thing in common; you know how important it is to keep moving, so much so that you may not have time to eat. Gemini here may exist on snacks rather that fully formed meals. Travelling light happens in a physical, bodily context too. Mentally, physically, emotionally - for you, stasis is anathema. You don't want to be weighed down. This must surely be the only zodiac sign whose bedrock is made from the shifting sands, blown this way and that, by a constant breeze.

It's a facet of your life that may manifest in an inability to stay in one place for any length of time. Home, for you, may be subject to regular change. It's possible that personal circumstances may mean you are unable to settle permanently in one place. However, you may simply get bored with your accommodation after a while, as curiosity drives you elsewhere. It's a similar impulse that may see you redecorate your home more than most people do; change and flexibility is built into your domestic situation. Some of you - finances permitting - may even have more than one home. Gemini on the Nadir may even find its outlet via an involvement in real estate, as a salesperson or negotiator, as it represents a fundamental need for variety and change in the domestic/environmental sphere.

So, if your roots are often subject to change, how do you avoid feeling cast adrift? Being grounded is, thankfully, an internalised state, so any vagaries in your external state of being can be accommodated at that level. Again, that's a reflection of the duality found with Gemini at the Nadir. The freedom to come and go, to follow where your mind takes you - and to refuse to be pigeonholed - is strong within you. When you look back at your early life - as I'm sure you do - you may reach the conclusion that your parents were right when they called you a strange child, one whose existence seemed marked by creating an more interesting universe in which to live However, you were never truly alone then - and you're not alone now. You always have yourself for company, so stop running away from yourself.

SAGITTARIUS MIDHEAVEN

Coming from a Gemini base means you aim for Sagittarius, and that's appropriate given that this is the sign of the Archer. If Gemini is information rich, Sagittarius is where that information is turned into greater knowledge and deeper understanding. That understanding may be philosophical or religious; intellectual or schooled at the university of life, but with a Sagittarius Midheaven, it will be something that influences your 'work face' and public image, and it will also influence where you see yourself fitting into society. So, with Sagittarius here, how does the world see you? The most fitting way to respond may be for you to ask yourself how you see the world.

Sagittarius is associated with a sense of perspective - it's where the sign's famed philosophical point of view originates - so your perspective is likely to be lofty. You look down on the world and, as you do so, you are able to see more in your peripheral vision than can be appreciated by more earthbound spectators - even if they use a telescope. Accordingly, the world may regard you as someone whose ability to take a broad overview is to be admired. Associated with Jupiter the king of the gods, you may feel that a Sagittarius Midheaven bestows not only an elevated outlook, but an elevated status too. As you may appreciate, that may be as problematic as it is beneficial.

Let's focus on your status for a moment. There is the possibility that, with this sign here, you will be a high achiever. One reason for this is that you display a great deal of positivity and optimism - particularly where your career is concerned. The possibility of failure may be alien to you. So is self-doubt. You also have a work face that is funny, charming, accessible and knowledgeable. It makes people like you; you get on well with all the people who it would benefit you to associate with - and that helps your ascent up the career ladder. You're also relatively flexible where your career is concerned, so whenever (or wherever) an opportunity appears, you're unlikely to remain committed to whatever you were doing previously. That busy, communicative and inquisitive Gemini base grows well into Sagittarius's worldly achievements.

You may be the one who gets 'the big job', or you may be the person who is a deeply knowledgeable expert in your chosen field. That's a positive expression of having Sagittarius here. You are also likely to be a good communicator because Sagittarius is expansive; if you have a career that involves specialist knowledge, it may seem like a logical extension for you to disseminate that knowledge. Sagittarius is well represented in occupations like journalism, broadcasting, education and publication; with this sign on the Midheaven these types of careers may be a natural fit for you. However, any role that has an expansive nature, involving large scale or distant connections, is likely with this placement. If your job involves international sales or extensive travel for example, that's Sagittarius's influence working well.

As with all astrological placements, there is a downside. There may be a certain amount of arrogance that comes with this placement. To be blunt, your view of your rightful place in this world as being a lofty one, may be your view alone. A sense of entitlement can come with this placement, and it may lead others to regard you as epitomising the less attractive side of this sign. The workplace 'know it all' or the 'barrack-room lawyer' - people who loudly proclaim they know more than the experts - are typical of the less attractive public images that are associated with this sign. Stubborn refusal to countenance anyone's opinion but your own may be a significant drawback to your progress in life.

Yet, Sagittarius here has the potential to do much good. You may respect tradition - yet be progressive in your aims. You regard the expansion of human knowledge as an important objective and, as a result, you may seek to discover more about the world and, in so doing, you may expand the sum of human understanding. Pushing further or pushing into areas that were previously unknown are challenges you relish; work that is exploratory in nature is exciting for you - and generally you prefer a level of change and excitement in your work to give your best work performance. However, a word of warning; you may not be in your career for the long haul. One hangover from your Gemini base means that frequent career changes may be a possibility for you. To avoid that, you may prefer to work on a shorter 'project' basis, thus giving you more frequent changes of scene.

So, with this sign, what are you aiming for? To go far and go high are the obvious answers, but there is more to a Sagittarius Midheaven than that. Ultimately, the Midheaven indicates that your aim is true. Truth, justice and an overriding sense of being free to become whatever you want to be, are strong with this sign here - and they are concepts that are just as likely to be applied in a social or societal sense. This is also a sign that is associated with the law; not the 'rules and regulations' we associate with Capricorn, but the search for justice that we associate with wisdom and understanding. It's the place where accumulated knowledge, gleaned from the information gathered in your Gemini phase, is given out (from on high, naturally) for the wider benefits of society.

When you consider that your reputation is aligned with the Midheaven, you can begin to appreciate how those with Sagittarius here are regarded as society's purveyors of truth. You may command a great deal of respect for several reasons; those who are perceived as generous, public spirited, often volunteering their time and energies in a way that benefits society, may have this placement. The route to social prestige may not be materially based - but that end is more likely to be reached if you are true to yourself - and submit yourself to the truth. That is the message of Sagittarius here.

Cancer IC - Capricorn MC

Security is everything; without security at work you will never have security at home.

Cancer Nadir

With Cancer on the Nadir, you will have a firm attachment to the past - more specifically, your own personal history, family background or place of origin. This bond may be so great that you carry the past with you throughout the present - and that's a lifetime. In the natural zodiac, Cancer is the sign associated with the fourth house and, as the Nadir marks the cusp of this house, Cancer - the sign associated with tenacity, defensiveness and vulnerability - is particularly strong. It's 'at home', so with this sign on the Nadir, home is where you may want to be. In fact, you may find it hard to leave. This does not mean you will spend your entire life in your childhood bedroom; people with this Nadir grow up, get jobs and develop their own independent lives in the same manner as the rest of us.

However, there will always be a deep need to take root, have a family-oriented lifestyle, become parents or nurturers or to feel that you 'belong' in a wider sense. It's that feeling of belonging (to somewhere or something) that makes you feel secure. It provides you with the firm base that you know will support you when things get tough. Let's not forget how vulnerable Cancer can be; it may be essential for you to address this vulnerability from the outset, as the urge to withdraw from life's challenges may not be the best place to be coming from. Insecurity is not a stable platform on which to build your life.

Personal security is vitally important when you have the Nadir in this sign - and our early life is where we establish our sense of personal security in its most basic form. The Nadir is an indicator of early life conditions and, when it's in Cancer, this indicates that your early life may have been family-oriented in a way that set the pattern for your later life. A closely knit family unit with well-maintained links to the wider family (however that is defined) is not unusual with Cancer here. It's the kind of family set-up that means your grandparents, aunts, uncles and cousins will have been part of your daily family life. It's what we tend to think of as a traditional family format - and it often extends beyond the family, out into the community. Cancer here can indicate that you grew up in a close-knit community where neighbourly bonds were almost like family.

So, in practice, how would this have been experienced? You and your wider family may have lived close to one other and the various family members may have been interdependent on each other. You may have been looked after by various relatives on a regular basis, as sharing family resources and responsibilities, such as childcare, is a feature of Cancer here. This is also the family that would have eaten together. Those broad emotional and familial bonds may have given you a sense of comfort as well as a sense of identity, place and belonging. There is no doubt that there will have been a lot of kindness and care in your upbringing, in what may have been a conventional - if old-fashioned - family unit. At best, you will have found this supportive, especially in an emotional context.

It may sound idyllic - and for some of you it may have been - but it's also the kind of background that could seem restrictive or suffocating to more adventurous or individualistic characters. Families are not always sweetness and light. Cancer is a sign that is also associated with less pleasant familial experiences such as emotional blackmail, moodiness, hurt feelings and being 'clingy' - the drive to hold onto something, even if that 'something' doesn't want to be held. If you felt the urge to break away, leave town - or leave the country - then it may have been wrench for you. Not only did you have to leave your home behind you, but your close family may also have made it plain to you that they didn't want you to go - and they are likely to have made it plain in a passive aggressive sense, using their 'hurt' to prevent you following your chosen path.

Leaving the family or community may not have been easy or well received, but the important thing for you is how you have responded to that shift (and whether it was problematic or otherwise) and how you incorporated it into your adult life - and there are several ways in which a Cancer Nadir can manifest here. First, you may not have left. Or, second, you may have left and then returned. Either way, you may see your role as being the next generation to carry the family traditions forward. Following in family footsteps may be a theme in your life - but it doesn't mean that you are destined to replicate the familial experiences that formed you - or remain bound to the community of your birth

To feel grounded is not the same as 'being grounded' - and I'm using that phrase in the sense of being held back or, as the pilots among us would say, 'prevented from flying', as opposed to being stable or well balanced. Clearly, the latter is a preferable place to emerge from - and that takes us to the deeper meaning of Cancer on the Nadir. Living with the memories of your early years, or actively maintaining familial ties and loyalties, does not mean that you must follow the same path as your forebears or restrict your own vision of the future in any way. Touching base with the best of the past allows you to do the opposite and reinterpret the past in a way that is meaningful to you - and with the Nadir in Cancer, that lies at the heart of the process of creating your own base.

Making yourself feel grounded - in the best sense of that word - means that you need to successfully internalise your own support system. Many of you will do this by creating a life that offers you the same kind of 'feel good' factor that you had in your childhood. Of course, in those instances where that may have been lacking, your challenge may be to create the inner emotional resilience that will enable you to have a safe space - emotionally - that will sustain you throughout your life. With this placement, many of you may need to consciously develop self-parenting skills in order to become your own nurturer and guide. Self-parenting means being your ideal parent - and not a replication of your birth parents. It enables you to care for your needs in the way that's best for you - and that way is the way that enables you to grow and fulfil your true potential.

Capricorn Midheaven

As Cancer is naturally attuned to the fourth house and the Nadir, so Capricorn aligns itself to the Midheaven. It's the sign associated with ambition, realism, gritty determination and hard work. As the Midheaven is where we are measured by our ability to face the challenges of the outside world, it also seems that this sign is a million miles away from the soft-centred, home loving crab on the other side of your chart. As with all the oppositional pairs on the 'Axis of Experience', it can take a leap of faith (if not imagination) to work out how to get from point A to point B. The truth is, as ever, complex; travel is rarely one directional and it's easy to forget the purpose of the journey. So, let's remember the fundamentals. You stand at the centre of your birth chart. Both ends of the axis meet in the middle. And that's you.

That same dynamic is at the heart of the opposition aspect; things must meet in the middle and, to do so successfully, there must be an area of common ground. With the Cancer-Capricorn axis, that common ground is security. The inner security you seek at an emotional level is made impregnable by achieving material status in the outer world. In other words, your outer achievements are designed to protect your inner vulnerability. Cancer's defensive base is the foundation for a Capricorn fortress. And, in the real world, how is that made possible? To answer that we need to look at how those dynamics manifest in your life as lived experience - which is, after all, what the 'Axis of Experience' is about.

With Capricorn on the Midheaven, you may be naturally ambitious and hardworking, however, it's more likely that you will have a 'common-sense' and realistic approach to whatever it is that you do to get on in life. You know nothing in life is free, so you work hard because you know it's the only way to be recognised as an 'adult in the room'. It grants you a certain status in the world and it enables you create that all important feeling of being in control of your own destiny. Being 'in control' is an important theme to those of you with Capricorn here; it's empowering because it enables you to keep your life steady and consistent. There will be few surprises - and that's how you want it to be. Your aim is to construct a place in life that is secure for the long term and that involves a degree of discipline on your part.

When you look back at that Cancer Nadir, it becomes clear how important Capricorn's discipline can be. Discipline provides the counterbalance to Cancer's restlessness and emotionalism, but it also provides a mechanism that enables those Cancer qualities of attachment, tenacity and instinct to have a productive, practical and orderly outcome. So, Capricorn here enables you to focus on the things that are important to you and be realistic about your own capabilities. You are prepared to take responsibility for your actions, and you expect others to do the same. You believe in taking care of life's essentials and you appreciate clarity in both words and deeds. Cutting through the crap (please excuse the phrase) is one way of describing your approach to the way you function best in the material world.

It's an approach that enables you to keep things in focus, but the downside is that it can be overly rigid and limiting. There is no doubt - in a career context - that this is a great placement for those who have managerial ambitions, or work in a business environment - or any field in which a clear focus on the detail or the 'bottom line' is required. To be recognised as a person of good judgement - regardless of your status in life or your career choice - is perhaps the ultimate accolade you can receive with Capricorn here. It enables you to assume a position of respect, and respect - as you will have noticed - is one way of achieving that all-important feeling of security. When you are respected, people tend to leave you alone.

Unfortunately, when this pair of signs on the 'Axis of Experience' are not working quite so well, 'alone' is what may result in an all too real sense. With Capricorn here, there is a risk that prioritising your outer life - such as your career and ambitions or devoting your time and efforts to running a company or your own business may result in the inner life - or the Cancer end of the axis - becoming neglected. So, when this happens, we see the outer life being prioritised over family life and personal relationships. In extreme cases, Capricorn here may indicate late marriage or a single life. It may be worth reminding you that in such cases, public image is derived from more than your career.

In a similar vein, it may be problematical for some of those with this 'Axis of Experience' to reach the level of authority and discipline demanded by Capricorn. Ruled by Saturn, Capricorn energy can be hard work to deal with. The limitation or fear that you feel internally may be experienced as a reluctance to engage with the outer world. The big, bad world may appear to be a harsh place - and that may be especially so if your Cancer attachments and defensiveness overwhelm Capricorn's autonomy and self-determination. That's not the result you want. Developing autonomy and self-determination are the key take-outs from your journey to the Midheaven; they enable you to be regarded on your own terms, rewarded for your own competencies and to realise your own ambitions.

In this type of situation, Capricorn here can result in issues like shyness, or other obstacles to be overcome, if you are to be successful in taking your place in the realm of life's winners. Thinking of that scenario in purely 'win/lose' binary terms may also be one of the problems you have. If you are feeling excluded from worldly progress, it's easy to think of your 'work face' or public status in negative terms or feel as if achievements are for 'other people' - and not you. That is a fallacy, and it brings us back to the nature of opposition - and a fundamental part of it at that. It's a question of balance. It may take you longer, it may require you to work harder, but rising to the challenge is what Capricorn asks of you - and if you run (or walk at a steady pace) towards that, you will find your place at the top table is well deserved.

Leo IC - Aquarius MC

It's so important to express yourself well, especially if you want a starring role on the stage of life.

Leo Nadir

So, you were born into royalty. That's a joke by the way; Leo may be the sign associated with aristocracy, but most of you who were born with the Nadir in Leo will have an ordinary family background. Unless you're a genuine aristocrat, Leo at the base of your chart will manifest in ways other than a full set of silver spoons in your mouth. The Nadir leads you back into history, both your personal history and that of your birth family. With Leo here, your roots may be humble, but your family may take pride in who they are and where they have come from. The family history may be dramatic, it may be courageous, or it may be entertaining, but one thing is certain - you will enjoy hearing about it. Even if your family is the most ordinary family on this earth, those stories will make you feel special in some way.

Feeling special is a theme that occurs regularly with Leo on the Nadir and that can have problematic as well as beneficial associations. Let's deal with the good stuff first. This is a creative and expressive sign; your life experiences - especially in your early years - may have seen you encouraged to develop your own creative talents. I'm not saying that you were a precocious or gifted artist, musician or sports star, but if there was something that captured your imagination, and you wanted to try it out for yourself, you may have been encouraged to do so. And you would have enjoyed it. Vitality is a solar quality and the Sun rules Leo; feeling vitalised and special is something that you will have discovered was essential to building your confidence. It's how you discovered your own capabilities and become the person you are.

When you have Leo here, feeling good about yourself is important; you need to have something to be proud of. That thing may be your family, your home, or your homeland, but in true Leo style that pride will be creatively expressed or even paternalistic in some way. So, you will want the best, as in the best home, the best family, the best kids - and I suspect you can see where we're going with this. Sun-ruled Leo does not hide away - even at the Nadir - so you may be keen to show off any of those things - and you may do so because it makes you feel proud of them. However, pride is a double-edged sword. Feeling proud of yourself may be an essential part of your foundation in life, but it can also generate mixed feelings in those whom you invite into your personal realm.

Many will simply appreciate your generosity and bonhomie. You may be a great party-giver, a flamboyant cook or an entertaining host. Some, however, may be envious and attempt to rain on your parade. To them, you may seem boastful or too proud in a negative sense. On some occasions they may be right. What makes you feel that your 'foundation' is better than anyone else's? It's a harsh lesson, but the fundamental issue is this; making your base a special place is your way of re-creating the feel-good factor you discovered was so important to you as a child. The words, "Look at me" or "Look what I can do" may not be articulated in the same way; in fact, they may be unspoken. Unfortunately, they are words that some people will not want to hear. Leo is a sign that is known for seeking attention - but that is not necessarily the best approach we need to take when it's found on the Nadir.

Attention will be part of your personal package, but it can surface in a negative sense. There will be people with Leo here who do not recall a childhood filled with encouragement; when they stood tall to express themselves the reaction may have been hostile rather than polite applause. This is the risk when you stand out from the crowd. It's hurtful. Especially because you don't mean to offend. Attention becomes a negative experience - and it may be one you shy away from. It's particularly hurtful if it happens in the home and comes from the people who are meant to love and support you most.

For some people with this placement, home may have been a 'Lion's Den' rather than the place they could call their safe space. It's not that you were in danger of being eaten alive (even if it felt like that sometimes) but there are experiences that are common and that some of you may recognise them. Your parents may have been proud of you - that's natural - but they may have expressed it in a way that made you feel uncomfortable. You may have felt like a prize exhibit rather than a prized child. Your parents may have boasted about your achievements or lived vicariously through you. They would have made you the centre of attention because *they* wanted attention. And the fallout would have landed on you.

'Tall Poppy Syndrome' is the name given to those who suffer from having their heads cut off if they get too tall - metaphorically of course. The results of that may prompt you to keep your achievements and creative impulses private - but it's hard to get the Sun to shine in the dead of night and your reluctance to allow yourself to shine may arise from having to deal with the fallout I mentioned earlier. Your parents' behaviour may have made you the object of hostility; some of you may have acted your way out of that, others may have retreated from putting your creative self on display at all. Criticism is painful and, to this day, you may find even constructive criticism hard to deal with because of the pain you experienced in the past.

So, if you hate that stomach churning feeling you get from waiting in the wings, the best way to counter it is to perform in front of an appreciative audience where a good reception is guaranteed. When you create that supportive base, your own home and family (or whatever you need to do to feel solid ground beneath your feet) that's where you can start believing in yourself once more. It gives you confidence you need to engage with the world, and it enables you to develop the courage to show a willingness to stand up and be counted. The great thing is, you have no shortage of courage; by inviting those you trust into your domain, you learn to trust the world outside a little more each time. You have a great stage on which to perform your greatest production - that special show called 'Your Life'.

Aquarius Midheaven

When you have the Midheaven in Aquarius, the most idiosyncratic of zodiac signs, your personal journey is concerned with claiming your independence and discovering your own genius. Before you wonder why you're not heading up NASA or discovering a cure for cancer, let's stop for a moment to consider the meaning of the word, 'genius'. In some instances, it may mean that you are intellectually brilliant, but what it truly means is that you have a markedly strong capacity or notable aptitude for something - and it really doesn't matter what that something is. That aptitude (whatever it is) is likely to be the thing that you discovered made your heart sing - even as a child. Also, it may not be, as you can unearth an aptitude or discover a capacity for doing something at any time in your life.

However, the important thing is that you will recognise the feeling that it engenders. You feel the same as you did all those years ago when something you engaged with made you feel alive. In that moment, you know that you're on the right track. However, the challenges you may face are as follows: first, you need to find out where the track is headed and, second, you must avoid losing your way. The answer to the first of those questions may seem easy - for some of you. You found your groove early in life and learned that it made you unique. Standing out (or being outstanding - they're not necessarily the same thing) gave you a confident and self-assured base to build on for the rest of your life.

That start in life enables you to have a 'work face' that is uncompromising and single minded - and you may be regarded as a maverick who does not necessarily fit in with traditional expectations. You may be someone who has succeeded because of your ability to look at life from a different direction. You may have an independent streak a mile wide, but that's okay with you. And it's okay because it's important for you to be recognised, in public, as 'your own person'. It's a phrase we hear used a lot, but what it refers to are those who are true to their beliefs, trust their own judgement and, above all, are independent in thought and deed. You don't need (or want) anyone else to tell you what to do.

When you have Aquarius here, that's your guiding light - and paradoxically, it may shine brightest for those who had to fight hardest to discover their genius. If you were one of the 'tall poppies' described earlier or grew up feeling the frustration of being unable to express yourself without being censored or ridiculed, you may feel some pressure to become independent and Aquarius on the Midheaven pulls you towards a destiny that involves putting your head above the parapet. Regardless of the job you do, or the direction you take, you will recognised for doing something unexpected or different. You may be regarded as different because your career choice or life path is at odds with that experienced by the other members of your family or community.

Making that break by being rebellious or being 'unusual' may be where you were destined to go, but it's a space where you may become recognised as independent, free and equal in a different way. Your own struggle to establish those things in your own life, makes those things are important to you. You need to express that through your life decisions and career choices - and you need to do so on a grand stage. Breaking away from limitation - or tradition - may be the best way for you to appreciate that restrictions also apply to other people - and not just you. The ideals of freedom, equality and independence may come to have a wider application than simply to your own life. Your egalitarian outlook enables you to move seamlessly in a variety of social circles.

There is something of the campaigner when you have Aquarius here; freedom and ideals are important and have an important place in wider society. A significant number of you will seek alignment with particularly groups or sections of society; that may manifest as an interest in politics or social causes, or with innovative, radical or even extreme opinions and ideas. In your career, that can lead you to be considered as quirky or eccentric. That's not necessarily a bad thing, depending on your job. A willingness to stand up and be counted reminds you that your own foundation was based on the premise that things can only get better. It's the belief you clung to when times were less secure - and it's the rock you will hold fast to forever.

You approach social integration from that standpoint; you no longer care what people think of you, nor do you care for other people's opinions. That may seem contrary, given this sign's essential humanity, but you are used to being the outsider who has no need to conform and to achieve that you need to have developed a thick skin - or at least the appearance of it. This is essential as you will always attract attention - whatever you do - and you may attract envy and criticism too. You may regard that as the price you have to pay to achieve your aims or ambitions. Being true to yourself - and being recognised as such - is more important to you that following the crowd.

It may be tough being a visionary, but it's never dull. You are future-oriented, and your mind is always one step ahead of where you are now - and it's several steps ahead of everyone else. If there's a major challenge you face, it's that of living in the present moment. The Midheaven is, however, a destination point; if you look around you, you will realise that your destination is the place where you can be creatively disruptive. You shake things up and the rigidity that is sometimes associated with this cardinal point is fractured to allow something new to emerge. The ultimate accolade for you is to be recognised as the agent of change in a moribund world - that is truly the Aquarian ideal.

Virgo IC - Pisces MC

You know that everything benefits from improvement; use your insight and empathy to inspire change and challenge the status quo.

Virgo Nadir

There is a reassuring feel to any of the earth signs on the Nadir - and Virgo is no exception. This is a sign that speaks of diligence, hard work, productivity, nurturing and reaping rewards, so when we look at your personal history in that context, some useful crops emerge from this deep and fertile earth. The Nadir is where we take root, and your roots may have been carefully tended. You may have been from a hardworking home where the values of discipline - in all things - will have been impressed upon you. When I say, 'discipline', I don't mean that your parents were necessarily overly strict - though that may have been the experience for some of you. Astrological symbolism can also be encountered by the lack of the thing being symbolised; in some cases, basic discipline may have been emphasised through its absence.

Discipline in its true sense is more about self-control and behaving in ways that are organised and thorough. You learn what is important in life - and what is not. Unfortunately, some form of punishment may be part of the learning process - particularly if you were held to an impossibly high standard. However, there is a more beneficial Virgo manifestation; you may have had a mentor figure in your life who guided you through your early years and taught you some important life lessons. That may have been one of your parents, but it's possible that this was another person. That person may have been another member of your family, but you may have found such a figure elsewhere.

Virgo on the Nadir can speak of a certain emotional distance or emotional chill in your relationships with your parents. This could have been for many reasons; for example, there may have been an emphasis on duty before pleasure in your home. In extreme cases, this may have been because one of the family members needed more care and attention - due to ill health for example - and this would have meant that your needs were subjugated to theirs. Alternatively, your birth family may have been populated with the type of people for whom emotional expression was difficult - or considered unnecessary. Robustly practical and earthy people may substitute 'doing' for 'feeling' with the result that emotional contact may have been limited. Or you may have been subjected to discipline for its own sake - and that would have been both cruel and unnecessary.

Whether you grew up in an overly disciplined environment, or the opposite - or somewhere in between - the onus would have been on you to make sense of it all. You may have learned to live with routines that were not of your own choosing, or you may have developed your own routines to turn chaos into order. Routines are both comfortable and useful; they provide shape to our lives, together with a sense of order and security. They become a way of fixing - or securing - yourself to a rhythm of life that makes you feel contained. Routines may be predictable - but that's how you prefer things to be. When it comes to establishing your own firm base, routine is an important building block to those with a Virgo Nadir.

The concept of fixing (or being able to fix) has wider implications, ones that go beyond the routine and, once more, we need to look back to where that comes from. If you came from a family where the phrase 'Make do and mend' had resonance, you will have grown up with experience of people being 'useful' with their hands in the most practical sense. Skills like carpentry or painting and decorating would have been carried out in the home, and handicrafts, such as dressmaking or knitting, would have been practised, either as hobbies or with a more serious purpose - that of providing an inexpensive means of clothing the family. Being able to do for yourself, the things you couldn't afford to hire other folks to do for you, may have been instilled in you at a young age. Becoming competent at life through developing your skillset applies here.

Being practical and 'hands on' is undoubtedly useful, but your experience of mending things may extend further than the material level. Many of you may practice the skills you learned in the family home to this day; even if you can afford to hire a carpenter you may choose to do it yourself because it makes you feel grounded and real. Repairing yourself - and others - emotionally, physically and psychologically, may also be a theme you encounter in your life when you have the Nadir in Virgo. In fact, it may be a way of touching that base that is so important to you.

I mentioned at the outset that this is a nurturing sign - but it's not the kind of sentimental, emotional engagement that you would experience, for example, with Cancer. Virgo is more robust and can be a proscriptive set of energies; you seek to 'improve' yourself (and others) by organising, perfecting and implementing systems and routines to improve your life by doing things like maintaining a tidy home, following a healthy diet, taking regular exercise, ensuring you have a good life-work balance and paying attention to your physical and mental health. These are the things that put you in your comfort zone - and it may be hard for you to see how you could function without them.

The downside to this that there are some things that are not fixable. When you look back at your early life, you may not have been able to fix that sick family member, or your parent's marriage; or you may not have been able to reach the impossibly high standards that someone else decided that you needed to meet. Guilt and self-doubt are the things most likely to weaken your foundation. Your challenge is to not allow that to happen. You have the right to a good, secure and productive life, and to achieve that you need to remember that, ultimately, you are responsible for sorting out your own life, rather than immersing yourself in the mess that is left behind by others. Virgo grants you the ability to draw that boundary. It's a gift to be treasured - and used well.

Pisces Midheaven

You're neat, tidy and organised at home and your inner life is a mirror of that domestic reality. In fact, if something's out of place at home, it's a red flag for your inner wellbeing. So, how does a person as mindful as you live with the reality of Pisces on the Midheaven? The answer to that question is that it's the only Midheaven sign that's available to you, so you're going to have to approach it from the sensible Virgo base that the universe has given you too - and it's a base that will have stressed the importance of making things work out. It's important for you, therefore, to find a place in this world that works for you -

something that perhaps enables you to escape from the routine concerns of your inner life.

Pisces is the sign of escapism, but to assume that Pisces on the Midheaven portends a lifetime of escaping from your career obligations, is somewhat wide of the mark. Pisces is gentle, unassuming and empathetic - and on the Midheaven these are qualities that you could bring to any profession. The external manifestation in those instances, has the potential to draw you to the healing and caring or charitable professions - and that's not out of line with the firm, practical, nurturing and 'fixing' qualities found at the other end of your 'Axis of Experience'. Channeling those qualities into something useful in the outer world, by using your fundamental 'hands on' approach in a way that helps others, seems to be a natural fit.

Of course, they are qualities that will fit other, more commercial, sectors too - but let's focus on the allegedly softer side for a moment. If we drill down into what it is that you do, a common thread could be that you enable others to improve their lives in some way - often through recovery, either from illness or bad situations. And it's also the type of work that does not project you into the limelight; in fact, you may be relatively invisible. Your 'work face' may be associated with a label; doctor, paramedic, care assistant, nurse, charity worker - or any other career 'label' that attaches to those whose individual status is overridden by the nature of the service they provide. Those careers are vocational in nature and vocation requires the dedication and application you learned a long time ago. They are also not materially based; your reward comes through the service you provide and the public esteem in which you are held.

So, did you aim to be invisible? Be honest; for some of you the lure of a public status shrouded in romantic myth may have been alluring - especially those of you whose artistic and creative sensibilities were honed by years of hard work and grueling practice routines. That's another legacy from that Virgo Nadir; at the base of your chart, it can imply that a lot of practice goes into what you do - and what you may do when you're aiming for that Pisces Midheaven is pursue a dream of perfection. Achieving perfection is worth the risk of failure - and Pisces here may take huge risks such is their belief that all will be well. You may be unassuming, yet you can be entrepreneurial; that sixth sense allows you to tune into opportunities that others would miss.

However, perfection, fame and fortune are hard to maintain because they require you to get real - and with Pisces here that's a short-cut to disillusion. Though Pisces on the Midheaven can be uplifting and inspirational, it can also lead to feelings of disappointment. Some of you with this placement may have experienced feelings of underachievement that do not accord with reality. Some of you may have what feels like eternal dissatisfaction with your place on this world and, as the saying goes, this may be accompanied by feelings of the grass being greener somewhere else. So, this placement could potentially undermine your professional achievements by making you doubt yourself - in more ways than one.

Doubt and disillusion can manifest at any time; you don't have to have been in the job for twenty years to experience the nagging realisation that life may have been better if you had done something else. The troublesome issue here is perfection - and perfection can cause paralysis. The stasis of perfection is a problem that affects this Midheaven sign in a notable way. If you grow up believing that everything needs to be perfect, then even choosing a career or having ambition may be blown apart before it even gets off the ground. If you can't achieve perfection, you may give up on having any realistic ambitions at all. You don't know what to do with yourself - and consequently, your dreams fade into oblivion.

To avoid this fate, you need to tune into one of Pisces most favourable qualities - and that's compassion. Compassion is a quality you may bring to your career - in fact it may be something you are recognised for - but it's more effective if you first learn show yourself some compassion. Beating yourself up for not being perfect or because you're not able to fix the world (a hangover from the Virgo Nadir) is something you need to tackle at source; use the hard work you learned at the base of your chart to achieve what you want to achieve and channel that compassionate energy from your heart to those who need it most - starting with yourself. That way, you won't lose yourself in the process. Be kind to yourself - and the world will be kind to you.

Libra IC - Aries MC

You have a gift for making everyone feel valued and part of the team. Use that to your best advantage by becoming team leader.

Libra Nadir

When the Nadir is found in Libra, life begins in a good place. We associate this sign with love, relationships, balance, harmony and a certain style, so those of you with the Nadir in this sign may feel blessed. You may be able to draw on memories of a childhood where creativity and artistic expression was encouraged. You may also have fond memories of a family where good relationships were prized above all else. The family home may have been tastefully appointed - regardless of how much money was available - and you may have been brought up to be always unfailingly polite and courteous.

It sounds perfect, in fact it sounds too perfect and, for some of you, that may have been so. Comfort, security and domestic bliss depend more on actuality than appearance. So, while some of you - hopefully the majority - will relate to the image of a fair, balanced and reasonable start in life, others may have felt that the appearance of family unity and togetherness was not much more than skin deep. As with the other 'dual signs' Gemini and Pisces, Libra is a sign with energy that can go in several directions before a happy compromise is reached - though with Libra the energy thrust is always geared towards compromise. So is that a good thing?

In traditional astrological fashion, it can be both good and less so. Let's deal with the problematic issues first. I'm going to start with the notion of compromise and how this works the context of Libra's traditional role as the peacemaker of the zodiac. There is an implication in this notion that suggests that, despite the harmonious things we associate with this sign, having Libra on the Nadir may indicate that your early home life wasn't so peaceful after all. There may have been an underlying threat of something rather uglier breaking out from time to time.

If you lived in a family where one of your parents had to act as the mediator in family quarrels, or who had to compromise and pacify other family members (or the other parent) to try and avoid a fight breaking out, then the image of Libra on the Nadir becomes rather more complex than we would normally associate with this sign. It may even have been you who took on this role of family mediator and, because of this, you may already be aware that Libra here is not inherently harmonious. Peace is an outcome that must be negotiated and bargained for, and it may not have been achievable despite your best efforts. Sometimes, you must live with an unhappy compromise because that's the only kind of balance that you're going to get.

If that's the background you have, there will have been a considerable psychological impact on you and that will have influenced how you create your own 'home base' or comfort zone. Libra on the Nadir suggests a deep emotional response that is more representative of how we perceive Libra here to be; a desire for peace and harmony in the home and domestic life that is more than simply a compromise between warring factions. It's likely to be fundamentally important to you to create a harmonious home - and that will be both a relational and, often, an aesthetic response too. Home - or the space where you feel the most 'at home' needs to be congenial.

There is no room in your house for discord; that is a red line for you. And remember, Libra is an assertive sign. You are more than capable of ensuring that rules are put in place - and kept in place. You will have negotiated the deal and ensured that your basic needs can be met in full. However, you need the agreement and support of those you live with. Having a supportive relationship that provides the framework for your domestic life is likely to be a priority for you - and that partnership must be a partnership of equals. However you divide the domestic responsibilities, fairness and equality are likely to be at the core of all decisions. That is likely to be an issue where there is little room for compromise.,

So, in the ideal world, what is the best outcome for those who have Libra on the Nadir? The object - as ever - is to create a sense of balance and stability, both emotionally and in a material sense. Creating that nurturing environment involves paying attention to appearances. When your home base looks good then you feel good, as Libra here shows there is a deep connection between external appearance- and how you feel on the inside. This is as true for those who recall their early years as 'a thing of beauty', as it is for those who may have had a more difficult experience. Regardless of the past, everyone with Libra here will feel the need to attach themselves to a beautiful and edifying present.

However, the Nadir also tells us that this desire stems from the past in more ways than one. It's possible that some of you will have inherited a sense of domestic good taste and style from at least one of your parents. It's also possible that this skill or desire to make the world look good will influence your career choice in some way - and that's something that your parents may have encouraged too. In this way, your private needs and desires may become the basis of outer success and, given that Libra is an ambitious sign, it's unlikely that you will ignore the opportunity to use that base to move up in life - and you may want to do so at speed.

ARIES MIDHEAVEN

I'm going to start where the previous section ended. Aries on the Midheaven is a powerful energy and it suggests that you don't waste time where your aims and ambitions are concerned. Usually, we think of the Midheaven in primarily a career context, but life grants us many ambitions - and not all of them are career related. So, it's worth reminding you of what the Midheaven represents in your natal chart. Career, status, public image, and public commitments (like marriage) are certainly among them. So are the things that are important to you because you perceive them to be high status, or they affect how you may judge - or be judged by - others.

So, having the Midheaven in the most impulsive of signs signifies that your approach to any of the things symbolised by this angle, is likely to be direct and to the point. As ever in astrology, the ways in which this plays out in real life may appear varied, but the core dynamics are always the same - and, in this case, they originate from the thing you may have found hardest to deal with in your private life; the de-stabilising, impulsive, aggression that is likely to have been suppressed in your past -

and in your psyche - is the thing that is going to power you into the public arena.

All the things we keep under wraps must emerge somewhere. That's true of all the polarities found on the 'Axis of Experience', however in your case, you're having to deal with an energy that's more explosive than most. That's not necessarily a bad thing; being able to direct your energy to attain the things that you want the most is a useful attribute, and it's likely you will have wasted no time putting it to good use. Let's think about the importance to you of partnerships in establishing that beautiful home base we talked about a moment ago. With Aries here, you may have committed to a life partnership at a younger age than many people do. You may have become a parent at a young age and had to deal with all the responsibilities that come with that status.

None of that is necessarily a problem, as you are also likely to be a person who rises to a challenge. However, you may also tend to rush into relationships or commitments. Rushing into marriage or other committed relationships is one way of achieving the balance and stability in your life that you need so deeply. It's when we get to this point that I hope you can begin to see where some of the issues with this placement may start to arise; being assertive, bold and courageous is one thing. Lack of planning or foresight is another. When it comes to the big issues in life - you have the potential for both.

Let's move on to career matters. You've probably read that having Aries on the Midheaven means you will join the army, prefer a physically active job or one that offers you the chance to develop your leadership skills. Of those statements, I think the final one is the one that may have most resonance with you.

Whatever you do in this life and whatever your vocation may be (and it could have an Aries flavour to it, there is no doubt) you will be the person who is most likely to get to the front and take charge of the situation. You tend to push yourself forward. Your 'work face' is assertive - but not belligerent (unless you sense there is a grave injustice happening in the workplace, in which case you will take up the fight).

Natural leadership ability is usually coupled with a great deal of confidence. You are not one of life's shy or retiring types (in the workplace at least) and you are usually a hard worker who is task oriented. You are likely, however, to have an aversion to dull and repetitive work and, temperamentally, you may be more suited to project-based careers that have a more rapid turnover of tasks and personnel, as that keeps you interested and focused on the job. Other factors in your birth chart also may be influential in that regard.

However, what is your core motivation when it comes to asserting yourself in either a career context or any other matter that affects your status? Once more we need to return to the Nadir and remind ourselves that Libra is essentially a collaborative, team-oriented sign. You will have honed your negotiating and team building skills to the extent that you are able to rise above being simply a team player. You are now the tram leader - and your public status is likely to reflect that - in whatever career path that you pursue. Your public image may, therefore, be one of someone who has made their way in the world due to their own singular efforts - and you may be regarded as a 'self-starter' whose talents and drive enabled you to get ahead of the pack.

Wanting to do things in your own way and being passionate about whatever you have chosen to do, is vitally important to you; that is what really matters. Unless you can be 'number one' in what you do then you may not consider it worth getting out of bed in the morning. Your aim may be to make the world a better place - but you will also be aware of the role that you need to play to achieve that aim. In that way, the oppositional qualities found at both ends of your 'Axis of Experience' may come some way towards meeting in the middle. No wonder you need that peace and harmony when you return home.

Scorpio IC - Taurus MC

Trust your own instincts and follow them; take your place in the world as a productive and respected member of society.

Scorpio Nadir

I'll come straight out and say this. Scorpio on the Nadir may not be the easiest of signs to have at the base of your natal chart. This sign is deeply existential, and it touches everything to do with your home, family and domestic situation with the hand of dread. If that sounds too 'doom-laden' to take in while you're having your morning coffee, think of it this way. Scorpio - more than any other sign - has an instinctive awareness of the fragility of existence. When Scorpio is the sign on an angle in your birth chart, that fragility becomes an issue that affects your life in a visible and tangible way. When it's on the Nadir, it means that the place you come from feels under threat. For many of you with this placement, that threat will have seemed like a real and present danger to you in your early life or family situation.

That sounds dramatic - and I know that many of you may struggle to recall such a potential horror from your childhood years. You may think to yourself, "was it really that bad?", or you may recall a few painful occurrences - but surely everyone experiences those kinds of things, don't they? You would be right to think that. Most of experience all kinds of things when we're growing up - both good and bad. However, with Scorpio on the Nadir, they stay with you - and you feel them more deeply than most. And the things that seem existential to you may appear to be completed normal to other people.

Let's get a few things out in the open here. Scorpio at the base of your natal chart does not imply that you suffered an abusive or violent childhood in a direct sense - though for some of you that may have been the major formative issue in your lives; it will have been a personal tragedy that had to live with and, hopefully, overcome. For others with this placement, there may have been something 'unspoken' affecting the atmosphere in your family home; perhaps your parents had issues in their relationship and although the issues did not affect you directly, you're likely to have sensed that all was not well.

It's also possible that you had a difficult relationship with one of your parents; bullying and power plays are not uncommon with Scorpio here. However, it's also possible that you developed a particularly close bond with one of your parents - the type of bond that may have been difficult to break away from. Either your parent may have found it hard to let go of you - or you may have found it hard to let go of your parent - extreme attachment issues may be associated with Scorpio here. The relationship may or may not have been painful yet facing the fear of letting go can transform something problematic into a deep and genuine bond that respects the autonomy of both parent and child - especially the adult child.

Transformation is the key to living with Scorpio on the Nadir, as attachment issues may go beyond your familial relationships. Scorpio is a fixed sign, and fixed signs like things to be fixed. I have often found that those with a heavy fixed sign emphasis in their charts do not like change. In the context of a Scorpio Nadir, change itself - at a fundamental level - may feel threatening and that's because you may have experienced change as a process you were subjected to against your will. If you're not in control of the process, then that fragile existence you've carved out for yourself can disappear without you being able to do anything to prevent it happening.

You may have experienced that feeling if your parents divorced - understandably so. You may have experienced it if circumstances meant the family needed to relocate - and suddenly the world you knew was taken away from you. Whatever happened to you - no matter how innocent or mundane - it may have felt as if your world fell apart. Scorpio here brings extreme emotional reactions; yet we are all subject to change. So, how can you overcome your fear of that existential threat that is, paradoxically, a far greater threat to your existence than change itself?

Making your internalised base secure is going to involve a major transformation in your approach to this issue - but it's the foundation you need to put in place in order to have a happy, healthy life. To feel secure and grounded, you need your own space, a place where you are in control and can direct any changes as - and if - you want to. The things that feel familiar will always challenge you emotionally, so you need to face up to those fears. Scorpio has a reputation for being fearless - but it's a fearlessness that comes at a price. You know that you must make yourself secure and provide a base for yourself that no-one can take away from you.

That may be a physical home, a family, a sense of belonging to a place, a relationship, an ideal or that deep sense of who you are, but the fundamental thing is for you to be secure in the knowledge of where you are now. The past made you, but you no longer live there - you live in the present. That is your reality. The great challenge for those of you with a Scorpio Nadir is to trust that the present that you construct will exist for as long as you want it too. If things need to change, you will be able to use your past experiences to create a new present that will serve you just as well. Trust in yourself. That's all you need to do.

Taurus Midheaven

The key word that applies to this particular 'Axis of Experience' is security. When you are coming from a place that acknowledges how fragile life can be, it makes sense to head for a place that reduces the risk as much as possible. Taurus is as risk averse as it gets. It's also a powerful energy that is creative, productive and controlled, and when it's on the Midheaven, it's important to you to be recognised as someone who is reliable, steady, trustworthy and dependable. That is risk management in action. You set your store by having a public image that is grounded and solid.

It may seem paradoxical but inner turmoil that can often accompany that Taurus Midheaven as, the tempestuous and volatile Scorpio Nadir will always lurk beneath. However, that's the place you are moving away from; the universe is asking you to become that stable, self-assured person you were intended to be. Material, emotional and social security (in the form of social status rather than welfare payments) mean everything to you; they are not only a badge of success, but they are also a measure of how far you have left the past behind. Of course, we never completely leave the past behind, but we can transform it into a more comfortable present - and this is something at which Taurus excels.

Comfort is everything to those of you with a Taurus Midheaven. That is why you may be drawn to those professions and occupations that make life more comfortable in some way. It may seem like a cliche but making the world a more secure and comfortable place is important to you when you have Taurus here. The world is your security blanket, so you engage with it on that basis. You may - quite literally - have a career in an industry or sector that provides people with food, housing, environmental or financial services. It's not difficult to see how such things - essential for our survival - are rooted in that Scorpio Nadir and the deep need to control the world around you.

Sometimes, Taurus may seem like having Cancer here - but the sign's core motivation is quite different; Taurus seeks physical stability through material and sensual engagement, rather than seek the emotional depths associated with the sign of the crab. Not that Taurus isn't a nurturing sign; physical and emotional comfort is important to you and, even if your career choice doesn't have 'Taurus' written all over it, it is unlikely that you would close a career that made you feel uncomfortable on the inside. To that extent, if your preference is for an occupation that has no stress, no drama, accords with your inner values, brings you a regular paycheck, some prospects for advancement and a good pension plan - that will suit you just fine.

Taurus is materially ambitious; however, your career ambitions are less about ambition for its own sake (leave that to Capricorn) and more about what that achievement can provide you with in terms of your material wellbeing. Less is never more when you have a Taurus Midheaven, and though you may not consider yourself to be a 'conspicuous consumer', your public image will contain as much understated luxury as you can afford. Those of you with a Taurus Midheaven may aspire to be seen as people of good taste and quality, just as much as you want to be regarded as sensible, professional, practical and pragmatic where your 'work-face' is concerned.

It's a combination that enables you assume a position of status in the society in which you live. Status confers security and it propels you towards success in business. The corporate world is often a natural fit for you, as businesses appreciate both your shrewd approach and your careful financial management skills. Running your own business often provides you with a secure structure in which to plan for your own future - and you also benefit from the security and respectability that being a business owner confers. With Taurus here, you commit to a career - whatever that may be - for the long haul and you expect a good return in exchange for investing your time and hard work.

So, does all of this make you feel reliable but dull? One thing that's easy to overlook is how closely Taurus is associated with pleasure. If your aim is to get the best out of life, then pleasure is part of the package. Taurus will not commit to anything that isn't pleasurable - no matter how worthy. There must be something in it for you, and that something includes the satisfaction of knowing that - whatever happens - your efforts have enabled you to have a life filled with plenty of high quality 'rest and relaxation' time. With Taurus on the Midheaven, your efforts are a means to an end - and that end is to be able to indulge yourself in whatever lifestyle choices you prefer.

You want to be seen as someone who has carved yourself an enviable and comfortable place in the world - and there may be many people who are not only envious of your success, but also your ability to appear so relaxed about your responsibilities. It's not that you don't take things seriously - in fact you are more serious than most when it comes to owning your choices and decisions. Above all, Taurus here needs to create something tangible and long lasting - and preferably beautiful too. Like the other Venus-ruled sign, Libra, your career or public status may be recognisable for its aesthetic, artistic or creative content. However, there is a permanence about Taurus that suggests that whatever you do, your intention is to leave a legacy for the benefit of others - and that may be your greatest achievement of all.

Sagittarius IC - Gemini MC

It doesn't matter what you believe as long as you have faith, but use your intellect to define how and why you made that choice.

SAGITTARIUS NADIR

Sagittarius on the Nadir is always going to give you an interesting backstory because of the huge number of potentials that Sagittarius carries within. Everything from extravagance to religion has the potential to have been part of your background noise; however, one thing is certain - less will not have been more. The Sagittarius influence on your family and early life may have been circumstantial (in that this sign is descriptive of your family history and circumstances) or it may be most evident in the character of one - or both - of your parents. In most cases, the wide-ranging nature of this sign may imply that all the above will be true, so let's begin by looking at your family history - because that may be a remarkable one.

Some of you will have come from families whose roots were far away from where you were brought up. You may have even been born overseas yourself. There are many reasons why people - and even whole families - relocate. Economics, persecution, an expansive attitude or a sense of adventure are just a few, but they capture the essence of Sagittarius, in that the impulse that made your immediate ancestors relocate on a global scale is likely to have been freedom. Freedom to shake off the restrictions of poverty and grasp the opportunity to make a better life; freedom to escape from religious or political persecution; freedom to escape from restrictive social attitudes in the hope of being able to live as they wanted to.

Somewhere in your family history there may be an element of this, yet not every family unit touched by Sagittarius will have travelled hundreds - or thousands - of miles to leave the past behind. Your roots may be distant - or even alien to you - but that can arise because your parents felt constrained by their own origins. Issues like social class, education - and the mobility that higher education can bring to people by opening a hitherto unknown world of opportunity. Your parents may have left behind their hometowns, their social class or their familiar world, for the chance of something better. Of course, 'better' is a relative term, so I would tend to look at Sagittarius on the Nadir as a signifier of an upwardly mobile family - though that may or may not be in the material sense.

Being upwardly mobile - or casting your eyes to the heavens - implies a positive belief in the future. That belief may relate to educational, spiritual or material improvements. Sagittarius tends not to distinguish between them, as they are the outcome of that positive approach, rather than the cause of it. Whatever the outward manifestation, you are likely to have experienced your birth family life as one that had moved on and become better for it. Yet, there may also have been an undercurrent of restlessness. Sagittarius here is not necessarily an indicator of stability; it's a mutable sign and the atmosphere in your home may have suggested that the family journey was not yet complete.

You may have experienced your own background as something you could not wait to escape from. Education or travel may have opened your eyes to future possibilities and, although

Sagittarius speaks of freedom, your early years may have not made you feel as free as you would have liked to have been. The desire to escape may have taken root in you at an early age. Your family may have been religious or had a particular perspective on life that you disagreed with, as it made you feel constrained; the paradox of freedom is that one generation's freedom to live as they wish is not necessarily shared by their children - especially if the parents views have been imposed on their offspring. An element of parental distance may also be experienced with Sagittarius here.

Your own personal space may, therefore, be important to you. You may have as spacious a home as you can afford, or you may prefer to live in an area that is surrounded by open space - such as a rural or coastal area. You may also like your space to be 'wild' or challenging in some way; being 'off-grid' may have a certain appeal. You may be fortunate if your family background provided you with enough material wealth to enable you to make that choice. However, even if your circumstances were more modest, you are unlikely to have been constrained by that. True freedom functions best at an inner level; your own sense of personal freedom is likely to have been a major component is establishing your own secure emotional base.

It's a base where your inner needs and outer reality will always meet in the middle. You feel most at ease with yourself when you're surrounded by the things that represent your deep need to explore life - and the world - in all its glory. So, some of you will 'travel light', preferring not to have too much responsibility or too many ties that would prevent you from travelling at a moment's notice. Others will care little for the traditional 'comforts of home', preferring to be surrounded by books, papers and ephemera collected on numerous voyages. Your home may be connected to academic pursuits, or, in some cases, the place you call home may be connected to a religious establishment. Setting up home in a disused church may attract you. A strong belief system is something that is a fundamental requirement for you.

So, however your own Sagittarius Nadir manifests, it will signify that being true to yourself is the base upon which all other aspects of your life will be built. Being true to yourself is the quality that underpins freedom in its deepest sense; if that means you remain free of the ties of being 'settled' in a way that more domestically oriented people would find disturbing, then so be it. If it also means you find your own comfort zone far away from where you were born, or you adopt a broad philosophy that enables you to take a more relaxed approach to your prospects - that's okay too. You will travel where the mood takes you; that is inevitable with a Sagittarius Nadir.

GEMINI MIDHEAVEN

The complement to that Sagittarius base is to have the Midheaven in Gemini. When you are confident that you have the freedom to explore life, Gemini here must seem heaven sent. Your aim is to share your experiences and knowledge with the wider world; however, the problem is working out how to do that. It's not that you don't know what to say, but you may have difficulty narrowing down your career options to one job as you seem suited for so many. Having a lot of options on the table is a particular dilemma with Gemini at the Midheaven and it can make it difficult to commit to a singular career path.

The problem may be one of indecision; it may also be due to flexibility or versatility. It may be due to all those things, but one thing is certain; you are likely to have multiple careers throughout your working life - and some of you may even run more than one at a time. Gemini at the Midheaven can imply that you are a Jack (or Jill) of all trades. That's a traditional view of this placement, but it's not one I entirely agree with. Although it's possible, it tends to portray you as someone who is inconsistent, or who is reluctant to engage with a career in depth - or with the application required to become an acknowledged expert in a particular field. To be labelled as a 'dilettante' or 'dabbler' is unfair to those with Gemini here, as you're about to discover.

The Midheaven represents the point at which you realise your potential, and the sign of your Midheaven suggests the ways in which you achieve that. With Gemini here, you may approach your career or social role with a degree of flexibility, but the key to unlocking your potential is to identify a role that enables you to incorporate that flexibility and 'space to breathe' into your public image and career. There is no doubt that many people with this placement will be attached to those careers that allow a degree of mobility (either mentally or physically) or make use of a talent for communication or academic ability. However, to suggest that that is all there is to offer is simply not true. It's about being connected, so careers in education, journalism, sales, or public facing roles where you enable others to access the information they need.

Any front of house or customer facing role - from a librarian to a taxi driver - may appeal to you, but the deeper (if it's possible to use that word in a Gemini context) rationale underpinning your career choice is that you need to be connected to the outside world - as well as free to make your own connections or make connections between other people. This sign at the Midheaven implies that you need to be part of the world around you - and recognisably so. Your role is to bring people and information together - what they do with it once you have performed that task is not your concern.

This is one of the reasons why many careers that require a Gemini approach have an air of being 'short-term' about them. Even those of you who have a sensible and stable long-term position will often discover that this is only possible because your tasks are subject to regular changes. Your role may involve project-based work - so there is always the level of change that maintains your interest. You may have a position that requires you to work flexibly - perhaps in more than one location (something that ties in well with your Sagittarius Nadir) or you may act as a consultant who is able to connect others to ways of working that are more advantageous to them. Having an appreciation for the ways in which things are connected may also have a practical application with Gemini here.

Though we usually think of Virgo, as the 'hands on' Mercury sign, Gemini on the Midheaven is just as adept at transferring information from one medium to another, for example, the information on an architectural or engineering drawing needs to be, literally, transferred to the ground or the machine. There is also a more generalised point that needs to be made; Gemini here shows an interest in making information accessible and widely available. You keep that information updated - old news is of no use to you. You see where changes need to be made and you pass that information to those who are best placed to put it into effect

- most likely your Virgo Midheaven cousins with their eye for detail.

So, with Gemini at the Midheaven, where are you headed? There is no one answer to that question - a fact that will leave you mightily relieved. However, even Gemini on the Midheaven needs a steer. When you're in two minds about your life's direction of travel - almost inevitable with Gemini here - remember what matters to you most. It's not where you end up, it's how you get there, and your journey will be more interesting than most. You may be the king or queen of multi-tasking; in fact, that may be the talent that you are noted for, and you may thrive on it. However, it's not the only thing you are recognised for. Your networking skills are superb. If you don't know something, then you will connect with someone else who has the information you need

Not that you're short of answers. Your thoughts, words and impressions count for something. In fact, they may make you more influential than you thought was possible. Why is that? The answer to that lies in the power of communication - and what it means to be the person who gives voice to the ideas that make a difference to people's lives. And you make a difference because you are one of life's problem solvers. You provide the answers to the myriad of questions that would otherwise remain a cause of mystery to those less connected to the world than you. Knowing what makes the world turn is perhaps your true ambition; you are driven by a need to know - and the supply of information is infinite.

Capricorn IC - Cancer MC

You may take your work home with you;
no-one senses the public mood as well as
you.

Capricorn Nadir

When I see Capricorn at the Nadir, it's often a signifier of a disciplined start in life. The traditional family. Old-fashioned family values. Those are the phrases that leap out - albeit in a restrained manner - when the Nadir is situated in the sign of the goat. Capricorn's influence extends over your family background in both an immediate and a more distant sense, and there are a variety of scenarios that carry the Capricorn imprint. I'll begin with the most obvious, your parents. One or the other of your parents may have the sign emphasised in their own natal chart. Of course, that can be interpreted that one of them is a solar Capricorn, but let's give astrology a little more credit than that.

The Nadir - in your case - is planted in the most ambitious of the earth signs. Business, authority, civic duty; all of those are themes that may have influenced your early life because of familial or parental involvement in those areas. Your family may have enjoyed a particular social status; maybe you were a 'respectable' or respected family. You may have been made aware of this at an early age - and even if that status was historic (and no longer applies) it will be something passed down in family history. The past and the present are closely aligned when the Nadir (the cusp of the fourth house associated with the Moon and the sign of Cancer) is found in the sign of Capricorn, the sign most closely associated with the tenth house, Saturn and the Midheaven.

What we have here is an inversion of qualities, and that theme of reversal may be one that has resonance with you when you look at your family history or familial lived experience. Your mother, for example may have been the more powerful parent. Although I tend to associate the fourth house with both parents, its maternal associations are well established. This particular 'Axis of Experience' can suggest a 'matriarchy', a family of powerful women who formed the bedrock of the family because they were sensible, capable, hardworking and tough. Maybe they had to be that way to survive - and to ensure the survival of the family. It's a selection of qualities that also speaks of a certain emotional resilience - and a lack of warmth.

It would be cruel to say that Capricorn at the Nadir is a sign of emotional frigidity or repression, though I know that some of you reading this may have endured that kind of experience in your early life. In most cases, I doubt that such behaviour was deliberate; it may have felt cruel to you, but most people respond emotionally to their circumstances. If your parent(s) behaved that way, it's likely they had a tough start in life too - though that doesn't in any way excuse cruelty or neglect. There is sometimes a sense of alienation with this sign - though it tends to arise from a marked sense of emotional distance rather than a sense of personal rebellion. Again, there may be a variety of reasons for this, even if the outcome is the same.

Capricorn is a lonely sign. With this sign at the Nadir, it's possible you were raised by a lone parent. Of course, that's not uncommon, but in most instances of single-parenting, order, discipline and material security can be big issues - not because your family life was disordered, ill-disciplined or insecure I hasten to add - but because there would have been an acknowledgement that these things matter. Capricorn is one of the proud signs; to succeed despite the odds may have been drilled into you at an early age. You may have been expected to work hard at school - or for your pocket money or allowance. You may have even been expected to get a job as soon as you were able to.

This may have been to help with the family finances, but I suspect it was a means of making you realise the importance of being able to take care of yourself at an early age. That is also a common theme with the Nadir in this sign. One reason for this is that Capricorn here can indicate your parents were older than the parents of your peers. You may have been a long waited for child and some of you may have been an only child. As ever in astrology, there are advantages and disadvantages to every situation, and I'll deal with the downside first. Those of you who were born to older parents may have had to come to terms with losing a parent sooner than most of us and that may have contributed to your sense of having to take care of yourself.

Singletons may have felt lonely, but your early socialisation would have been done in 'adult mode'. As a result, you may have had a mature outlook at an earlier age than your peer group. Another potential upside to this placement is that you will have experienced an upbringing that was big on realism - and keeping your feet on the ground is the place that you come from today. You never get ahead of yourself because you know how important it is to live your life fully engaged in the present. Of all the Nadir placements, this is the one that knows, instinctively, how important it is to build a secure base. When you're on your own, you only have yourself to rely on.

So, for those of you with Capricorn at the Nadir, you feel grounded (and earth signs need to feel grounded) by following in the traditions of your family. Whether you like it or not, you come from a place where being 'down to earth' is a way of life. You are disciplined, responsible and you know that hard work is the best way to get a good start in life. If there is a danger with this, it's that you may repeat with your own family, the emotional distance you experienced as a child. And some of you may choose not to have a family - or you keep your family small - better to produce offspring of quality rather than quantity. You're likely to devote considerable time to ensuring your children enjoy a good start in life and you may be ambitious for them.

CANCER MIDHEAVEN

At first glance, Cancer and Capricorn on the 'Axis of Experience' is one of those pairings that seems poles apart. Steady Capricorn and emotional Cancer seem so far distant in terms of experience that it seems hard to imagine how one could inform the other. However, what they have in common is something called tenacity. Both signs are persistent, determined and never give up. They are qualities that may have defined your start in life, and they are how you intend to make the best of your time this Earth. The Midheaven in Cancer shows that you have been quietly ambitious about achieving a certain status in life. No matter who you are and what you do, you are aware of the importance of not only achieving your aims, but to holding on to what you have achieved.

The background that emphasised the importance of a solid start in life was undoubtedly a benefit to you. It may have helped you to hone your instincts and develop a feel for the best route to take - especially where your career is concerned. Knowing which moves to make - and when - is, for you, the best route to success. Outer displays of naked ambition are not your style. You prefer to identify your target and move towards it in a way that may seem imperceptible to those who have a more direct focus. The crab may move sideways - but that doesn't mean that you take your eyes from the prize. So, how does that work in practice? If you appear quiet and unassuming, how are you going to stand out from the crowd? That's a tough question to answer with Cancer here, because your instincts will be telling you to not stand out from the crowd at all.

The Midheaven is the place where we are recognised for our public status and identity, so remaining hidden may seem a strange way to approach this most impersonal of spaces. Yet, there is a method to your apparent madness. You fit into society by having a work face that connects with people at an intensely personal - and often emotional - level. In the workplace - or in any public position - you have an ability to connect with people as individuals in a way that makes them feel appreciated. If you're the boss, for example, you're likely to make time to get to know those who work for you. You may take an interest in their wellbeing, and you are likely to want to be appraised of any concerns that they may have - at both a work and personal level.

This public facing care and compassion is certainly genuine - but it's also a shrewd move. By creating a familial feeling in the workplace, you aim to get the best out of people by making them feel comfortable. In your world, emotional satisfaction is more conducive to achievement than conflict or aggression. In a position of authority your work face is, therefore, likely to be parental and, if those in your family do the job they are supposed to do, then all will be well. That same dynamic applies regardless of where you sit in the corporate structure. There is always someone in the office who personalises their workspace, making it a comfortable extension of their home. That person is likely to be you. Cancer Midheaven is the person who will remember everyone's birthdays and will even supply cake; after all every workspace needs a mother.

Cancer is a protective and nurturing sign and those are the qualities you are recognised for. This may be so at an individual level, but your public identity is more likely to be hidden within a structure that enables the real you to remain out of sight. By responding to people's needs, the focus is not on what you do, but on what you do for others. This Midheaven is well represented in the nurturing professions - and that can be anything from nursing, early years teaching and childcare to providing homes or working in the food supply business or catering - a form of feeding the masses. What those careers - or vocations - have in common is that they create safe spaces and a feeling of comfort. They also create a space where those with a Cancer Midheaven can achieve a deep sense of emotional satisfaction through a public facing social or work role.

Work that includes an emotional or feeling element may be important to you, especially if you have found personal emotional satisfaction hard to access or express. Past experiences may have contributed to this, and it's something that may continue to impact on your private life. However, taking care of people in a public sense is a way of bolstering your own emotional security - and security in a wider sense may also play a role in providing you with a career outlet. We tend to think of assertive signs like Aries as being a natural fit with roles in our defence forces and security services; it fits the image we have of machismo and courage. Cancer, however, is a defensive sign; an emotional connection to home and homeland will often prompt a similar career choice - but for very different reasons.

The core issue here is one of how you feel about the things that are important to you. The Midheaven in Cancer is likely to feel deeply bonded to matters connected to homes, family matters, social bonds and issues affecting the country in which you live. Cancer on the Midheaven gives an ability to connect with the public mood in ways that make those with this placement effective diplomats and politicians. Even if you don't engage with those careers on a professional basis, you're likely to share the same skillset; again, it's down to wanting to protect and create a safe space at a social or societal level. You may be attracted to working for organisations that do that - they may be charitable or non-governmental, but they enable you to secure your emotions by securing the lives of other people.

Like the other water signs, Scorpio and Pisces, Cancer is imaginative. When placed on the Midheaven, the ability to tune into what people want gives you the potential to create and satisfy the public mood in an artistic sense. Creating art is a process that involves the emotions - and it involves emotional release in an indirect manner for the creator. That suits the dynamics of this sign in the public arena. Comparatively few of you will become professional artists but working in the arts in some capacity may provide a similar sense of emotional engagement, and in true Cancer style, you may engage with art in public yourself - and find it satisfying to do so. Those visits to public museums and art galleries? They may be more important to your emotional wellbeing than you care to admit.

Aquarius IC - Leo MC

You know that you're different and you want to live by your ideals; use your creative powers to make that possible. For everyone.

AQUARIUS NADIR

Aquarius at the Nadir is, perhaps, not the easiest of IC placements to live with. On one hand, it's a sign associated with innovation, independence and originality. On the other hand, it can be chaotic, destabilising and revolutionary in all senses. So, has this sign given your personal and family history a radical emphasis or has it helped to make you the independently minded, progressive yet unconventional person you are today? The answer is likely to be both, so let's look a little closer at the reality for those of you with Aquarius here. The first thing to note is the presence of something fundamentally unconventional at the heart of your home and family life. The place you have come from is likely to be a 'one-off'; not everyone will have had a family life yours.

In astrology, all placements can come with a variety of interpretations. They will share the same dynamics of the sign involved, but there will be a variety of outcomes that are either positive or otherwise. With the Nadir in Aquarius, it's possible that the differences between the two positions could fall at the more extreme ends of the spectrum. For example, the Nadir in Aquarius could place your origins in a family who were markedly socially aware, politically active, intellectually engaged or idealistic.

They are traits that blend well together, and if your family background fell at that end of the Aquarius spectrum, you may have been well versed in all those things as you grew up. They may have been a notable feature in your family history - and you would have considered such things a 'normal' part of your upbringing.

Aquarius is a socially concerned sign. It's future oriented, but it's also an impersonal sign. Yet the Nadir marks the most intensely private and personal part of your natal chart. If you have this placement in Aquarius, the convictions and ideals that influenced you in your early years are likely to be deeply held; they form the bedrock of the way in which you are likely to experience the world and wish to be seen by it too. All that sounds logical - this is Aquarius and logic plays a starring role - but what are the downsides to this Nadir? The depth of feeling with which you hold onto your ideals may make you a revolutionary at heart, but there is more to life than waving a placard.

The Nadir is the place where you establish your own base. It's where you feel most safe and secure. It's deeply emotive - and as Aquarius is an unemotional sign, that may signify there are some serious issues that need to be addressed. If the background emphasis was on things outside of the home - which it may have been with this sign - it's possible that at a deeply personal level, you may have felt overlooked. When I wrote about the Nadir in Capricorn, I mentioned that it was often a sign of being emotionally cool. Traditionally ruled by Saturn, Aquarius shares this feature, but I would describe Aquarius's emotional distance as being one of alienation - more in keeping with the influence of Uranus, this sign's co-ruler. Alienation is a sign of 'disconnection' and, whether by choice or otherwise, a certain emotional disconnect is often a feature with the Nadir in this sign.

Emotional disconnection happens when we detach from issues that may be too difficult to process. The placement of the Nadir suggests that your background may have contained emotional experiences that were difficult to deal with. They may appear in a variety of guises and, as with all matters that are intensely personal, who am I (or anyone else for that matter) to tell you what those experiences are or how you should respond to them? The important thing is that they happened, and you need to adjust and make yourself emotionally secure in response. Detachment is simply one way of doing that because, ultimately, it enables you leave the past behind. This is, perhaps, where you find your sweet spot. Of all the signs, your base needs to be defined by looking forward - and never back.

This can make you something of a pioneer who does things in your own way. Even your definition of family is likely to differ from what many would consider to be 'the norm'. Family - to you - will be those you feel most comfortable with. Being with like-minded souls may be preferable to associating with your blood relatives, in fact your birth family may make you feel stressed or uncomfortable in some way. Aquarius is a fixed sign, yet it is, paradoxically, associated with instability and change thanks to its relationship with Uranus. If you endured chaotic living conditions in your early years, or your life was subject to rapid and destabilising changes such as those that result from parental divorce for example, then you may relish the freedom to set your own rules, standards and timetable. No-one is going to tell you how to live your life.

So, let's assume that you've achieved the level of personal freedom that is so important to you. What happens next? What do you do with it? What you need to bear in mind is that the dynamics of Aquarius don't stop affecting you – and you cannot leave the past behind completely - no matter how hard you try. The denial form of detachment is emotionally unhealthy. The best outcome is to incorporate a re-imagined version of the past into the present and use it to plan a better future. In practice, that means you need to incorporate all the independent, progressive features of your Nadir's sign into your private life. The things that inform your comfort zone need to be unique and unlike anything you experienced growing up.

Whether you live in a modern house, fill your home with the latest gadgets, or live in a domestic situation that reflects your own free-thinking and independent needs, those things will reflect the way in which you feel most secure. Inner security is a personal thing, yet it manifests externally in the way we arrange our personal and domestic lives. If your personal and emotional reality is forward looking, that may reflect in your personal living preferences; you're unlikely to favour old homes over new - except in those instances where an old building may be re-purposed in an unusual way to provide accommodation. That's simply one example but I'm sure you get the idea; when it comes to your private life - and your own personal emotional foundation - you dance to your own tune.

Leo Midheaven

The freedom to be yourself on a grand stage is something that you may aspire to when you have the Midheaven in the sign of Leo. Of course, how you achieve that aim will be personal to you, and the ease (or otherwise) of your journey will be dictated by the way in which you have secured your foundations as described above. It's our foundation that prepares the way by instilling in us a sense of certainty. Knowing that you have a safe space to return to - should you need to re-trace your steps - is an important part of anyone's reality, regardless of the pair of signs on the 'Axis of Experience'. With the Aquarius-Leo axis, many of you will have a head start.

Aquarius at the Nadir has an independent and, some would say, bloody minded approach to becoming centred; the focus on independence and personal freedom at one end of this axis is a great base on which to secure those things you are motivated to achieve. With any luck you will have secured a great deal of confidence - even if it was hard won - and confidence is the key to making the best of a Leo Midheaven. Like Aquarius, Leo is the sign of the individual. Associated with the most creative forms of personal expression, Leo at the Midheaven brings those qualities to the public arena. So, when we look at how this sign influences your career choices, your 'work face', ambitions and public status, it's Leo's qualities of positivity, courage, warmth, generosity and sincerity that govern your approach. A certain theatricality also helps.

Leo has a sense of fun. When this is applied to its influence on the Midheaven, one thing is clear; you are regarded as someone who knows how to enjoy yourself. Whatever career you are drawn to, it needs to be enjoyable to you and you won't countenance taking on a job that is anything less than that. Dull, routine and mundane are not your thing (unless you truly get a kick out of them…) but it would be lazy astrology to suggest that all of you with Leo at the Midheaven seek fame and fortune above all else - particularly the 'fame' part of the equation. However, you are unlikely to be happy in a position where your contribution is ignored. You aim to be recognised for what you do and, while some of you may have a talent for self-promotion, I suspect most of you will work hard at ensuring it is the quality of your work that gains the applause.

Leo is a proud sign. On the Midheaven, it tells us that you take pride in your achievements. You believe in setting a good example and that is one of the reasons why many of you will have good leadership skills. The confidence that is sustained by your independent, spirited base travels well to the public domain; whether it's a workplace, a social enterprise or a civic entity, your positivity can inspire others to follow your lead. You are likely to be a good public speaker, as Leo is an expressive and performative sign. We tend to associate communication with Gemini, but Leo has a flair for presentation of all kinds; it's likely that this will form part of your skillset in any career you choose. It's also a skillset that makes you persuasive and entertaining; you know how to put people at ease.

So far, so good. There is no doubt that a Leo Midheaven is one to be admired. It gives you a platform from which you can look down at the world and direct your considerable energies to make it a better place to be - for all of us. That's the considerable upside of this placement. In astrology, as in life, there are always downsides too. The lofty position you may attain because of the recognition of your skills or talents, may lead you to believe that you were entitled to that destiny. On occasions, there may be those with this placement who doubt the need to earn their elevated status. Conflating your personal ambitions with automatic success is not a wise move. It can lead to arrogance, entitlement, domineering or vainglorious behaviour. Just because you have a Leo Midheaven, it doesn't make you the first choice for boss.

Learning to tailor your ambitions with the realities of the situation in which you find yourself is a challenge you will have to face. The concept of 'face' also may be something of an issue for you, as you are someone who will live or die by your reputation. If that sounds dramatic, it's because it is - or that's how it may seem if you have the Midheaven in Leo. The thought of any form of failure (real or imagined) equates to public humiliation in your eyes - and it's a fate you will do anything to avoid. It may prey on your mind, yet you are unlikely to let your concerns show in public. Your public image is, therefore, something over which you exert considerable control. Appearance and reality may be at odds - yet the show will go on.

With this Midheaven sign, what the world is asking you to be is an example to us all. To lead with humility, to follow with grace and to be proud of your achievements - whatever they may be - is the way to achieve status and admiration. Use the qualities of your Leo Midheaven to guide and inspire others; this is the sign that puts you in the spotlight, so use that light to lift the spirits of those of us who need to be reminded that life is not all bad. What this achieves, is more than simple appreciation; it reminds you that you are no longer the child who is overlooked. You are no longer detached or alienated; you as an individual have been validated in the best sense. By being free to be yourself you have become free to express your best self without shame or fear.

Pisces IC - Virgo MC

You are an open book, receptive to the undercurrents that flow through your veins. Let competence and humility carve a path to your place in the world.

Pisces Nadir

I'm not saying your family was a boundary free zone but there is something ill-defined at the core of Pisces at the Nadir. When things drift or when they are uncertain, we find ourselves having to adapt. The phrase, 'to go with the flow' is somewhat overused - and though it appears to describe the reality of a Pisces background, the truth is always more complex than it first appears. Pisces is a multifaceted sign, so the most straightforward way (if that's possible) of looking at your personal history, your family and those things that make you feel secure is to acknowledge that security, for you, may have an entirely different context than it does for more unimaginative souls than you. To appreciate where I'm coming from with that, you're going to have to use your imagination…

Fortunately, you'll find that easy to do. One of the things that may have marked your early years - regardless of your family situation - was the ability to lose yourself in another world. You may have been the family daydreamer. You may have appeared shy or hesitant to engage with the rough and tumble of the world around you. It's something that may have set you apart from your siblings or peers, but it's a quality that will have perhaps puzzled your other family members - and even your parents - so while they may have remarked on it, they may also have chosen to ignore it as much as humanly possible. After all, a quiet and reflective child is far less to worry about than a total tearaway. However, still waters run deep; you will have noticed all the currents and tides that surged around your family home - and it's likely your escapist tendencies evolved for a reason.

Personal circumstances often dictate how we respond to our immediate surrounds. With Pisces - unlike Sagittarius - the desire to escape is directed inwards, and an inner desire to transcend - or simply be elsewhere - can indicate that the outer world is troublesome to deal with at an emotional level. Being overwhelmed by issues that you cannot resolve - or simply do not understand - is a frightening experience. Pisces at the Nadir can indicate a background that included some of those experiences; problematic (and often hidden) family issues such as alcoholism or drug abuse may have affected some of you. At the time, you may not have been overtly aware of what was happening, yet you will have sensed that all was not well. That feeling may have been reinforced by adult behaviours intruding into your childhood in ways that you should not have had to experience.

Children should not have to be confronted by - or deal with - the fallout from the grown-up world. Yet that may have impacted the early life of some of you. Neglect, instability and insecurity come in many forms, but with Pisces here, you will have had your own way of dealing with that - and it's called hope. Pisces is perhaps the most adaptable sign; whatever comes your way, you can shift and become whatever you need to be. Pisces remarkable positivity and optimism are often overlooked qualities, but with Pisces at the Nadir, they are often the bedrock of your existence;

they are the things that get you through - no matter what life throws at. you. And that's because experience has taught you well.

If your life has been subject to shifting tides, you will have learned to let go. It's your way of dealing with the uncertainty of the world around you and it enables you to face the future with rather more confidence than you would otherwise have. There is, however, a downside to this. There is the possibility that you may gloss over the past, pretending all was well when it was rather less so. You may also find it hard to maintain clear boundaries between yourself and those who may have let you down in the past - and who may let you down in the future. Pisces at the Nadir suggests you may struggle to draw the line between your own interests and the demands of family members or the people with whom you live. Sometimes it may be self-inflicted, as you may struggle to respect the boundaries of other people too. With Pisces, it's always a two-way street.

The issue here is that you come from a place of empathy and universal love. You are the person who will walk a mile in someone else's shoes - and that makes you susceptible to the very issues you had hoped to escape from in your early years. One of the reasons for this is that you may have been brought up to always think of others needs before your own. With Pisces here, that may have been an unconscious process, rather that diktat from on high. You may have been subliminally aware of other people's needs because you absorbed the emotional signs more effectively than most. Those signs would have been subliminal; passive aggression and emotion blackmail are insidious because they turn your emotions against you. One way of avoiding difficult emotional reactions is to head them off at the pass.

Pisces is one of the great peacekeeping signs; Libra will keep the peace through negotiation, but Pisces does it by anticipation. That sixth sense works to avoid confrontation - and confrontation is something you cannot deal with at all. It's too emotionally upsetting, and your background may have honed your sixth sense to the extent that you tune into other people's needs even when that works against your own interests. However, the needs you really need to tap into are your own. Developing some compassion for yourself is where you truly need to be coming from and, by the way, doing so does not come at the expense of your empathy with others. Without that self-compassion, the stormy, moody and self-defeating tendencies of the Pisces Nadir will drown you before you set sail.

Self-compassion enhances your sensitivity in a much more productive way. That is the outcome you need to be aiming for, as it takes you on the journey towards the other end of the 'Axis of Experience', the Virgo Midheaven. However, before you take your first steps, you need to ensure that your base is as stable as it can be. That can be a challenge for all of those with a water sign at the Nadir - and Pisces especially. When the base of your natal chart is fluid, you need a sturdy ship, a vessel that allows you to sail to the destination of your choice without being blown off-course. You also need to be able to find a secure anchorage, as there is nothing worse for you than being cast adrift. Perhaps the keynote of a Pisces Nadir, however, is this: you are at your most emotionally secure when you know you belong to no-one but yourself.

VIRGO MIDHEAVEN

Let's assume that you are to become the captain of your ship. You have a background that is, as we have seen, rather flexible in nature. This means that you're adaptable. You know how to make the best of any situation and your sixth sense gives you head start when it comes to working out which direction to take. You're keenly perceptive and your imaginative faculties enable you to visualise outcomes, solutions and possibilities that would seem impossible to those less visionary than you. However, to achieve status in society, you need to be more than a dreamer. You need to turn your visions into reality - and do so with a degree of competence that proves you are more than the dreamer everyone assumed you to be. That is the challenge of a Virgo Midheaven.

The assumption that many would make, is that the elements of dreaminess, boundary issues and a less than stable background would make it difficult for you to even know which way to go, let alone set foot on the path towards the ultimate prize. To assume that would be to underestimate you - and where you are coming from. Overcoming such issues is likely to have made you a strategic thinker who knows the value of planning and foresight. Avoiding disaster will have become a priority for you in your personal life - and it's one that serves you well as you move out into the professional arena. You have become adept at problem solving, personal organisation and making things work out - and those are the qualities you need to focus on to prove your mastery of the game of life.

And those are the qualities that make your practical and realistic about your chances of success. You are where you are, and you're determined to make the best of it. That involves having a vision of where you want the journey to take you, that is both achievable - yet it also involves a great deal of self-improvement. Self-improvement is a core motivation when you have Virgo at the top of your natal chart. You know, from experience, that without it, you'll be destined to remain in subservient roles that fail to maximise your potential - yet many people with this Midheaven take on service roles in a professional capacity. However, there is a world of difference between expected to service other people's emotional needs and making a conscious decision to provide a competent, professional service that finds solutions to specific problems.

With the Midheaven in Virgo, you are likely to be drawn towards roles that capitalise on your organisational and managerial skills. It's an externalised expression of the Virgo impulse 'to make things work' and it draws on the experience of the Pisces Nadir where you learned how to make things work for you at a deeply personal level. This outward application is, of course, less personal than that, but it enables you to ensure that your outer world in kept in working order. Many of you are more likely to work for an organisation than be self-employed - though self-employment can't be ruled out. So, while some of you will create your own business entity, most of you will fit into existing organisational structures with ease; in fact, you're likely to thrive there because you are always willing to take responsibility for your own actions - and those of others too.

Virgo at the Midheaven has a distaste for chaos and this makes you focused, analytical and somewhat functional in your approach to your work and career. You may even be regarded in that way, as the person in the organisation who 'gets things done'.

In either scenario, you're likely to develop new skillsets to cope with changes or future challenges that come your way. Many of you will also gravitate towards career sectors that involve practical, 'hands-on' skills as Virgo, like Gemini, is a dexterous sign. However, the Virgo impulse is directed towards being useful and making things better than they were and, because of that, many of you may find your place in the healthcare, training, 'problem solving', consultancy and teaching professions. It's not difficult to see how Pisces 'universal love' can be channeled productively.

The Midheaven is where we find our place in the world, and that involves developing your confidence to a level that enables you to pursue your ambitions. That process involves identifying the things that are important to you; it's a process of prioritisation. With a Virgo Midheaven you are great at process, because it involves logical progression based on your critical evaluation of each stage of the process itself. This enables you to tailor your adaptability to suit any shifts in circumstance, and it allows you to be flexible without appearing to be out of control - and being out of control is likely to be your greatest fear. 'Out of control' is a place you do not wish to return to; many of you will have to work hard to avoid being dragged back to the place where you began.

Perhaps the ultimate experience of the Virgo Midheaven is to direct your critical faculties in a constructive manner - and that is not always easy. Just as it is easy for you to be critical of your own performance, it is easy for you to be critical of other people too - particularly in the workplace. You may be great at solving problems, but you don't want to become the problem. Strained relationships with those in power, or with those who work alongside you or under your direction, does not a happy workplace make. One issue may be your need to control and that's a reaction to the 'out of control' scenario we discussed earlier. Control freakery is not necessarily the best antidote to this; it's far better to take a systematic approach and appreciate that everyone has a useful role to play. Try and avoid getting a reputation as a whining, hyper-critical perfectionist who sets standards that no-one can meet.

Avoiding being dragged down must be a conscious decision. It's not a given that you will find the competence required by a Virgo Midheaven easy to achieve; in fact, the opposite is likely to be true. There may be something in you that needs to be healed before you can begin to heal other people or the world in which you live. Any outer ambitions you may have will often need to be framed by an inner need to overcome what you perceive as your own flaws and limitations. However, this Midheaven placement may enable you to heal yourself by enabling the healing of others. By becoming an educator, providing healthcare, mental and physical therapy, or by ensuring your 'work face' (regardless of your profession) is that of someone who is recognisably competent, your own healing process is assured.

Chapter Four

Planets Conjunct the Angles

One thing that can't be ignored is the presence of any planet close to a cardinal point. Planets conjunct angles and, to a certain extent, any planets that fall in the angular houses, are particularly elevated in your chart, as their energies are integral to whatever is represented by the cardinal point that they are connected to. So, a planet close to the Ascendant will be a key influence on your self-image; a planet close to the Descendant will influence your partnership complex; a planet close to the Midheaven will play a significant role in your career choice or public image and a planet close to the Nadir will have a significant role in how you view your home and family - and how you form your own personal foundation.

For the purposes of this book, I've focused on the planets that are conjunct the cardinal points and, in accordance with astrological convention, planets that are conjunct the Descendant and the Nadir are listed as being opposite the Ascendant or Midheaven. I have also assumed that any planet in aspect to a cardinal point will be 'in orb' if it's within 8°-9° of the angle (I would give the Sun and Moon that extra degree). Of course, even that simple exercise throws up a few questions. First, you may have planets in the angular houses of your birth chart that are 'out of orb' to the cardinal point. How much weight should these be given when you're working out how your own 'Cross of Matter' functions?

In response I would say this. The planets in angular houses should certainly be interpreted by their house position. They will be prominent and influential in your chart to a certain extent *because* they are in angular houses, but they will not be so influential as they would be if they were in orb to the house cusp itself. As I've said before in this book, the devil is in the detail, as things aren't necessarily as straightforward as they would first appear to be. For example, a person with an 'out of orb' stellium in an angular house may find that it is a much more powerful influence than a single planet conjunct a cardinal point. As with many things, it depends on the 'flavour' of the natal chart and the patterns it contains.

This brings me to a second point. When planets are conjunct a cardinal point, they may be in the house either side of that cardinal point. For example, a planet conjunct the Ascendant may be in either the first house or the twelfth house - and they are very different places to be. The nature of the house influences how and where a planet's expression is experienced - and when a planet is conjunct an angle, I think we must take a really nuanced view of this. I would tend to interpret the expression of the planet in an angular house as being more outwardly directed. If the planet falls in the house behind the angle - a cadent house - the planet's expression may be more reflective or internalised, or it may become more cerebral or intellectualised in some form.

For example, Mars in the fourth house conjunct the Nadir may indicate someone who is coming from a place where assertion or aggression forms part of their family history (military service, active in sports or, sadly, even domestic or sexual violence) or it may have played a formative role in how that person learned to stand on their own two feet - for example, they may have focused their energies towards creating a home and family life. Place that angular Mars in the third house and the expression becomes associated with verbal assertiveness (a sharp tongue), mental incisiveness or maybe an inner drive to keep busy - even hyperactively so.

The planet that conjuncts the angle may be in a different sign to the angle, particularly if the angle falls close to an early or late degree of the sign in which it falls. The planet will express according to its sign, but as part of the angle complex it has a role to play in how you frame your personal narrative. Imagine a situation where you have, say, Venus conjunct the Midheaven and they are both situated in Aquarius. In this example, you would enjoy a noticeable degree of independence in matters like career choice and social status. You may be recognised as someone who is 'different' from the norms of your social background, and this could manifest in an unconventional attitude towards career choices, relationships, partnerships and even the kinds of creative or stylistic choices that would get you noticed in public.

For example, a person whose achievements in life were closely tied to their ability to do things their own way - even to the extent of loving the 'shock value' that is associated with their public image - may have this kind of placement in their chart, for example, such a placement could signify an 'avant-garde' artist, musician or designer. What happens, however, if you place that

Venus in Capricorn? Venus is more serious, restrained and conventional when it's under the influence of Saturn's sign. The independent Midheaven in Aquarius is still there, but Venus in Capricorn may be more business or conventionally oriented. A self-made businessperson may 'take a risk' in setting up their business, but with this Venus placement, they are certain to have carried out a full risk analysis. They may be future oriented and original, but they will be business-like and are likely to have financial acumen thrown into the mix. They may be regarded as seen as both independent and innovative, yet conventionally successful in the material world.

Those are just a couple of small examples, but they demonstrate that when a planet is conjunct an angle, the sign and house placement matter because they influence the 'fine tuning'. They transform the placements in your birth chart into the complex and subtle reality that is your personal lived experience. So, when you read the descriptions of the planets in conjunction to an angle, do keep in mind that there will be additional subtleties that arise due to house position, sign and any aspects to the planet itself.

In the following descriptions, I've looked at the planetary placements from 'both sides' of the angle, so I hope that gives you an idea of the subtle (and maybe not so subtle) distinctions this can make to your angular complex.

The Sun

When the Sun is conjunct an angle in your natal chart, your solar traits are a key part of the angular complex. The ego, your vitality, creativity, motivation, confidence, core identity and sense of self are bound up with the affairs of the cardinal point in contact with the Sun. In astrology, the Sun also represents the father or paternal line, so the Sun conjunct a cardinal point may indicate certain qualities that are recognisable in your father or his birth family.

Sun Conjunct Ascendant

Born with the Sun conjunct your Ascendant? The Sun plays a starring role in how you create your self-image and how you project that image. It's easy to assume that the warm qualities of the Sun are projected outwards - regardless of your sun sign - and for those of you with the Sun on the **first house** side of the Ascendant that tends to be so. The Sun infuses your personality with its light and warmth. It helps you to approach life with self-confidence; you appear charismatic and motivated. Your solar traits come to the fore - especially if the Sun and Ascendant share a sign - and this makes you a powerful presence among your peer group.

You have natural leadership qualities and a sense of your own importance; however, this may be something you need to control. the strength of your personality may make it easy for you to become egocentric and domineering. This may be more of an issue with the 'fiery' or outgoing signs (though not exclusively) and it's something you may have to become conscious of in order to present the best attributes of both your sun and ascending sign. It's an aspect that can be challenging, as you usually need to grow into it in order to get the best out of it. You need to use your power and influence to benefit others rather than yourself.

The **twelfth house** placement of the Sun conjunct the Ascendant is a more self-conscious affair. We tend to assume that the Sun conjunct the Ascendant shines brightly regardless, but on the twelfth house side it needs a little encouragement to do so. Although the Sun is part of your Ascendant complex, it's in a house that is more reflective and quieter than its first house counterpart. So, although your personality incorporates your solar traits, those traits may be more subdued, or they may be affected in the following ways. For example, your solar qualities may be evident to other people - but not to you. You may appear confident but suffer a little from 'imposter syndrome' on the inside. You may find it a challenge to assert your natural authority, or your inner motivation may remain vague or mis-directed.

This can make it difficult for you to access your sense of self with the ease you would expect from a Sun-Ascendant conjunction. However, it can give you a deep awareness of the motivations of those around you, and it can be a remarkably creative placement as the imaginative world of the subconscious is likely to be a major part of your personality. It's a sensitive placement but beware of it being oversensitive; it can be just as easy for the ego to be pricked with the Sun on the twelfth house side of the Ascendant as it is on the first house side - perhaps even more so - because of the hidden insecurities that often come with this placement.

Sun Opposite Ascendant

When the Sun opposes your Ascendant, it is conjunct the Descendant and plays a key role in how you approach and form relationships of all kinds. The Sun here signifies that relationships are of primary importance to you - but that is especially so when the Sun falls in the **seventh house**. You identify not only with your partner, but with your relationship to the extent that it may become difficult for you to maintain a sense of your own individuality. Relationships are such an important part of your identity that you may feel incomplete or 'lost' when attempting to function outside of your primary partnership. The partnership itself may also have a strong image that dominates the identities of the individuals in the relationship.

What you may also experience with a seventh house Sun opposite the Ascendant, is a drive to relate that underpins many other areas of your life. All kinds of interactions, including career or professional ones, will be informed by this Sun-Ascendant aspect; you will assert your identity by bonding, negotiating and mediating your way through life. You will be acutely aware of the benefits of bringing people together and you will appreciate both sides of an argument. Finding mutually acceptable solutions to all kinds of problematic situations is something that comes easily to you. You have a natural inclination towards justice, collaboration and equality; this provides you with a natural and enviable social skillset. However, you must try to avoid being 'all things to all men', as the saying goes.

With the Sun opposing the Ascendant but falling on the **sixth house** side of the Descendant, your primary relationship may be a working partnership. Relationships will be important to you as they form part of the image you project into the world, as well as being a constituent part of how you see yourself. In a sixth house context, you want a partner who will reflect well on you, so you set high standards - and that applies to both personal and professional relationships. In this scenario, professional relationships may turn into personal ones; those with this placement may meet their partner in a work or other sixth house setting. You may also find that you need to 'work at' your relationships to improve them. You may find it hard to ignore relationship flaws and you may have to accept that, ultimately, no relationship is perfect.

This is also one of the nurturing placements of the Sun, and because it attaches itself to your relational and social life, there is the possibility that your natural orientation will be towards 'looking after' those with whom you form close partnerships. This can lead to an imbalance in some relationships, though other outcomes are also possible. The organisational principle that underpins the sixth house may mean that you and your partner have clearly defined roles within your relationship. That sounds fine, as it may be the most efficient way to organise the partnership, but it can lead to feelings of one (or both) of you feeling taken for granted by the other, if your respective roles become too 'mutually exclusive' or imbalanced in any way.

SUN CONJUNCT MIDHEAVEN

With the Sun conjunct the Midheaven in the **tenth house**, your identity, creativity and confidence are bound up with your achievements. It's often suggested that this is the placement that signifies 'fame and fortune'. I wouldn't go that far, but I would suggest it shows a character that is at ease with being in the public eye. However, that's not always indicative of celebrity status; career, ambition and social status are part of who you are, and you are likely to identify with what you do. The Sun here may show that your personal identity also has a public image. There may be an involvement with a family business, or your family (through the paternal line) may be well known in some way. You may also be identifiable because you have some form of public office or socially recognisable role - such as a teacher or doctor - or any other job that has a socially responsible and recognisable 'label'.

A person with a tenth house Sun conjunct the Midheaven may be particularly 'goal-oriented'. That's great in a professional sense, but too much of an emphasis here may lead to imbalances in other areas of your life. The Sun here may lead you to identify with your own power, expertise and authority to a marked degree; this can lead to arrogance, as you take any challenge to your authority in a deeply personal sense. In other words, if someone questions a decision at work or challenges your status as a self-appointed leader, you may regard it as a threat to your core sense of self; it seems to undermine who you are. That's not to say you don't have great leadership potential. You are a person who assumes responsibility with ease and, whatever you do in this life, you are likely to assume a role that confers the kind of responsibility and status that is expressed in a traditional manner.

The **ninth house** side of the Midheaven sees the Sun in the house of expansion and, with this placement, your identity is informed by your understanding of the world around you. You may be motivated to succeed academically, or you may be recognised for your intellect. However, for most people with this placement, identity and vitality is often expressed in a desire to experience as much of the world as possible. You may regard yourself as an eternal traveller or you may be seen as someone who is 'foreign' or alien in some way. Perhaps you needed to leave your past (or your origins) a long way behind you to get where you wanted to be in life. Your identity and sense of who you are is tied to both ambition and distance - and that distance may involve a symbolic and/or a literal journey

At a deep level, travel enables you to see 'the big picture'. You are always able to keep things in perspective. You may have come far, but you rarely lose that sense of who you are. You are progressive by nature and naturally optimistic, however, the ninth house is associated with 'inflation' and it may be easy for you to assume an inflated sense of your own importance. So, this placement highlights the importance of your identity; it's for you to decide whether that's based on merit or if it's simply an egotistical thing. What this placement does suggest is that you are highly motivated, and that your motivation is best expressed a positive and idealistic manner. If your journey takes you to wisdom, that may be the best outcome of all.

Sun Opposite Midheaven

The Sun opposite the Midheaven in the f**ourth house**, places a great emphasis on your origins. Your sense of who you are is intimately connected to your roots - and that may lead to identification with your birth family, ethnic group or birth community, or your homeland. It's tempting to say that those with this placement rarely stray far from home, such is the strength of home and family connections. For some people that may be so, but for others the opposite may be true. Those who have been displaced often feel a conscious desire to 'root' and the

Sun here may shine a light on that. So, your identity may be bound up with patriotic fervour, or it may be connected to your birth family or the family you create. In whatever form it manifests, a deep sense of belonging is crucial to your identity formation.

That sense of belonging binds your identity and motivation to your roots. Whether those roots are represented by your birth family or your country of origin, you know where you have come from. However, the important thing with this placement is not to live in some (often imaginary or sentimentalised) past; with the Sun on the fourth house side of the Nadir, it's essential for you to build your own firm foundation. Having your own base will be important to you. Creating your own comfort zone and acknowledging your own need to have a space to call your own is important to you. You need a space that you identify with and that enables you to create a family, a home, a sanctuary or even a business in your own image. If the latter is the case, it's likely to have a domestic focus.

With the Sun opposite the Midheaven on the **third house** side, your identity is linked to how you think and communicate. The connection to your Nadir, the place you came from, also implies that your origins may have been influenced by mental processes rather than emotional considerations. Your family home may have been a place of intellectual stimulation with access to books, some vigorous debates and even a few arguments. It may have been an active place, but it could also have been one where your emotional needs were secondary to your educational needs - or even to the needs of your siblings. The third house can be a crowded place You may have needed to articulate who you were just to stand out from the crowd. Your early environment may have taught you the importance of effective communication, and that will have provided you with a skillset that is useful in all areas of your life.

With this placement, creating a foundation is also important to you, but it is likely to be based on your ability to adapt to whatever the prevailing conditions are in your life. The third house is a place of movement so your own home life may be one that is subject to regular change. You may become bored and need a change of scene, or you may experience relocations due to frequent job changes, or you may have a career that involves being on the road. Regardless of the cause, the underlying message is one of a certain instability that may reflect your early years experiences. You learned to adapt so change holds no fear. A flexible, mentally stimulating, fast-paced environment is where your core strengths find their most natural outlet. Wherever you reside, you will always become part of your neighbourhood, as you need to be busy and involved.

The Moon

When the Moon is conjunct a cardinal point in your natal chart, your emotional nature is one of the ways you connect with reality. You form an attachment to the parts of your life represented by the cardinal points - and it's an attachment that will be rooted in your subconscious. The Moon is sensory, instinctive and works on gut feelings. With the Moon conjunct any of your angles, your feelings and memories will be in play - often visibly so. The Moon in astrology also represents the mother and maternal family line, so the Moon conjunct a cardinal point may show areas of maternal influence in your life.

Moon Conjunct Ascendant

The Moon in the **first house,** conjunct the Ascendant, binds your identity to your lunar side, and this may be expressed in several ways. You may physically resemble your mother or her family or be named after a family member on the maternal side. As far as your appearance goes, you may have that characteristic 'Moon face' (it happens). You may be a person whose emotions are easily and visibly triggered, such as a 'touchy' person or a 'heart on your sleeve' type of person. You may see yourself as a caring, nurturing person - and that's how you come across to other people too. The Moon here puts your lunar traits up front and personal - and it doesn't get more personal than the Moon, representing (as it does) your innermost, private and deepest attachments. And speaking of attachments, you may be a person who clings to people, objects and situations - and that may manifest in many ways.

Your identity is firmly connected to the Moon in your natal chart. Your sensitivity is pronounced and, regardless of your gender or parental status, you have a caring and maternal approach to life. That is simply who you are, so it's unsurprising that many with this aspect are the 'go-to' people for those in need of tender loving care. Kindness is your middle name. However, you can be moody. Being so emotionally exposed to your environment does often result in emotional inconsistency or instability. You shift with the tides, and it's something you can't hide, as the unconscious side of you may dominate. You are impressionable and reactive; things move you, yet you have an inner strength that can be surprising. Outwardly warm, but inwardly private and protective of your own image? That's the Moon right there.

With the Moon on the **twelfth house** side of the Ascendant, many of the same features described above are recognisable. However, in the twelfth house the Moon shines inwards and that's where some of the major differences between the two placements are found. Your emotions are prominent, but they are likely to be kept under wraps - most of the time. It's surprising, therefore, when you have an emotional outburst, as you usually present as a warm, kind and caring individual that everyone knows and loves. With a twelfth house Moon your persona is less emotional than your first house Moon counterpart, but it's much more difficult for those feelings to find an outlet. So, your persona has to look for the best routes available - and they are found in the twelfth house realm.

This is an imaginative and creative placement and your identity and sense of who you are is likely to be 'at home' in that world. It's your comfort zone and you may have escapist tendencies; the world of your fantasies may feel like an emotionally safe space. It's more constructive for you give such feelings concrete form and, though some of you may enjoy artistic and creative pursuits, others may need to be aware of the dangers of losing yourself in other ways. You are likely to have instinctive insights into issues such as mental health problems - or even health issues in general. This may be because of personal experience, but the Moon's capacity for empathy and sympathy gives you an emotional connection to those in need. Shyness is not uncommon with the Moon conjunct the Ascendant, but it is more pronounced when the Moon is in the twelfth house.

Moon Opposite Ascendant

The Moon opposite the Ascendant is conjunct the Descendant. On the **seventh house** side of the cusp, it shows that your emotions are tied to your partner. Of course, many of us would assume that to be so in a relationship, but for those of you with this placement, a relationship is an essential part of your emotional support system. You function better as part of a pair, and you're emotionally geared towards that. You enter relationships readily and you are adaptable to your partner's needs. You make a kind and generous partner but take care not to overlook your own needs; the relationship may be your comfort zone, but your partner is not responsible for your emotional wellbeing. Feelings can run high when the Moon is placed here and there may be dependency issues on both sides.

The Moon here may also indicate that partnerships in general are important to you and, regardless of gender, you may have close ties to the women in your life in both a personal and professional capacity. Taking that forward, the Moon here shows a gift for reading other people. It's easy for you to anticipate the needs and responses of others; that's an intuitive skillset that may be useful to you throughout your life as it clearly has many applications. One thing to be aware of, however, is your need for reciprocity. You need your feelings to be validated through your relationships and if appreciation or acknowledgement does not come your way you are likely to feel deeply hurt. You may be a nurturing soul, but your relationship needs to be a nurturing space - and that should be your aim with this lunar placement.

With the Moon on the **sixth house** side of the Descendant, emotions and relationships are closely connected, but they are expressed in a practical and productive manner. The sixth house is the place where we seek to 'improve' and your instincts are aligned in that direction. As your Moon is bound to your relationships, then they too are an arena where 'improvement' is played out. You will be concerned with making your relationship 'work' in an emotional sense and that means that the relationship's focus will be on making it a nurturing space where the wellbeing of both partners is paramount. However, unlike the seventh house Moon, this focus is likely to be onto things that make you 'feel good' in a tangible sense. So, things like diet and nutrition, exercise, domestic organisation and self-care are likely to be on the agenda.

Your feelings are often expressed via the things that you do for each other. Easing the burdens of the day is as valid an emotional response as a hug or sweet words. The Moon here appreciates emotional honesty and, as you share the gift of insight with your lunar seventh house cousins, this makes you a natural at working relationships that use this quality. The sixth house is the house of work and working within the field of emotional relationships (counselling, psychotherapy or other therapeutic professions) may come naturally to you. Even those of you who do other things for a living will appreciate a workspace with supportive and emotionally aware relationships. One more thing. You may be an emotional perfectionist, so beware of that. To feel good, your relationships do not need to be perfect. Good enough will suffice.

Moon Conjunct Midheaven

The Moon conjunct the Midheaven elevates the Moon in your natal chart, particularly when it's on the **tenth house** side. The Moon here aligns your emotional needs with your career, ambitions, public status and your sense of being part of the world in a 'grown-up' sense. You are sensitive about your reputation, and this means that you try to get along with people, as you are risk averse to being a social outcast. This means that you are generally a well-behaved and responsible person and, depending on other factors in your birth chart, that may work well for you - or not. One factor in this may be related to the influence of your mother. She is likely to be an important - even dominant - figure in your life and, depending on the nature of your relationship, this may also work well - or not. Female members of your wider family may also be influential in shaping who you become.

The tenth house is influential in career matters; you may take your career cue from your mother, so you need to ensure that your decisions are made for the right reasons and not to satisfy any un-lived maternal aspirations. It will be extremely important for you to separate your emotional needs from outside pressures to maintain mental and emotional stability - and to succeed in life to the best of your ability - as that is the most emotionally healthy outcome for you. At best, you may have great sympathy with social issues and the ability to empathise with others in the public domain. In fact, the public arena may become your comfort zone. Careers that capitalise on this and emphasise your lunar qualities, or are vocational in nature, are likely to be a good fit.

With the Moon on the **ninth house** side of the Midheaven, your emotional needs are still bound up with your career, ambitions and achievements in a social sense - but you may be slightly more relaxed about it. The ninth house is a place of travel, expansion and philosophical contemplation. Your comfort zone, especially in terms of your career or personal ambition, may take you overseas - or at least far from your place of birth. You think of yourself as fitting into a big picture and you tend not to be limited by the small-minded opinions of others - or mundane responsibilities. Your attachment is to emotional freedom, not emotional bondage. You need travel and adventure and that need comes from a deep inner restlessness that seeks constant emotional satisfaction from new experiences and a changing environment.

Change is important to you, but you need to appreciate that this may originate in restlessness; to be at ease with yourself you feel that you need to be 'somewhere else'. The notion of things always being better elsewhere is one that may ultimately be self-defeating, as emotional security is something that can only be found within. As you are so emotionally connected to your career, it's possible that this may provide you with an avenue for emotional release. Intellectual restlessness and a deep need to know more, do more and be more may take you along some routes that are out of the ordinary and that may provide you with the emotional stimulation that you seek. One issue you may have to think about with the Moon here may be a tendency to intellectualise your feelings. You may run away from - or avoid - deep emotional engagements or commitment, as you feel such things limit your freedom.

Moon Opposite Midheaven

The Moon opposite the Midheaven on the **fourth house** side of the Nadir, resides in its most comfortable place. The Moon rules the fourth house and its placement here is powerful indeed. With the ultimate in lunar placements, you have a deep emotional connection to the place of your birth. This may be a bond to your birth family or your wider homeland. Those with this placement may not stray far from home - however 'home' is defined. Home is the place you go to to 'touch base' emotionally with yourself and it may be important to you to create a comfortable home. Your instincts are geared towards nurturing and self-care; regardless of your moon sign, you know how to make yourself feel good, though you may cling to habits, or cling to the past, more than is good for you. You also have a strong preference for things that are familiar to you.

With this placement, are you more likely to be tied to your mother's apron strings? Not necessarily so. Yes, you will feel an affinity to home and family matters, but all aspects to the Midheaven impact on your life direction and should be looked at in that context. With the Moon here, issues to do with the past may influence your career choice. You may also work in a career that is associated with themes such as nursing or childcare, or any of the nurturing or caring professions. Careers in any of the 'landed' professional are also a possibility and you may be drawn to horticulture, agriculture or real estate/property development. Your career choice may be influenced by family responsibilities, so trying to balance professional and domestic responsibilities may be a challenge. Ultimately, you will always do whatever it is that makes you feel as if you truly belong somewhere.

With the Moon on the **third house** side of the Nadir, the feeling side of life is something you feel just as much as the fourth house side, but you are more able to articulate your feelings. Talking about things comes naturally to you; you are a sensitive and intuitive communicator, and you may be able to help other people to access their feelings too. With the Moon in aspect to the Midheaven, this opens the possibility that you could use this ability in a professional context. Psychological insight, or the ability to sense what people are thinking or feeling, may be useful in a variety of professions. For example, counselling, teaching, sales and marketing and public relations draw on such skills - but beware of your own sensitivities. This is a placement that can lead to a 'thin skin' and you may, at times, be oversensitive to the words and opinions of others.

With this placement, your thoughts, words and ideas are heavily influenced by your emotional state. This may result in emotional outbursts from time to time - particularly with the more expressive moon signs. Even for the more emotionally introverted, this placement can lead to an emotionally excessive or sentimental communicative style. The Moon's expression here can be variable. Emotional changeability can emerge as mental restlessness and, with the connection to the Midheaven, you may need a career that feeds on this restlessness. This is, therefore, a great placement for research and intellectual pursuits that require your emotional engagement - but enable you to communicate your knowledge too. You feel 'at home' doing that - and that's what matters to you more than anything.

Mercury

When Mercury is conjunct one of the cardinal points in your natal chart, ideas, communication, mental process, physical and mental co-ordination and organisation are an important part of the life experience represented by the angle concerned. Mercury in your natal chart represents connections of all kinds; in an information rich world, Mercury is the conduit that enables what we know (or think we know) to be transferred from one person or place to another. Transport and physical movement are as much a part of the Mercury brief as the more mental and cerebral associations of this planet.

Mercury Conjunct Ascendant

Mercury conjunct the Ascendant - and on the **first house side of the Ascendant -** aligns your self-image to that of the messenger god. I'm not suggesting you invest in some winged-heeled boots (though they do look cute), but there will be something noticeably 'mercurial' about you. Regardless of your ascending sign, there will be a certain flexibility in the way you present yourself and you may be one of those souls who others see as permanently busy. This is the placement of the packed schedule or the well-ordered diary and, depending on your Mercury sign, this can make you appear to be either the most scattered - or the most organised - individual. You may be mentally or physically restless and you are likely to be well-informed. Here, Mercury absorbs information; you like to be recognised as someone who is 'in the loop'.

There may also be a nervousness about you. Some with this aspect tap their feet or fingers constantly. Your hands often need to be occupied as fully as your mind; many with this placement will be skilled at handicrafts of all kinds. You may be recognised for your skill and dexterity and perhaps also for your sense of humour. Mercury is as quick verbally as it is mentally and physically, so a ready wit may be part of your persona. Your natural orientation will be towards the mental or intellectual side of life. This is one of the intellectual placements and, even if you don't consider yourself an intellectual in the academic sense, you will be regarded as 'bright' or knowledgable. You may be a natural teacher - even if that's not your profession.

With Mercury on the **twelfth house** side of the Ascendant, you have a mercurial persona, but it's much more retentive. Expressive Mercury is much more intuitive here, so you are more likely to be a deep thinker or someone who keeps your opinions to yourself - unlike your first house cousins. Mercury close to the Ascendant always affects your self-image and those with this placement may be noticeably shy. It's not that you don't know what to say - in fact you may be extremely sensitive and tuned into information and detail - however, you may simply prefer to listen. Mercury here is a good listener, and you will feel more confident about expressing yourself when you have appraised a situation (something you do well) rather than jumping straight in. Your mind tends to work in tune with your senses.

It's no surprise that this is the placement of the poet. You may be regarded as someone who knows how to say the right thing at the right time - yet your mind may seem to be on other things. There is something of the daydreamer about you, but with Mercury here this appearance may be deceptive. It's possible your thoughts are not taking you in to a world of dreams, but to a world where you are plagued by insecurity and self-doubt. This placement can be where overthinking, and moodiness reside, and this can lead to a personality best described as 'changeable'. Developing a positive inner dialogue is often helpful for those with Mercury here; it will help to combat your more irrational thoughts and encourage the creative mercurial talents often present with this placement.

Mercury Opposite Ascendant

Mercury opposite the Ascendant in the **seventh house** puts Mercury in the realm of your partnerships. Planets conjunct the Descendant influence your approach to partnerships and your partner may carry one or more of the signature traits of this planet. This fast-moving planet often indicates that you need a meeting of minds - or a partner who is clever, communicative, speaks well and has their own set of four (or two) wheels. To maintain your interest the relationship needs to be interesting, and this placement shows that you need to be busy - together. A relationship that doesn't provide you with an active social life or intellectual stimulation or 'witty banter' is going to feel like a dull place to be. Mercury here can be easily bored. Mercury here may indicate more than one marriage - or the need for a 'twin soul'.

This Mercury placement may point towards relational issues. Mercury on the Descendant may be reluctant to commit when there are so many options available. Mercury here may be inconsistent or play the field - or you may be the one on the receiving end of such behaviour. That's more likely to happen with Mercury projected onto your partner, with your partner acting out your own unaddressed Mercury needs. 'Develop some relational awareness' is the message you'll be getting here; spending hours analysing or talking about the relationship is not the same as emotional bonding. That may be the issue you need to think about most.

With Mercury on the **sixth house** side of the Descendant, Mercury and relationships come together, but the emphasis may be much more practical. Mercury is the ruler of the sixth house, so this is a placement that lends itself readily to professional or working relationships - or simply making your relationships work. With this placement, Mercury's analytical and organisational attributes may be put to good use. Partnerships may be communicative and supportive, in fact that's probably the outcome you are looking for. When I see couples, whose lives are 'dovetailed', i.e., they fit together well, I often think of this placement. Why? They pay attention to the details of their everyday lives together. Little things matter in relationships - and being able to talk about them helps more than you think it does.

This is also a Mercury placement that can reveal some inequalities in your partnerships, and this may say more about your own Mercury expression than it does about your partner. Inequalities can manifest in many ways - and they are not always a bad thing. There may be an intellectual gap, or one partner may be neater and tidier than the other - and as a result do more of the household chores. One partner may have health issues (or a bad case of hypochondria), so the other partner has the burden of looking after them. This dynamic may exist in many relationships, but with this Mercury placement such things may be (or become) a dominant or defining feature of the relationship - and those issues may feature in your workplace relationships too.

Mercury Conjunct Midheaven

Mercury on the **tenth house** side of the Midheaven elevates Mercury in your natal chart and gives it a particular importance in connection with your career. Before you rush off to enroll for that journalism course, Mercury may imply you have a career where words, thoughts, ideas and communication are important, but it may also show that you are concerned with your public status. Being 'well thought of' may be something you seek with Mercury here. The Midheaven represents your public image so 'writer' or 'teacher' may be on your CV or resume. Whatever you do, you may be regarded as an authority, or you may communicate with authority regardless of your chosen profession. Mercury here also may make you think you are important. Beware of being seen as a braggart with this placement.

With Mercury conjunct the Midheaven, career matters may be flexible or changeable. You may find it difficult to choose between career options or you may actively seek a profession that allows you a degree of flexibility in your role - such as regular travel, or the ability to work shifts, or the need to alter your working hours to suit the demands of your other commitments. However, there is another side to Mercury with this placement. Job insecurity may cause frequent shifts in your career - and you may change your profession as a result of that. Having more than one career trajectory, or being recognised for multiple abilities, is also possible with Mercury conjunct the Midheaven. This may lead to you taking on multiple roles within one organisation.

With Mercury on the **ninth house** side of the Midheaven, your career focus, your ambitions and public status is, in many ways, even more likely to be 'mercurial' than it would be on the tenth house side. In this position, Mercury's academic or 'clever' traits come to the fore, as the ninth house is a forward looking, intellectually oriented domain. Mental processes are expansive with Mercury here. You achieve your ambitions because you have the intellect and mental capacity to do so, or the position you reach in life requires you to have a certain intellect because it's associated with the job that you do. As with your tenth house Mercury cousins, being an authority on a certain subject is a possibility - particularly in an academic or teaching context.

However, Mercury here is not always destined for academia. This placement is highly analytical and shows you have an enquiring mind, but it is also subject to the changeability or flexibility we associate with the messenger god. If you were thinking of enrolling for that journalism course, this placement would be helpful as the ninth house is where you search for the truth. Mercury's energies are best deployed in places like the media and broadcasting organisations, as well as in teaching and lecturing. Getting information 'out there' is the object with Mercury conjunct the Midheaven, and 'out there' may also involve a significant amount of travel - either literally or metaphorically - as the ninth house takes you a great distance from where you began.

MERCURY OPPOSITE MIDHEAVEN

We come to Mercury conjunct the Nadir. On the **fourth house** side of the cusp, Mercury adds a mentally lively layer to your foundation in life. Your family background may have been academic with ample access to books and intellectual stimulation. Your natural curiosity may have been encouraged by your parents and lively debate may have been encouraged within the family home. However, your family life may also have been chaotic; Mercury here can be disruptive, and you may have seen a few changes of residence during your childhood, or you may have had to split your time with your parents if they ran separate households. That restlessness and flexibility is something that may still be a feature of your domestic life or home base. Your home may be 'multi-purpose', especially if it's also your work base.

Mercury on the fourth house side of the Nadir connects your Mercury energy to your home and family life, but there is more to it than that. The fourth house has deep roots, and your mind may have the same depth. A retentive memory and excellent research skills are a feature of Mercury here, as is an interest in fourth house concerns like family history, local history - or the past in general. And though Mercury is a rational energy, it may be less so when situated here. This is a place steeped in emotion, so you may have the ability to connect emotionally, intuitively and imaginatively. It's a great placement for a therapist or counsellor, as you are highly perceptive. However, it may be hard for you to think outside of your mental comfort zone, or deal with ideas that challenge orthodoxies, so beware the narrow-mindedness that can also be a feature of this Mercury placement.

Mercury on the **third house** side of the Nadir, finds Mercury in its own house. This is a restless, mentally agile and active (some would say hyperactive), intelligent and communicative Mercury energy that needs vigorous expression. When combined with your foundation - the place you come from - it shows that your base is likely to be a clever and talkative one. This tends to suggest you sought out mental and social stimulation from an early age - regardless of whether that fitted with your family background or not. With Mercury here, you will have had your own ideas and asked many questions. You are naturally curious, so you may have realised - at an early age - that a good education was going to be your springboard to the future. You acquire languages and information quickly - and you may have grown up in multi-lingual family or environment.

As such a mental live-wire, you are smart enough to know that you won't get anywhere in life without using your intellect or communicative abilities - or the network of contacts you have built up over the years. You know how to open doors and you are not shy of doing so. Regardless of your Mercury sign, this is a strong and assertive Mercury energy, and it makes you 'good with words' in a wide variety of contexts. Professions such as journalism and other word-based careers such as interpretation, translation or language teaching may be a good fit for you. Words are your comfort zone when Mercury is on this side of the Nadir. You may 'talk the talk' but lose interest in more mundane matters that don't provide you with that essential stimulation. You may be a thinker, rather than a 'doer', as your practical side may not be so well-developed as your mind.

Venus

With Venus conjunct an angle in your natal chart, it would be easy to assume that Venus would impart beauty, grace, material benefits and a desire for indulgence and pleasure in those parts of your life represented by the cardinal points. In some instances that may be true, however, there is so much more to Venus than the rather superficial surface gloss we often associate with the goddess of love. Venus is fundamentally concerned with our value system and how we relate in a broad sense, as well as more abstract concepts such as balance, equity and harmony. 'Fair Venus' may have more to do with equality and justice, rather than the colour of your hair.

Venus Conjunct Ascendant

Venus conjunct the Ascendant in the **first house** is often considered a most fortunate placement. Venus is visibly part of your persona, so the fortunate among you may be genuinely beautiful in appearance. I always maintain that looks are something we inherit; appearance is something else entirely. With Venus here you are likely to be concerned with your appearance - and in some cases overly so. Venus is associated with vanity, as much as it is with beauty, so a pre-occupation with self-image may result. In most cases, Venus in this position will add a sense of style. Elegance, grace and charm are likely to be found, but remember that 'charm' works both ways. Genuine charm is a great thing, but it's manipulative cousin, exercised in the pursuit of personal desire (Venus again) may be less so. Either outcome is a possibility with Venus here.

A Venusian personality may be charming (in all manner of ways) and is likely to be comfortable in the world of culture and the arts. Not everyone with Venus here will be an artist, but there will be a sense of balance and refinement, socially as well as in a cultural or aesthetic sense. Your self-image needs to represent you in a beneficial way and those benefits may be connected to your own personal advancement. Venus is a material girl; your personal desires mean a lot to you, particularly if they can be translated into material gain. I doubt many of you will rob a bank, but you may be prone to excessive spending if other factors in your natal chart point in that direction. This can be an indulgent placement. You may spend a lot on your appearance - and 'appearance' may have a broad interpretation.

Venus on the **twelfth house** side of the Ascendant is interesting because it may result in behaviours that are completely different to those experienced with a first house Venus. A few degrees may make a big difference, and that difference occurs because twelfth house planets are in the shadows. Venus here may be no less beautiful, graceful, elegant or charming than her first house sister. However, she will have a hard time seeing that - and that has real implications for those who have this placement. Your self-image is bound to a planet you find hard to see or own and that may play havoc with your self-esteem. Venus represents the things we value. A first house Venus conjunct the Ascendant may have no issues with self-regard; on the twelfth house side that may seem like an existential issue.

How do you value yourself when you cannot appreciate your own worth? It's an issue that may manifest in several different forms. Downplaying your Venusian charms may be one outcome. Self-esteem issues are also at the heart of relationship problems;

if you cannot recognise your own worth, you may have problems recognising the worth of potential partners. Venus in this location may result in an inability to see lovers as they are. Self-deception - or deceit - regarding the nature of relationships can occur. This may result in secret (or secretive relationships) or relationships that are based on fantasy rather than reality. Somehow, imaginary love is more accessible - and maybe preferable - to the real thing. Venus here can be addictive, so some of the indulgence issues associated with this planet may be problematic, because you are more likely to be in denial about them.

VENUS OPPOSITE ASCENDANT

Venus conjunct the Descendant on the **seventh house** side, places Venus in her own house. Venus is strong in this position, yet those with this placement may project this planet onto their partner rather than own its qualities for themselves. However, that's not always a bad thing. Venus in this position shows a willingness to compromise and a desire to please. It also indicates a deep desire for your relationships to be harmonious. You hate conflict; disagreements have a disproportionate impact on your emotional wellbeing. You are likely to be the person who reaches out to resolve disputes - or tries to avoid them in the first place. You have natural negotiating skills and a diplomatic manner. There is a risk, however, that you give in too easily to 'keep the peace'.

With Venus here, the challenge may be to find balance in relationships. That is important to you because you value your relationships - and your partner. They reflect yourself and your own core values. Too often you may prize a partner's physical attractiveness or material wealth as a measure of your own worth, and you may use the partnership as a means of personal validation. You value your partner because of the companionship that they provide, as you would struggle to spend life on your own. You are likely to be sociable and your relationships may be notably so; your social life together may be more important than it is to most people, but you may need to ensure that its outward focus does not obscure the more intimate bond between you. Appearance is not always the most important thing.

With any planet on the **sixth house** side of the Descendant, the focus is often on making relationships work, so with Venus here you have an in-built advantage. You have the same negotiating and diplomatic skills as your seventh house cousins, and you are happy to put them to use in both personal and professional relationships. This is also one of the planetary placements where both types of relationship combine. You may meet your partner at work, or you may both work in the same business or industry. At a more personal level, you may also share similar lifestyles, habits and daily routines. They may seem like small issues, but a harmonious relationship, - where one partner's habits or preferences don't clash with the other's - is often a deal maker rather than a deal breaker.

This is a placement that favours business partnerships and harmony in the workplace generally, as you will tend to establish good relationships with your colleagues. However, there is another side to Venus here. It may show that you are fastidious about choosing a partner who will be right for you. You want relationships to be perfect, so you set the bar high - sometimes too high - as no mere mortal can ever be good enough for you. With Venus here, you may have to avoid being critical of your partner. You are a deeply loyal person and having a partner who is also loyal to you can act as a great confidence booster. One last thing; this can be a surprisingly indulgent placement and it may be tempting to blame your partner for leading you astray. You may have to work hard to keep yourselves - and the relationship - healthy.

VENUS CONJUNCT MIDHEAVEN

Venus conjunct the Midheaven on the **tenth house** side is one of those prized Venus placements. The world looks at you - and sees Venus. Public popularity, or being well known for your charm, grace, beauty, style, good taste, wealth or artistic accomplishments is to live the dream; but what's the reality? As ever, that may be more complex that it first appears. You may have a notable gift for any of the things we associate with Venus, to the extent that they form the basis of your life path or career. More generally, however, Venus is associated with success. This may be in any career that requires you to foster good relationships, have financial acumen or a good aesthetic sense. However, it may also mean that you are successful in any career you choose to pursue - largely because you find it a pleasure rather than a chore. It's easier to succeed when you enjoy what you do.

Regardless of her position at the top of your chart, Venus may still be associated with your most personal relationships, as public status and public image may be defined by more than your career. Your own public image (or reputation) may be tied to that of your spouse, as marriage is a public commitment. Venus here may mean it's your significant other who is recognised for those Venus traits you read about earlier. They may be wealthy, accomplished or gorgeous and, of course, you benefit from that association. However, there is more to this placement than reflected glory. You're likely to be attracted to power in some form; this is a placement that speaks of your own ambitions and, with Venus here, those ambitions will be materially based. A love of visible wealth or public recognition for your achievements is likely with Venus in this placement.

Venus on the **ninth house** side of the Midheaven brings a great deal of enthusiasm to your career ventures - and those career ventures may be adventurous too. Whatever you do, it will need to incorporate the desire to expand your sphere of experience - and your sphere of influence. Venus here is associated with wanting more; in the context of your work face or public image, 'more' can mean you desire to be well rewarded for whatever it it that you do, or you need the freedom to create a career path that aligns with your intellectual or ethical interests. Rewards in this context may be more than materially based. Venus here may have a particular interest in philosophy or the law; careers that are in tune with your own value system or have an educative or spiritual bias may also attract you.

A love of education will always be associated with your public image and status. As I mentioned earlier, the Midheaven is the point at which our public commitments are visible. Venus here suggests you may meet your spouse through higher education or while travelling - though any other ninth house setting is also a possibility. As a couple, you may be recognisably intellectual, religious or well-travelled. One of you may be from a different cultural background. You may share - a great Venus word - a career connection. Either share a career path or your careers share a ninth house connection. Shared values will be important -

and may be the basis of your commitment to each other. Commitment itself may, however, be an issue; the ninth house is the house of excess, and more than one marriage may be indicated by this placement.

Venus Opposite Midheaven

The Nadir marks our most private and personal space, so Venus on the **fourth house** side of this point is often regarded as a fortunate placement. What better to have the goddess of love and happiness at the base of your natal chart? Some of you with this placement will have been born into a happy family and some of you - regardless of your background - will desire to create that on your own terms. This Venus placement can, however, suggest a start in life where family values may have been materially based rather than emotionally supportive. Your desire may be to create your own loving and supportive base to make up for that lack - and you will usually be lucky in doing so. Family values are important to you - and you tend to place a high value on tradition. That conservative approach may extend to your value system too.

You are likely to have good relationships with your family members, in fact you may be the person who is seen as the family mediator. You are also likely to be the person who hosts family parties - and that is something you are likely to enjoy. It may be that you are more financially comfortable and it's a way of spreading the love. Comfort is important to you, but so is a home that is visibly appealing. You need a home that is stylish and well-appointed, and it may be more expensive than the homes of many of your peers. You are happy to spend money on the right property and you may make money from property. Venus here often has an interest in real estate, home interior design or architecture. A family background in any of these may form the basis of a future - and successful - career.

On the **third house** side of the Nadir, Venus loves to communicate - and communicates well. In this position, Venus uses words to foster good relationships, particularly in the home and local community. Venus here is happy in its neighbourhood and is unlikely to stray far from the home base. It's an engaging and sociable placement and may result in a person who knows everyone else around their home area. If that sounds like you then you are probably the person who knows everyone and who organises the local flower show or yard sale. Like your fourth house cousins, Venus here can show an interest in real estate, as the third house placement is associated with trading and exchange. However, Venus here may show a certain restlessness when it comes to your own home; you may fall in love with a new home and move house more frequently than most.

You are likely to be a natural negotiator as you are charming, persuasive and eloquent. Many of you will have a good singing voice, so it's a great placement for a local choir member too. At a personal level - and the Nadir is personal - music and the arts in general may have been an interest that was encouraged by your parents. You may have come from an artistic or creative home - and it's likely to have been a happy home too. I say 'likely' as for some of you may not have been so fortunate. Venus here has a gift for mediation, and it may be a skill you had to develop in your earlier years. You may have been regarded as the family peacekeeper, the one who attempted to keep life pleasant - and that may be a skill you use to this day. You love a well-mannered debate and a stimulating home environment, as you are easily bored.

Mars

Mars conjunct an angle in your natal chart is likely to result in a great deal of energy being directed towards the affairs represents by the cardinal point touched by the god of war. Mars is a pro-active and impulsive force; though we often think of Mars in an 'angry' context, it's a planet that can also have beneficial results if well controlled or directed. Mars's influence will always be directed by the sign in which it is found. It goes without saying that some Mars signs will be easier to deal with than others. It's with the fire and air signs that the more 'combustible' effects of Mars will be most noticeable.

MARS CONJUNCT ASCENDANT

Mars conjunct the Ascendant in the **first house** is an extremely powerful placement, owing to the planet being both conjunct an angle and being placed in the house that it traditionally rules. Powerful, punchy and direct, Mars adds a real drive to your personality that is similar in effect to having the sign of Aries here - and if you do have Aries here then you will truly be a force of nature! Mars conjunct the Ascendant is, however, not just forceful; it's also highly competitive. Your strong personality means you regard those around you as competitors - and that applies in every field of endeavour, not just in the sports arena. You are ambitious, direct, independent and courageous. You will almost certainly regard yourself as a leader and will tend to flourish in situations where someone needs to take charge.

There is, of course, a flip side to every placement. Though you are likely to be open and friendly, adventurous and good humoured, the words 'me first' may be used to describe your approach to life. Mars is often associated with sharp implements, however the sharpest thing about you may be your elbows. That's an old saying and it generally means that you do not hesitate to push yourself forward at every opportunity. There is a difference between being confident - and you will certainly be that - and being pushy. It is far better to be self-confident than to approach life as if everything is a fight. Mars here can make you fight-prone and accident prone. You have a lot of energy that needs careful direction, so your challenge with this placement will be to use that energy constructively rather than destructively. Anger management issues are not uncommon.

Though Mars is conjunct the Ascendant, when it's found on the **twelfth house** side of the line, the dynamic is very different from its first house cousin. Mars here is not just more restrained; it's hidden from view and if you have this placement you may struggle to access or acknowledge the qualities of the god of war. Where Mars on the first house side directs energy out into the world, Mars here directs it towards the self - and you may find that hard to deal with. Dealing with anger is not easy - particularly so when it's suppressed or turned inwardly against yourself. It's not uncommon to feel ineffective or powerless with Mars here; the energy is there but you may not recognise it or know what to do with it.

From this, you may deduce that this is often a problematic placement. It may certainly feel that way if you were expecting Mars conjunct the Ascendant to always be the dominant (or domineering) personality that it's reputed to be. However, Mars on the twelfth house side is more subtle than that - and those of you with this placement may have to consciously develop Mars's qualities as they won't come naturally to you. Yet they are as available to you as they are to anyone with Mars conjunct the Ascendant - you just need to approach them from a different direction.

Mars Opposite Ascendant

Mars conjunct the Descendant on the **seventh house** side, places the god of war in the house of love. That may sound as if it's going to be a major problem, but if you think of Mars as the energy that gives you drive and initiative - as well as the force that gives you assertiveness - we can start to give this placement of Mars some context. Mars is dynamic and its residence in this location suggests you will be forceful in relationships. That means you are likely to take the initiative and you are most likely to be the hunter, not the prey. You may be impulsive in relationships Sexual attraction and excitement may override your judgement - especially when it comes to the suitability - or longevity - of the relationship. Both personal and business relationships will have an active, energetic and masculine flavour.

Leaping into a partnership situation with enthusiasm may have much to recommend it - after all fortune favours the brave - but proximity to the Descendant brings with it the issues of projection you will have read about earlier. Projecting your own Mars qualities onto a partner may carry certain risks - particularly when we look more closely at the more unsavoury qualities associated with this planet. I am sure you would find it hard to admit that you habitually attract bad temper, volatility and even violence into your life in the guise of the person you love most, but this is a risk with Mars here. The challenge you face is to assert yourself in relationships; sadly, those with this placement sometimes learn to stand up for themselves the hard way.

When Mars is found on the **sixth house** side of the Descendant, your enthusiasm and energy is directed towards the practical aspects of relating. The sixth house is where we make things work and Mars is always happiest when working out. So, a vital part of your partnership may be the things you do together - and those things are likely to be physical. A shared interest in exercise may be important to you. An active lifestyle - however it manifests - will be part of your relationship. However, you may be competitive with each other. You may both put a lot of effort into your work, so a team effort may be required to ensure your daily lives function well. Unfortunately, Mars may indicate a certain willfulness and unwillingness to compromise, so arguments about 'who is responsible for what' are more likely with Mars here.

It's worth recalling that the sixth house can be a place of inequality, so you may find yourself in a partnership where it takes a great deal of your energy to make things work between you. You may feel as if the partnership is one-sided - with you taking on the burdens and responsibilities - and that may make you angry. Of course, that may occur for many different reasons. Your partner may have a health issue or they may have a a job that means they are simply not there for a lot of the time. Mars could imply that you have a partner who has a job in military service or their career 'comes first' in the relationship. You may need to establish your own form of independence within the relationship. Separate lifestyles may be a possibility with Mars here.

MARS CONJUNCT MIDHEAVEN

If there's one thing about Mars on the **tenth house** side of the Midheaven, it's this; it fires up your ambitions. All the competitive and leadership qualities of this planet are reinforced by this placement and those with it are often career oriented and hungry for success. Even if Mars is in a 'quiet' sign, this energy will act as a spur to achievement. Mars wants to be the winner and, as the Midheaven is the signifier of public status, you want to be seen as a winner in the eyes of the world. Winners are competitive, so you're likely to assert yourself in order to reach the finishing tape ahead of everyone else. It's a sporting metaphor, but it applies to your career or any other position that enables you to be seen as 'somebody'. The ego is strong with Mars placed here.

However, there is more to Mars on the Midheaven than a raging sense of entitlement. You are notably pro-active, and you can make rapid decisions that can affect not only the course of your own life, but the lives of other people around you. This can manifest in both positive and negative ways. Public impulsiveness can make you seem reckless or brave. It an also make you appear full of initiative or pushy - particularly as you prefer to take the lead in all things. You have natural leadership qualities that are undoubtedly useful in a career or public context, however you may need to learn to moderate a tendency towards behaving as if your way is the only way. A downside of this placement is that you are not a team player. There is only space for one achiever in your life - and that's you.

Mars on the **ninth house** side of the Midheaven adds a more cerebral cast to this placement. Your public image may be associated with a formidable intellectual energy, or a great enthusiasm for pushing the boundaries of human understanding; you may even be a pioneer in your chosen profession or area of expertise. Even mere mortals with this placement may be recognised for their intellectual passions. You grow your ambitions through your own well-directed efforts and your sense of adventure. You believe that all things are possible, and you set out to make things happen. Mars on this side of the Midheaven has a great sense of purpose; when you put your mind towards something you don't stop until you have achieved your goal. This is not only an intellectually forceful placement, but it's also a highly motivated one.

You may be a 'force of nature', but there are also some downsides to this placement. Intellectual enthusiasm may become intellectual arrogance. Though you are likely to enjoy a mental challenge, you may not like to be challenged. The same sense of superiority that we saw on the tenth house side of the Midheaven also exists here, so your challenge may be to avoid being regarded as aggressive or argumentative if your views, opinions or beliefs are questioned. However, you are also capable of fighting for your beliefs. This may result not only in career choices that involve vigorous debate, but the fight may also be more literal. The military or religious ministry are examples of Mars acting due to a belief system. 'Career activism' or an active career - of all kinds - is possible with Mars here.

Mars Opposite Midheaven

When Mars is found on the **fourth house** side of the Nadir, Mars's energy is directed towards your private life, home and family. Mars in this position can be problematic, given the nature of this planet; it's a self-centred, assertive and aggressive energy that may not sit well in a domestic environment. The Nadir relates to our past, and Mars conjunct this point suggests that the past may have been troubled. Domestic violence is an extreme occurrence, but many with this placement may have experienced a home life marred by arguments and a troubled atmosphere; a troubled or difficult relationship with a parent is not uncommon. This may result in difficulties with self-assertion. Mars is 'hidden' and shyness is one of several outcomes, as is an inability to express anger. There may even have been such issues in your homeland.

You are coming from a place where you felt your safety (physical and/or emotional) was compromised, so one outcome of this placement may be that, in your adult life, you direct your energies towards making yourself secure. Mars here is best applied to making your own home and, as it's a physical energy, you may be passionate about gardening or DIY. You may even build your own home or be passionate about creating your own family - and you may feel the urge to do so at an early age. An active and positive outlet for that Mars energy - however it manifests - is essential to your wellbeing. You are a private person, but that reluctance to be visible may be useful in career matters. Self-directed and highly focused careers involving research, lone working or sensitive/secretive matters may be suited to your deep need for personal safety and self-sufficiency.

Mars on the **third house** side of the Nadir emphasises some of the aggressive situations I've just described but places them in a third house context. For example, you may have come from a violent or troubled neighbourhood. You may have fought or argued with your siblings. You may have brothers rather than sisters. In a boisterous household, you may have had to fight to be heard. So, you will have become verbally assertive and most likely quick witted. Mars here can be humorous, though it's more likely to be sharp, pithy banter that sophisticated comedy - think rapid fire one-liners rather than a sketch show. You may have discovered that staying ahead - mentally and verbally - gave you the edge. It's important that you articulate your needs in a direct manner - it's how you protect your own interests and feel most secure.

The sensitivity associated with the Nadir can make you seem thin-skinned, as you tend to take criticism personally and meet it with verbal aggression. One of the downsides of the placement is a tendency to speak and react without thinking; it's a defence mechanism, yet it doesn't always act in your best interests. Being easy to trigger has its drawbacks, as anger can make you seem like a bully. In such situations, your responses reveal your own vulnerabilities rather more than you realise. Education, however, may be your saviour. You are likely to be passionate about learning and you are acutely aware of its benefits. Information is also something you pursue with a passion, and this may push you towards careers where contacts and communication are a vital part of the job. However, beware of inflaming others with your words. You can be provocative, even if you don't mean to be so.

Jupiter

Jupiter makes things bigger. It's a fact. So, Jupiter conjunct an angle in your natal chart really amplifies the message being played out by the cardinal point according to its sign. We also tend to think of Jupiter as lucky or beneficial; that may be so on occasion, but we must be careful about making that assumption. Sometimes Jupiter's luck manifests in ways that do not seem particularly fortunate at the time. When Jupiter is connected to the cardinal points in your birth chart, you need to think about things like expansion, distance, things that are foreign or alien to you, wealth and intellect - but you can't discount greed, inflation or excess. Jupiter is best approached with an open mind.

JUPITER CONJUNCT ASCENDANT

Jupiter conjunct the Ascendant on the **first house** side is often considered to be a most fortunate placement and those with it often present with a 'jovial' personality. Jupiter here may warm even the coolest of ascending signs and it enables the shyest of personalities to be more outgoing than they otherwise would be. However, Jupiter on the first house side of the Ascendant may also amplify the characteristics of the ascending sign; whatever your Ascendant's characteristics may be, Jupiter will make them more visible. Think about it. It was never going to be the opposite. However, Jupiter here may also produce someone who appears not to take life too seriously - and that may have both positive and negative forms of expression. Optimism is one thing; carelessness is another thing entirely.

Regardless of your ascending sign, you will generally have a positive approach to life, and you may appear to be luckier than most people. Some of you may appear to have the Midas touch. Positivity, an expansive attitude and an openness to new experiences will enable you to embrace opportunities that less adventurous souls would shy away from. It's not luck, it's an abundance of self-belief that takes you on that voyage of discovery, or in a beneficial direction of travel. It's that self-belief that enables you to develop a philosophical outlook and a sense of perspective that less sanguine souls would struggle to understand. Jupiter here is undoubtedly useful when it comes to boosting your self-image, but that can have a literal meaning; those who struggle with their waistline will understand exactly how Jupiter works in that way.

With Jupiter on the **twelfth house** side of the Ascendant, Jupiter's effects may be more internalised, yet they remain a key part of your outer personality. That may sound like a contradiction in terms, so I'll explain. Through its traditional rulership of Pisces and the twelfth house, Jupiter is at home in the shadows. If you think of Jupiter solely in terms of its expansive, outgoing qualities, then you invariably miss out on the deeper more reflective and philosophical qualities of the king of the gods. On the twelfth house side (and regardless of ascending sign) those qualities may come to the fore. You may be noted for your generous spirit, as Jupiter here may be used to benefit others. In that sense, you 'give away' a twelfth house side Jupiter, but because it's connected to the Ascendant, it accords with your self-image.

Jupiter here is no less a part of your self-image than it is for those who have it on the first house side, however, you may have difficulties recognising it as such. The twelfth house often represents a blind spot, so having a twelfth house Jupiter conjunct the Ascendant may result in you failing to recognise the potentials of your ascending sign - or undermining them in some way. Jupiter here may manifest in ways that self-sabotage your efforts. Jupiter's classic laziness - or extravagance - may be examples of this, as are the classic Jupiter traits of gambling or general irresponsibility. The main issue here (however it manifests) may be an inability to distinguish between your own self-image and an overwhelming desire to escape. The urge to escape from yourself - or at least lose yourself in some way - may be strong with Jupiter here. Self-discovery is a more positive outcome.

JUPITER OPPOSITE ASCENDANT

Jupiter in the **seventh house** side of the Descendant is often a coveted placement. After all, who would not want the god of good fortune in the house of relationships? As with many placements, it can be a mixed blessing. Jupiter - in relational terms - has a mixed reputation. So, let's deal with the good side first. Once more, Jupiter here can be literal. In the real world, those with Jupiter here may marry more than once - it's not uncommon - and those with this placement may be philosophical about that fact. There may be similarities to having Sagittarius on the descendant, i.e. partners may be connected to higher education, religion, the law, foreign countries or be wealthy. Regardless of your descending sign, Jupiter may indicate an advantageous marriage - and that may be financially so. Good humour may be the greatest benefit of all.

Of course, we need to look at the other side of Jupiter. The legends of old tell us that Jupiter was serially unfaithful to his wife, so infidelity may be an issue when you have Jupiter here.

Naturally, that may lead to the multiple partnerships I mentioned earlier. However, the deeper issue may be one of commitment generally. Jupiter's expansive and restless nature may result in issues like boredom, 'wandering eyes', and a belief that (in terms of your relationships) that the grass is always greener on the other side. There may be a reluctance to be tied down at all. Jupiter here may indicate that, where partnerships are concerned, you prefer to keep your options open and may never commit. The message overall is, however, one of cultivating a positive and optimistic approach towards relationships; it's better to have adventures together, rather than apart.

With Jupiter on the **sixth house** side of the Descendant, Jupiter affects your relationships in a practical, working sense - and this may include the work you do for a living. The connection between relationships and mundane daily life is often a problematic one, as it seems to imply that relationships will somehow be dull or, thanks to Jupiter's influence, overburdened by the responsibility. That's not necessarily so. The emphasis here is on making relationships work and Jupiter can be helpful in that respect. You may experience beneficial working relationships with colleagues - or you can establish both personal and professional relationships through your work. In both instances, you may bring knowledge, enthusiasm and a positive outlook to both your work and your personal relationships.

Clearly Jupiter is often more of an asset than otherwise. In purely practical terms, it can indicate that you and/or your partner have an element of Jupiter in the work you do. Work options may include the health and education sectors, or it may involve long distance travel. It's also possible that at least one of you may be well paid - and you may even run a profitable business between you. Establishing good relationships may be a key element of your work. However, either you or your partner may be prone to overwork or have more than one job. This may be essential, or it may be because you're that way inclined. Jupiter here can also indicate a need to take care of your health. Over-optimism can lead to neglect, and you may need to work hard to ensure that both of you take care of your health and make good lifestyle choices as a fundamental part of your relationship.

Jupiter Conjunct Midheaven

Jupiter conjunct any angle is often a good thing, but in career terms, Jupiter connected to the Midheaven on the **tenth house** side is often seen as the golden ticket. But is that always so? Jupiter here certainly inflates ambition and confidence. The world will often regard you as an exemplar of whatever it is you have chosen to do, but that does not mean your public image is automatically associated with success. There is no doubt that Jupiter here can be successful. In career terms, you possess a natural enthusiasm that delivers results, but you are also recognised as someone who can see the big picture. You have the intellectual capacity to understand how business operates and you can spot an opportunity from a mile away. That's the upside. However, there are also drawbacks to this placement that come from Jupiter's less positive attributes such as the habit of biting off more than you can chew.

Ambition is one thing, but it needs to be backed up by talent and hard work. Hard work - or the lack of it - may be the issue here. It would bruise your ego to be regarded as lazy or indolent, but you may run the risk of gaining that reputation unless you take steps to prove otherwise. Fortunately, the ability to spot a good career opportunity and a positive approach can help you to overcome that trap. You need to be genuinely enthusiastic about what you do, so your vocation may have a Jupiter flavour; law, academia, journalism or anything that involves culture or long-distance travel. If you follow your inclinations, you may find yourself in the position of making your own luck. Success often comes easily to those who find their work to be both interesting and effortless; it's certainly a more rewarding route to travel.

Jupiter on the **ninth house** side of the Midheaven finds the planet of expansion positioned in its own house. This puts Jupiter in a comfortable place and that's no bad thing when it's expanding your ambitions. Jupiter here has a natural affinity with some of the adventurous and expansive occupations you see when Jupiter is found in the tenth house, but on this side of the MC, Jupiter's influence works in a slightly different way. Where the tenth house Jupiter expands ambition from a worldly perspective, Jupiter conjunct the Midheaven on the ninth house side puts your ambition in perspective. You may be philosophical about your prospects. However, it's often a well-travelled placement and you may travel far to achieve or find success. It's also an intellectual placement, so knowledge-based industries may be of significance for you in terms of your career.

Your quest is to know more (or be more) regardless of the sign on your Midheaven, and this gives you the ability to visualise exactly where you want to go. Serendipity - being in the right place at the right time - may also play a part in the direction you take. You regard your life direction as a great adventure, and you are generally flexible enough to be receptive to any opportunity that presents itself to you. You may be taken far from your place of origin; your public status may even be one of 'migrant' or alien. However, it's likely that you have chosen that status and will benefit from it. Those benefits may come in many forms, but the most important one for you may be connected to freedom. If your origins made you feel constrained, Jupiter here will have the effect of enabling you to shake off those restraints - be they physical, moral, ideological or intellectual.

JUPITER OPPOSITE MIDHEAVEN

Jupiter on the **fourth house** side of the Nadir places outgoing Jupiter in the most private part of your birth chart. Regardless of the sign on the Nadir, you will associate your home and family of origin with the kind of Jupiter influences that have influenced the way in which you take root. However, Jupiter and taking root somehow don't seem to go together. Taking root implies that you are fixed to the spot and, as Jupiter is known for itchy feet and a need for space, the place you root may be far from your place of origin. Your comfort zone may be defined as a wide-open space - and you may be unable to live somewhere where you can't get fresh air or be stimulated by a cosmopolitan environment. You need somewhere you can appreciate culture - and cultural differences.

So, what brought you to that point? Was there some restlessness in your early life that you're re-living now? Or was there simply an overwhelming desire to strike out on your own? Many with this placement see the world as 'home'. This expansive feeling may be due to having a well-educated family background that made you appreciate the importance of having a solid intellectual foundation. Some of you may have had a wealthy or financially 'comfortable' family background that enabled you to experience more of the world than your peers. You may have had parents who suffered from 'wanderlust'; family bonds may be loose. It happens. Whatever your personal backstory may be, it enables you to create an open and comfortable space of your own. It's a space that you may share with others, as generosity and conviviality will be part of your domestic life.

With Jupiter on the third house side of the Nadir, the educational and intellectual Jupiter traits are forever associated with your past - and maybe with the past in a more general sense. Jupiter here has a big appetite for knowledge and that may include a desire to know more about the past. It's also possible that Jupiter is well represented in your family background. As one of the signifiers of intellect, one or both of your parents may have been well educated, worked in academia or those professions that require high level education. You are likely to have been encouraged to learn and develop your own academic capabilities. Home may have had an academic 'hot-house' atmosphere where you were encouraged to join in debates on a wide variety of subjects. Both breadth and depth of knowledge would have been considered important.

So, a house filled with bookshelves, conversation and most likely an expansive open-minded perspective on life. What more could you ask for? Jupiter here increases mental enquiry and communicative talents; it often signifies proficiency in more than one language and, when conjunct the Nadir, Jupiter implies you began life in a multi-lingual household or were raised in a country where the dominant language was different to that of your birth family Even if that was not so, your mental enthusiasm may take you far. A philosophical mind-set and a jovial and positive attitude make you one of life's more engaging characters. You are likely to be someone who always has something to say, as you are rarely - if ever - lost for words. You have a wide variety of interests, and most likely a great sense of humour too.

Saturn

With Saturn conjunct an angle in your natal chart, the affairs that are related to that cardinal point are going to present you with a challenge. That challenge - in common with any Saturn placement - will be to overcome fears, limitations and negativity and to eventually develop a sense of confidence and authority. Saturn always demands that you put in some hard work, so it won't be an easy ride. However, Saturn's rewards for your efforts fall in the long-lasting to permanent category - even if they are a long time coming. Patience is a virtue where Saturn is concerned.

SATURN CONJUNCT ASCENDANT

How do you feel about having Saturn conjunct the Ascendant? When you have this placement on the **first house** side, it may be a placement you have had to take seriously. Saturn here can make you a rather serious person. Or, at least, that's how you appear. Regardless of your ascending sign, Saturn conjunct the Ascendant makes you take life seriously. You will be seen as the responsible one, the person who can be relied on to be always the 'adult in the room'. Convention tells us that you may be overly cautious and plagued with worry and self-doubt. For some of you that may be so. Caution or, as some would call it, due diligence, is certainly part of your approach to life. You don't rush in or make rash decisions - and for those of you with your Ascendant in the more spontaneous signs, that may be a bonus.

However, Saturn here can be limiting. The self-doubt that I mentioned above, can manifest as shyness, especially in your younger years. You may lack confidence, but your fears are often misplaced and may result from your habit of being overly self-critical. You are hard on yourself, and while that may eventually give you a stern and uncompromising attitude that can be useful in certain situations, your habitual hesitancy and reluctance to take a risk can trap you in a state of inertia. That may be the cause of the despondency and negativity that are also associated with this placement. Those feelings are a message that you need to work hard at overcoming your self-limitations. You have the self-discipline to do this - and Saturn here shows that you can construct a secure and realistic approach to life that will not disappoint you.

Saturn on the **twelfth house** side of the Ascendant is not the easiest of placements. Saturn lives within the limitations of cold, hard reality and the twelfth house is a place of boundless dreams. It's not an easy combination. With this placement, you will share all the issues of self-doubt and self-criticism, but these will be overlaid by unconscious fears and a liberal dose of guilt. The problems with this Saturn twelfth house placement are that it (a) functions at an unconscious level and (b) it's so closely allied to your self-image that you find it difficult to have a positive view of yourself and your own potentials. Rather than confront those issues, you ignore them, and this can lead to feelings of victimisation, isolation or being misunderstood. Saturn builds walls - and the biggest barrier you face is the one you have built for yourself.

So how can you stop being your own worst enemy? You may feel unable to reach out for help. Saturn often works in ways that make us feel helpless. When that happens, the solution is often to do the counter-intuitive thing. Fears exist to be overcome. Barriers are there to be dismantled - and that is exactly what you must do. Fortune favours the brave and there is no lack of courage with this placement. You need to be courageous and ask yourself some difficult questions. Have that awkward inner conversation and allow yourself the time and space to work out how to respond to the challenges you seem to have set for yourself. Of course, some of those challenges will have entered your sub-conscious from elsewhere. Working through your anxieties is preferable to being overwhelmed by them - and you may need professional help to achieve that outcome.

Saturn Opposite Ascendant

Saturn on the seventh house side of the Descendant casts Saturn's stern gaze in the direction of your relationships. This is a placement that often carries a certain stigma, but is it a bad thing to have the God of reality situated here? I don't think it's too bad, though it does - like any placement - have its downside and I'll deal with that first. Saturn may make you lack confidence in this area of your life. This may be because you have experienced criticism from those you thought were your close friends. Such things are painful - and not easily forgotten. You may have direct experience of failed relationships (perhaps your parents divorced) and this may make you hyper-critical of your own partner(s). It's a self-defence mechanism that seeks to shield you from further harm, but it doesn't lead to relational satisfaction - especially in the short term.

So far, not so good. Add to that a propensity for being attracted to strict or controlling figures and you can begin to see where Saturn's dubious reputation in this area comes from. However, what is not in doubt is your own serious approach to relationships - and all that this entails. You may be cautious, but you have high standards. You learn from your early relationship mistakes and, as you age, you gain control by making the right choices and decisions. With Saturn here, you don't like wasting your time and you will reject those who are not going to be a worthwhile long-term proposition. Your relationships need to be long lasting and loyal. So, you may commit at a later age than your peers, or there may be a significant age difference between you and your partner. With Saturn here, you're often prepared to wait for the right person.

Saturn on the **sixth house** side of the Descendant ties your relationships to the house of work. The emphasis here is on making relationships work, but with Saturn it can be so much more than that. Saturn is connected to career and status through its rulership of the tenth house, so Saturn here shows that business or professional partnerships may play an important role in your life. This is a comfortable place for Saturn, and even in a personal relationship, elements of work and discipline will be found. Your romantic partner may be your business partner. Perhaps you are both career-oriented, and maybe you both have a 'business-like' approach to the relationship. What Saturn here does suggest is that the relationship is well ordered; your life together has a certain routine - and that may not be true of your life outside of the partnership.

Saturn here also suggests the need to work hard to keep the relationship healthy. One way of making a relationship work is to ensure that it is structured to ensure the maximum satisfaction for both parties. Given that the sixth house can be a place of inequality, achieving that objective may be a challenge you have to face. Although Saturn works well on this side of the Descendant, you will face many of the challenges that Saturn poses when found on the seventh house side. In addition, Saturn here is also connected to health. Given Saturn's associations with limitation, it may be that some of you will be in a relationship where health issues are a problem. Maybe healthcare in some form will be the focus of your business, in which case you would benefit from Saturn's association with health and hard work in a more positive sense.

Saturn Conjunct Midheaven

We come to Saturn on the **tenth house** side of the Midheaven, the place where Saturn is right at home. However, does Saturn here bring automatic success in your career, or recognition as an 'authority'? The answer to that may be 'all in good time', as Saturn here may work to frustrate your ambitions - particularly in your early years. The self-doubt associated with this planet may undermine your ambitions or your effectiveness. You may experience critical bosses or have bruising encounters with those in authority - and that may include your own parents. You may feel as if you have achieved in life without any visible support from others. This is the 'self-made' placement, and it owes that fact to your self-reliance and your disciplined and persistent climb to the top. You are likely to be deeply loyal to your employer or you may experience long service in a public or civic role.

So, how do you define, 'getting to the top'? For you it's about demonstrating that you have learned from experience and earned the respect that you receive from others in your profession or trade. There are no shortcuts with Saturn here, so you are unlikely to have had a meteoric rise in your career. Career success may not occur until later in life - or it may require you to work on your own towards a specific goal. However, patience is a virtue that is often rewarded. Becoming respectable, authoritative, capable and trustworthy may be reward enough for some of you. For others, being recognised for running your own business, or achieving an executive position will be your defining ambition. Saturn here does suggest that you may work too hard on a regular basis. Your ultimate challenge may be to take a time out before you suffer burn out.

With Saturn on the **ninth house** side of the Midheaven, structure is found in the house of abstract thought, and it's allied to your career. The ability to organise thoughts and concepts - and make them real - is a blessing indeed. Those with Saturn here may (or may not) be found in academia and research, science, business or the arts, but the thing they will have in common is this; the ability to translate ideas into something that can have a material impact on the lives of the rest of us. Saturn implies 'mastery' of your subject and, with it in this position, you would make an excellent teacher or lecturer. It's a career that you are likely to be involved with long-term - or you may have entered the profession in your later years. Saturn is consistently associated with age and time. You are likely to be an authority on your subject and will be regarded as such.

However, the association with higher or further education may manifest in a different way. Saturn's reliable caution - and some self-limiting beliefs - may have made you wary of further study, particularly in your youth. You may have attended the 'University of Life' but realised later that your lack of a formal education restricted your career opportunities. Sometimes we need to make hard decisions and recognise where we went wrong. Saturn here suggests that it's never too late to change your mind. However, as usual with Saturn the danger is you become narrow minded and negative in your world view. A 'fear of flying' (sometimes literally so) may keep you from exploring your full career potential. That is the Saturn challenge you will need to overcome. Sometimes we put mental barriers in place and then complain that the world seems to agree with our limited perspective…

Saturn Opposite Midheaven

Saturn on the **fourth house** side of the Nadir implies that structure and form is found within the home - and usually it suggests that the birth family may have been heavy on discipline and light on love. That sounds emotionally bruising - and I can see those of you with this placement nodding in agreement. Saturn is associated with restriction and limitation, so typical life experiences may include being raised in a family with strict religious beliefs, or traditional cultural practices, or perhaps your family kept themselves to themselves and discouraged social interaction outside of the home. With Saturn here, it's also possible that the family unit was a small one. Being raised as an only child or having 'older' parents or a single parent - usually the mother - is also a possibility. Saturn is also a watchword for responsibility, so you may have assumed some family responsibilities at an early age.

It can be tough, but it's not the only option with Saturn here. Family bonds may be tight but that's not to say they're not loving or loyal in a Saturn kind of way. There may have been encouragement for your ambitions and an emphasis on hard work, but it may have been that your parents were concerned with setting a good example rather than being deliberately harsh towards you. Your background may have also seen your home used for a family business, or you may have gained your first working experience alongside one or the other of your parents. That may have given a 'business-like' feel to the family home and you may have followed your parents career footsteps by working in the same business or industry. Following a family tradition - in whatever form - is suggested with Saturn here, as is the likelihood of creating a solid and enduring base in life.

Saturn on the **third house** side of the Nadir places all those Saturn connotations in the house of the mind and communications - and they are forever linked to the place you come from. In a broad sense, this may mean your home and family, homeland or even your personal memories, so let's look at how Saturn's influence works here. Your family may not be that communicative or communication may have been functional rather than engaging. There may have been communication or educational issues in the home too; your parents may have been poorly educated or they may have had a negative view of education, considering school a 'waste of time'. You may have had siblings with speech or educational issues, or even mobility issues - or it's possible you are affected in that way. Saturn here can restrict more than the mind.

Again, it seems like a severe placement to have at the heart of your home, however - as with any placement - that's not the only outcome. Saturn here can indicate that your parents considered education to be very important indeed - and you may have been encouraged to view it that way too. You may have had parent who was an educator or who was involved in the communicating professions in some way. The home was likely to be a place of learning, but it may have had to be so. Saturn also suggests restriction in communication in another sense; the language spoken in your home may have been different to the language spoken outside. If your family were from another country, you may have needed to learn a second language - and that may not have been easy. It may have delayed your progress through school, and you may have needed to work harder than your peers.

Uranus

When Uranus is close to an angle in your birth chart, you can expect the unexpected in the area of your life that is touched by the 'shock jock' of the solar system. Uranus is considered the 'higher octave' manifestation of Mercury and often shares that planet's intellectual and communicative concerns. However, it is a far more progressive and independent force than the messenger god. Uranus conjunct an angle challenges you to do things differently. Whatever the norms and values of your family or society are, you will be determined to challenge them. Whether that is provocative or visionary - only you will know. Either way, you won't care what anyone else thinks. That's Uranus.

Uranus Conjunct Ascendant

Uranus conjunct the Ascendant in the **first house** is going to get you noticed. It's often said that Uranus here makes you physically 'different' in appearance. Some may be born that way but given that you usually have some control and a degree of personal choice about how you present yourself, Uranus here usually shows that your appearance is different from the norm because you want to be seen that way. Uranus is the most independent and individualistic of planets. It's also often the most contrary and rebellious, so you will rebel against any attempt to get you to conform to other people's notions about what is sartorially acceptable. You embody your own unconventional inclinations; not everyone with Uranus here will have green hair, but you will know exactly what you need to do to make an impact.

Uranus's impact is not always visible on the surface. It's one of the intellectual planets - some would say nerdy - so the impact is likely to extend to your personality. You may look normal but have something of the 'geek' about you. Uranus here can create the kind of intense and focused personality that is often seen in the archetypal loner who is happiest on their own, doing their own thing. A sharp, unwavering focus is part of the Uranus package as is a strong persona. Uranus is magnetic, charismatic and opinionated. You love your personal freedom and hate any challenges to your right to be yourself. Energetic, fierce and unemotional, you have little time for those who are not as progressive or forward thinking as you. It's an impulsive energy and adds a nervous excitement to even the gentlest of ascending signs.

When Uranus is found on the **twelfth house** side of the Ascendant, Uranus is expressed in an inward and reflective manner. Given the nature of this planet, that's not always easy, so I must ask, how well do you sleep? Uranus keeps you awake at night, as it has a well-deserved reputation for speeding up the mind - think Mercury with rocket boosters. If you're the type of person whose mind races in the dead of night? Blame Uranus. However, flashes of insight, the ability to process problems - and find radical solutions to them - can be the result. The problem may be that you remain misunderstood. Your ideas may even be too difficult for you to own, so you suppress your own genius. I'm using the word 'genius' here in its true sense to mean your own special qualities, aptitudes, capabilities or creative impulses that, if expressed, would mark you out from the crowd.

We often find it hard to own a planet in the twelfth house - and that's even more of an issue when that planet conjuncts the

Ascendant. Uranus here may be projected at an unconscious level, so if you are recognised for some special quality by others, you may fail to see that quality in yourself or you may try to play it down. You may, deep down, want to be free to express who you are in your own way, but you fear that will prove to be a lonely experience. Underlying feelings of alienation can result with Uranus here. However, there are more positive outcomes. Uranus is concerned with society and social issues. You may 'give away' Uranus and become involved exposing social problems that should concern us all. That way, your identity connects with 'the masses' - especially the hidden or marginalised groups in society. Uranus enables you to identify with everyone and that may be its gift.

Uranus Opposite Ascendant

Uranus on the **seventh house** side of the Descendant places the planet of extreme individuality in the part of your natal chart that defines your relationships. Regardless of the descending sign, Uranus here is the mark of individuality in relationships. You may have an unconventional approach to relationships (by the standards of the culture in which you live) or you may want your partner to appear to be different from in some way. Uranus is thus projected onto your partner; they may have an unusual sense of style or appearance, or they may be 'Uranian' in some way - perhaps they have a career in science or technology - or maybe people simply think that they are weird. It may be that the two of you together present as an 'odd couple'. The two of you may be perceived as a mismatch in some way, but that - to you - may be the thing that makes the relationship work.

There are often issues of commitment when Uranus influences partnerships. Uranus loves freedom and is uncompromising. As partnerships are about give and take, you may have to negotiate your way around that one. Fortunately, you understand that relationships are based on equality. In fact, that may be the most positive influence of Uranus here. Equality, fairness and excitement are as much a part of the Uranus imprint as detachment and rebelliousness. Injecting positive Uranian qualities into a relationship is the message you need to understand, as with all Descendant issues, it's the relationship that needs to embody the principles of the descending sign and any planetary placements close to the Descendant. With Uranus here, you need to be honest and uncompromising in your quest to achieve that objective.

With Uranus on the **sixth house** side of the Descendant, your relationships are bound to the space where we seek to improve our lives. The sixth house is the house of mastery, a place where skills are perfected, and with Uranus here opposed to the Ascendant relationships are tied not only to our lifestyle choices, but also to our routines. A relationship here is not going to be 'run of the mill'; it runs to a different timetable to the lifestyles of most of the rest of us. So, what does that imply? What is a non-routine relationship? Uranus's freedom issues may surface even more markedly than on the seventh house side of the Descendant. Couples who are together but have separate lives, or partners whose working routines (like shift patterns or travel for work) mean that establishing a regular lifestyle is difficult are examples of this in practice. The partnership may need to embrace irregularity in some form.

It takes a certain type of person to endure chaos, but with Uranus the partnership may be chaotic in some form. That does not mean either of the partners are badly organised people; external influences - work related, health related or simply things that you didn't see coming - may disrupt the relationship from time to time. However, Uranus here may indicate you have a certain genius for making partnerships work - no matter how unusual or unlikely the partnership may appear to be. One reason for this may be your ability to look at the relationship from a different angle - and that applies to business and professional partnerships too. It may suit you to have a more distant relationship, or one where you maintain your own space within the relationship. You may simply work together in a Uranian-type business. Or freelance. Together.

Uranus Conjunct Midheaven

Uranus conjunct the Midheaven on the **tenth house** side of the cusp suggests a certain amount of independence or rebelliousness in career matters, and it also indicates that your work face or public image will be unusual in some way. Regardless of the sign on the Midheaven, you are likely to follow a career path that is unusual in the context of your family, social or cultural background. So, you may do something different - even if that difference isn't immediately apparent to the rest of the world. Of course, the thing you do may be unusual. An unconventional career or one that requires an independent and radical approach is likely to be a career route that interests you. However, you may need to avoid the temptation to be different for its own sake. That may not get you anywhere.

With Uranus conjunct the Midheaven you will find it difficult to accept social norms. Any attempt by society to define you will result in some reactive behavioural issue that may undermine your ambition or potential. Attempting to shock those with whom you must co-exist is not always a smart move, and yet you are likely to be a smart cookie - even if unconventionally so. You see your role as one of re-defining society's rules; whether society agrees may be another thing entirely. So how can you get this placement to work to your advantage? Allowing your originality to shine may be one way of doing it. Using your intellectual gifts is another. Uranus has an affinity with society, so rather than alienating it, you would do well to understand social concerns. Your contribution to that debate could be powerful - you 'get' the issues and will not shy away from articulating them.

On the **ninth house** side of the Midheaven, Uranus has an intellectual focus - even more so than in the tenth house where its rebellious traits may dominate. That's not to say that Uranus here isn't capable of contrariness. The ninth house is where we gain perspective on life. When Uranus is conjunct the Midheaven on the ninth house side, that perspective may be taken from a strange angle. A unique world view, a tendency to give voice to jarring opinions and an incisive mind may make for a political extremist. Even if you don't see yourself that way, I suspect you will be recognised as one who challenges mainstream opinions and who is more than willing to offer an alternative perspective on what you see as the way ahead. It's not that you have all the answers, you simply believe in asking questions - and some of those questions may be difficult to answer.

Intellect and enquiry are wedded to your career and public image; many of you will find a great outlet in higher level education or those occupations that require hypothesis, analysis or a scientific mind - and I use the term 'science' to include the full range of social sciences too. You are likely to be a natural student and need considerable mental stimulation. A downside of this placement may be that you are easily bored by people and situations you feel have nothing to offer you intellectually or have nothing to offer society other that the same worn-out attitudes that you generally despise. For such a proponent of freedoms - freedom of thought and speech in particular - you may be surprisingly intolerant. However, there is a silver lining; you are genuinely friendly, and it is not impossible to get you to change your ideas. Radical reform appears to start in the mind.

Uranus Opposite Midheaven

Uranus opposite the Midheaven - in the **fourth house** - places the god of disruption in the family and home. Most people like to be rooted to a family or to a place, but with Uranus here, the Nadir may represent a point of instability rather than the reliable anchorage we suppose it to be. As this placement is a private and inner space, Uranus may manifest at an inner level and that instability may be felt emotionally. However, unstable feelings and uncertain responses come from somewhere, and Uranus may represent some tangible, chaotic or disruptive events in your lived experience - particularly as it relates to your childhood, home and family. Patterns set in our early years tend to repeat, so Uranus in the fourth house side of the Nadir may indicate a lifetime of domestic disruption; frequent house moves, and relationship changes are often typical.

So, is this such a deeply buried placement that it's hard to deal with it in a conscious manner? The answer to that is complex;

Uranus here is an unemotional placement in an emotional place. You may intellectualise your feelings or detach from them as a way of coping with things that were uncomfortable in your younger years. Feeling alienated from your family, being the 'odd one out' (or being made to feel that way) or coming from a family where emotional contact was either rare - or of the 'wrong' kind - is not uncommon with Uranus here. You may have experienced emotional distance or volatility from at least one of your parents. Unsurprisingly, you may have always felt a need for independence, and you may have decided to live on your own from an early age. Personal independence and self-reliance may have given you a stable base from which to move forward in life.

With Uranus on the **third house** side of the Nadir, the impact of this planet is more likely to be experienced at a mental and intellectual level, though with Uranus you must always expect the unexpected; some of the domestic and familial issues associated with the fourth house placement may also be experienced because of the proximity to the Nadir. Uranus here suggests you will come from a family background that was intellectually or academically stimulating. However, the opposite may also be true; you may have been the genius in a family where educational attainment had always been average at best. Whether you fall in either of those camps - or anywhere in-between - you may have been precociously intelligent and surprised your parents by learning to speak and read in advance of your peers.

So, did that make you a model student? Uranus can be opinionated, contrary and bloody minded; you may have been able to communicate and process information at an early age, but you are likely to be impatient with mere mortals who cannot compute as fast as you. Mental intolerance is also a mark of

Uranus here. You are easily bored when you're placed in an environment that doesn't provide the stimulation you need at the pace you need, and where you're also likely to be subject to rules that simply make you want to rebel. If that sounds a lot like your school experience, then that's not surprising. Working in groups is not for you as you hate to be held back by others - you prefer to study or work on your own, unfettered by unwelcome input. This may be interpreted as intellectual arrogance; it's often a quarrelsome placement for Uranus - yet it's a friendly and funny one too.

Neptune

Neptune conjunct a cardinal point in your birth chart is, like the presence of the other outer planets, a challenging one. Neptune may inspire but it also obscures. Maintaining a grip on reality is hard with Neptune close to a cardinal point. One of the major Neptunian issues concerns defining and maintaining your boundaries; with Neptune lines are often blurred. However, Neptune is also responsible for artistic and creative inspiration - though for this to achieve its greatest potential, Neptune needs to be firmly anchored to avoid being lost at sea.

NEPTUNE CONJUNCT ASCENDANT

Neptune on the **first house** side of the Ascendant is a placement that sensitises, obscures and may even undermine the persona that you try to create - regardless of what your ascending sign may be. The extroverted signs are softened end the already introverted signs may fade into obscurity - at least that's what conventional wisdom would have us believe. Neptune here is outwardly expressed. When it's connected to your self-image, you may be sensitive about your appearance and how you feel other people may react to you. This can lead to the famous Neptunian 'shape shifting', as you re-imagine your personality to blend in with whoever is in your immediate environment. You may not want to stand out in the crowd, so Neptune may be shy or evasive. The art of disappearing is one you may have perfected over the years.

Yet there is a paradox. Like the other outer planets, Neptune is a big player. You can't hide its influence - though you'll try hard. Work with it in the positive sense and you will regard yourself as creative and imaginative. Others may call you a daydreamer, a fantasist or simply unrealistic in your approach to life but fantasy and imagination play a huge part in how you feel best able to express who you are. Life for you is best experienced with you at the centre of your own dream world. It may be glamorous and escapist at times, but sometimes it simply enables you to let go of the things that would drag you down. You are conscious of all kinds of influences coming at you from all directions; the trick with Neptune conjunct the Ascendant is to allow yourself to go with the life's flow - and not be caught up with the currents and drown.

Neptune on the **twelfth house** side of the Ascendant is completely at home in the house that it rules. The twelfth house represents our 'hidden enemies' and, with Neptune conjunct the Ascendant here, the hidden enemy is most likely to be yourself. Neptune taps into your unconscious and, when allied to your self-image, it can obscure your sense of who you are and how you can best express yourself. You may be uncertain about how to best present yourself. Inner fears and complexes may become visible for all to see - except you. You may be blind to your own abilities and as a result you may lack self-confidence. You may feel isolated, self-conscious, shy and misunderstood. This is often not an easy placement. Getting in tune with yourself (a good night's sleep or time out from other people) is essential to those with Neptune here.

So how can you lighten the raw vulnerability and anxiety that comes with Neptune? The urge to escape is always huge with Neptune - and this can be seen in the addictions and dependencies that abound with Neptune on either side of the Ascendent. The twelfth house side is particularly vulnerable because it's the unconscious side. It's hard to deal with something you cannot see. However, that same vulnerability and sensitivity allows you to look within. Acknowledging your own frailties enables you to develop great empathy for those who suffer and using this gift to help others may be one way of dealing with your own issues. This is also an inspired, artistically creative and spiritual placement. You are tuned in to the realisation that there is more in this universe that the logical and material - and that is this placement's greatest gift of all.

Neptune Opposite Ascendant

With Neptune on the **seventh house** side of the Descendant, Neptune enters the realm of your relationships - and once again it's not an easy placement. Neptune idealises - and that takes the partner (and the relationship) into the realm of fantasy when all concerned need to be rooted on Planet Earth. So, how does that manifest? Regardless of the descending sign, the temptation is to see the partner, not as they are, but as who you want them to be. It suggests that in your younger years you created a fantasy of what relating would be like - and that may cause problems finding a partner who can meet that ideal. So, you may experience relationships with people who are not what they seem, or who vanish when you desire commitment. Relationships founder on contact with reality - and that leaves you hurt and alone.

Chasing rainbows always ends in disappointment, so how can you learn to overcome any negative Neptune influence here? First, you need to address your own complicity in the situation. Being unrealistic about relationships may be something you need to work on, as is your own undressed need to remain detached, or any issues you may have with working out just who you really are.

Neptune here can make it difficult to establish deep intimate connections; the need to escape does not sit easily with the desire to relate. All that sounds like a big ask, but when Neptune is the problem, Neptune is also the solution. Use your instincts to work out what is real - and what is not. What you don't need is to become a relationship victim, so use your talent for soul connection to connect to reality. It's the only place you will find that soul mate you desire.

Neptune on the **sixth house** side of the Descendant is also concerned with relationships, but the emphasis here is often on dealing with the practical side of relationships. Our daily lives are the nuts and bolts of relational reality - so you can guess what happens when we find Neptune here. Organisation is a challenge, and a disordered lifestyle may form part of your relationship picture. This means that your life together falls on the messy side of the spectrum, but it can also mean that accommodating Neptune in the relationship has a more idealistic cast. Coping with a partner's health issues may be one outcome. So may a shared interest in a spiritual approach to your daily lives. Shared spiritual practices such as prayer, meditation, yoga - or even shared occupations in areas related to health and wellbeing - may be the mark of Neptune here.

The sixth house is can also be a sign of unequal relationships and some of the things I have already mentioned point towards that being a relational issue. Caring for another person, whilst done with love, puts the burden onto their partner, as does coping with the everyday impact of addictions or unreliability. This is also a placement that suggests partners may be subject to separation - not necessarily in a divorce kind of a way - but as a result of one partner's work obligations. Every sailor's partner will know what I mean by that. In this kind of situation, one partner will be primarily responsible for the daily chores. If you didn't know how to stand on your own two feet, then you will need to learn how to do so, otherwise it could get messy. Literally. Neptune here uses the relationship to help you learn to manage your life - though at times it may seem rather unfair.

NEPTUNE CONJUNCT MIDHEAVEN

When Neptune conjunct the Midheaven falls on the **tenth house** side, Neptune affects your career and your public image or status. If we look at your career options first, Neptune may be variously creative and artistic, caring, empathetic and spiritual - or have a leaning towards maritime or liquid/gas occupations. Much will depend on your Midheaven sign to determine how you approach your workplace and 'work face', but one more thing to be borne in mind is this. Neptune here may make it difficult for you to decide on a career path at all. Neptune obscures and idealises, so you may experience problems seeing a way ahead, or you may be wholly unrealistic in your expectations. Neptune here may also point to Neptune-type parental issues that may influence you in your eventual career choice. It's often a sign that you need to be emotionally attached to what you do.

Neptune in this position attaches a Neptunian label to you. You may be identified by your career (see above), but you may also be arrested for public drug or alcohol offences. Addict and drunkard are also labels in Neptune's Midheaven collection and there is the risk of glamourising 'alternative' lifestyles. Neptune here may also signal periods of unemployment. Escapism and work are conjoined, and, in some instances, your career may slip away from you. If, or when, this happens? You may find it difficult to get back on track. Neptune and victimisation also go hand in hand. You may feel like a victim of a bad employer or become dependent on public aid - either on a temporary or permanent basis. If it sounds like Neptune gives you a hard time here - that can happen. Cultivating belief in your own abilities and ambitions is often the key to living with this Neptune placement.

Neptune on the **ninth house** side of the Midheaven may be slightly easier to live with - though it does share the same propensity for escapism and illusion. That aside, Neptune on this side of the Midheaven benefits from being in an expansive, hopeful and optimistic domain and while this may lead to career matters being unrealistic, it may also lead to a vocation that is rooted in faith, spiritual enquiry or a quest to discover more about the meaning of the universe - in all its forms. Not everyone here will be an academic; academia or the contemplative life may offer an escape from the rigours of corporate climbing, but so does travelling in search of universal truths of another kind. Dropping out of higher education or mainstream society or taking time out to 'find yourself' on distant shores is not uncommon with this placement.

So how can you deal with Neptune on this side of the Midheaven in a productive manner? In truth, you may not want to. The allure of the mystical world may prove too overwhelming. However, there is always the potential for the Midheaven to stabilise Neptune's influence without negating it. The intuitive and visionary gifts of Neptune are strong in this house and, when allied to the Midheaven, creative, inspiring and visionary ideas can be the result. Many a successful businessperson has combined Neptunian inspiration with the solidity of the Saturn-ruled

Midheaven to great effect. Neptune's intuition and 'feel' for what the public want (when allied to the MC) can lead to successful businesses and careers that depend on having your 'finger on the pulse'. For all its problematic associations, Neptune conjunct the Midheaven can be both shrewd and successful.

Neptune Opposite Midheaven

When Neptune opposes the Midheaven on the **fourth house** side, the planet of clouds draws a veil over your private life. You may look back on your early years with an imagined fondness, or you may fantasise that things could have been different somehow. Wisdom tells us that this placement often indicates a dysfunctional family. This may be true for some. Issues with substance abuse in the home may have been an issue in your early life - and patterns set then may replay throughout your life in a home and family context. Loss of a parent or negligent parenting may also be issues with this placement. However, many of you will have genuinely fond memories of your early years. The IC reminds us of the past - and even if your memories are rose-tinted, it doesn't mean that they are false.

If you spent happy holidays at the seaside or learned to sail because your parents were keen on outdoor activities, or maybe you lived near water - then Neptune is working well for you in this position. There may be maritime ancestry in your mother's family. You may feel more attached to your mother than to your father. Boundaries are blurred with Neptune, and you may have experienced problems detaching from your mother. Forming your own secure base is the challenge we face in the fourth house and that may feel more threatening to you than most. However, if Neptune is working well, you will want your base to be your 'ideal home'. Having your own space to retreat to will be important to you - and you will be conscious of making your base as life-enhancing and beautiful as possible. It's your refuge from life's storms.

Neptune on the **third house** side of the Nadir is often associated with some forms of mental disorder and in combination with the IC, there is the potential for this to run in the family. There may have been a certain 'nervousness', particular in your mother's behaviour. Perhaps she was 'highly strung' or overly worried - and those feelings of insecurity may have transferred themselves to you. Neptune is porous and thoughts have remarkably effective wings when Neptune is around. However, it would be a mistake to ignore the more positive outcomes of Neptune here. These include having a family background that was, perhaps, notable for inspiring your imaginative and creative mental faculties. If you were encouraged to play - and enjoyed - games of 'make-believe' as a child, then Neptune will have helped you to realise the value of learning through play.

Of course, imaginative play is a great escape valve. Other worlds are often less threatening than the one we inhabit. In the real world, you may be ignored, go unheard or unseen or simply find interactions with others threatening in the extreme. The vulnerability associated with Neptune here can lead to shyness and active seclusion - perhaps as a response to bullying or childhood cruelty. There may even have been issues with your siblings that caused you to withdraw into your own, more soothing and congenial world. As the family 'dreamer', you may have been reminded of your inability to pay attention or your oversensitivity to the words of those around you. Perhaps it's a pattern that persists today; a positive attribute of Neptune here is to use your imagination to inspire others. Your words have a magical quality. Use them well.

Pluto

With Pluto conjunct an angle of your natal chart you could be forgiven for feeling as if the universe is punishing you in some way. Pluto is associated with things like power and power games, existential angst and cataclysmic change, so it seems you may experience some tough challenges in the parts of your life represented by the cardinal point aspected by Pluto. However, Pluto also represents the power of transformation; recognising and reclaiming your own power is likely to be a big issue for those of you with Pluto in aspect to a cardinal point.

Pluto Conjunct Ascendant

Pluto conjunct the Ascendant in the **first house** is a powerful placement. Much has been said about Pluto here producing a persona that is deep, secretive, complicated, intense and intimidating - and for some with this placement, that may be true. For most of you, your identity is bound up with your personal transformation and that means your persona is oriented towards being in complete control of how you wish to be seen in this world. You create and re-create your self-image as you feel is required. You have a charismatic personality and a great deal of self-control. That doesn't mean that you're necessarily as dark and dangerous as Pluto is reputed to be. You present yourself according to your ascending sign, but there is a hint of something more under the surface. You have presence and you are likely to be able to command the room - and read it too. Your intuition is finely tuned.

Why is the power of transformation so important to you? You are acutely aware of the need to adapt to the world around you.

Dramatic change may be a feature of your life - and personal growth and transformation often occurs through the medium of 'a drama'; you may even initiate such events in order to push yourself forward. You fear being engulfed in a tide of challenging emotional responses. Jealousy and fanaticism are not unknown to you. However, you fear losing control more than anything else. You are emotionally resourceful and highly analytical, and this may help you to overcome those self-destructive moments. Transformation occurs when you realise you have the power to make your own choices and the freedom to be your authentic self - without damaging either yourself or those you love.

With Pluto on the **twelfth house** side of the Ascendant, you may be unaware of the extent of your own power. Regardless of your ascending sign, you may be difficult to get to know as there is part of you that remains unavailable. You may strike people as secretive and this hints at one of the issues that those of you with this placement are more likely to experience - and that issue is trust. You may present with a perfectly pleasant personality, but you tend to keep people at arm's length because, fundamentally, you don't trust them. This often arises because you have a great awareness of your own vulnerability - and an equally deep awareness of the 'soft underbelly' of other people too. This ability to see into another's soul can work both ways. You can sense hidden motivations and whether they are telling you the truth - or downright lies. This can make you a natural detective.

Your self-image is something you are adept at hiding - but not necessarily in a bad way. Yes, you may suffer periods or shyness or keep yourself to yourself but having a persona that can be so effectively masked enables you to access your own unconscious - and that of other people to a marked degree. You can be remarkable sensitive and empathetic to the concerns of others - in some ways that's a deflection of your own insecurities. In this context, you may appear fearless and capable of helping those with real psychological struggles from a position of deep understanding. To reach this position, you may have had to heal your own trauma. Pluto here may signify someone who has had to transform themselves - mentally and emotionally - in order to survive. Your natural orientation is towards meeting life's challenges - without being your own worst enemy.

Pluto Opposite Ascendant

Pluto on the **seventh house** side of the Descendant brings Pluto into your relationships, and it's a demanding placement if not handled well. Let's explore why this may be so. There's something I'm going to call the 'freedom-closeness dilemma' and it works like this. You yearn to merge with your partner, yet you resist the loss of autonomy and control that this would entail. Pluto can transform a primary relationship into a battleground, a contest of wills, as you and your partner find yourselves having to work through issues of jealousy, possessiveness, trust (or lack of it) and control. With Pluto here, you may meet your own Pluto issues through your partner; coercive and controlling relationships are a possibility with Pluto opposite the Ascendant. At the very least, you may experience some form of emotional abuse from time to time.

When such problems arise, they demand a response. Often, difficult relationships maybe the route to personal empowerment for those with this Pluto placement. You may need to confront your fears of rejection, loss or betrayal and recognise that any Pluto issues you project in a relationship may be due to your own

Pluto issues. Dealing with relational matters as basic as equality and sharing, may be a feature of Pluto on the Descendant. As with all Pluto placements, there is much to be learned before a situation can be transformed. Relationships are your vehicle for that and, as Pluto also connects you with regeneration and healing, acknowledgement of your own complicity in those intensely painful episodes may lead to a complete transformation of your partnerships.

Pluto on the **sixth house** side of the Descendant brings those same partnership issues to the fore but it may be easier for you to deal with them in a therapeutic context. This is a Pluto placement that lends itself to deep analysis and healing, yet you may also have to contend with obsession and problem solving - or even an obsession with problem solving. So, there is a chance that you analyse your relationships to death, rather than simply enjoying them. Pluto here may also show a connection to relationship counselling; if your obsession is to make relationships work, then you may encounter this as a client or a practitioner. The deep insights you have into *how* relationships work may lead to a 'relating' career, and this may be a passionate and healing vocation for someone with Pluto here.

As with many sixth house conjunctions to the Descendant, Pluto may also be influential in business and professional partnerships. A partnership here may be plutonic in nature - but it may be the line of work that resonates with the Lord of Darkness. In personal relationships, Pluto here may indicate that your partner is a workaholic or works in a business that deals with taboo subjects, such as death, wealth or taxes. If this placement describes a business or professional relationship, the business itself may deal in matters that are private, sensitive and where absolute trust is vital. Research and investigative industries also fall under Pluto's remit. A business partnership may, incidentally, suffer from some of the same relational issues as a personal relationship. Power, trust and financial issues have the potential to destroy the relationship.

PLUTO CONJUNCT MIDHEAVEN

When Pluto is so elevated in your birth chart that it conjuncts the Midheaven, it is a powerful planet indeed. On the **tenth house** side of the MC, Pluto grants an immense determination to achieve in life - preferably in your own way. Single-mindedness and ruthless ambition may accompany this placement, but before you start making plans to become an oligarch, for most of you, Pluto here makes you a determined and responsible professional whose 'work face' is likely to be tough - but fair - and committed to improving your organisation, workplace or career prospects. You may also be a high achiever because you stand out from your peers, though things can work the other way too. Sometimes standing out can lead to the wrong kind of attention and, with Pluto here, issues like dealing with bullying in the workplace are not unheard of.

So, how do you avoid having a target on your back? Mostly by having the sense to keep your head down and avoid the situations that could make you vulnerable. As with all Pluto placements, you're highly sensitised to the environment around you and this enables you to side-step the pitfalls of office politics more adeptly than most. It also helps to have an eye for detail, work hard and have considerable leadership potential. Many of you will know how to work the system - in a good way of course - yet there is the potential with this placement to stop at nothing to get your own way. Mostly this will manifest as a gift for persuasion that comes in useful as you negotiate your way to the top. At a deeper level - and Pluto is deep - your ambitions may originate from your relationship with your dominant parent. Proving something to the world (father) is often a factor with Pluto here.

With Pluto on the **ninth house** side of the Midheaven, your mind is powerful, and you may have great depth of understanding; however, that depth of understanding is likely to be tightly focused. The expert whose understanding of a particular subject or specific issue is a notable feature of their public status, may have this placement, but what they are unlikely to have is the breadth of understanding that would enable them to pontificate on other unrelated issues. Expertise in one area does not necessarily confer great knowledge about everything else, and those who are tempted, by the power of their own belief system, to impose their beliefs on others may be revealed as narrow minded or dogmatic. Pluto here may be a charismatic crusader or have messianic zeal - and be recognised as such.

What this placement may also confer, is a deep interest in understanding how religions and other ideologies (such as political beliefs) affect human nature. You may be deeply philosophical and driven to understand more about the world in which we live - and beyond. This quest for a universal truth - or truth in a more earthly setting - may reveal itself in your career choices; the law (in a judicial sense), academic research or any other occupation the has 'investigation' at its core, are likely to feature in your public profile. One other thing with this placement is that it may mean travel is important to you. The Midheaven is often a signifier of 'importance' and, with Pluto nearby, this may be mean that travel has been life changing for you or is connected to your own personal renewal in some form.

Pluto Opposite Midheaven

With Pluto opposite the Midheaven on the **fourth house** side of the Nadir, your personal, home and family life are going to be affected by the planet of destruction and renewal. It may seem as if the universe has a vendetta against you. Many of you with this placement may be nodding in agreement with that statement, as your life may have been affected by issues such as bereavement, divorce and financial loss. Deep churning feelings arise when your security or the stability of your base is threatened in any way. The events that prompt those feelings may not be as drastic as the things I've mentioned above. It's your responses that may be the issue here - and if you have this placement, you're likely to understand - at a deep level - what it means to feel threatened, helpless and out of control.

That deep understanding is possibly the greatest gift you can receive from, what can be, a difficult placement in your natal chart. The drive to be in control of your own life and secure your own base is strong with Pluto here. This may mean you need to make difficult choices, often involving leaving your birth family or homeland behind you. This may be because your original home life was problematic in some way; a domineering mother or parents who were overly controlling may have been an issue. Those issues may even remain a problem in your life if the deeper emotional impact of them is not addressed. To break the pattern of 'family troubles' requires conscious emotional resilience and the ability to recreate your own secure base. In milder cases, this may translate as an ability to physically create and recreate 'homes' and transform the lives of others too. It's surprising how often those two extremes are connected. That's Pluto.

When Pluto falls on the **third house** side of the Nadir, there is an intensity to your mental processes and often in the way you communicate or, more to the point, don't communicate. Dark thoughts and an element of secrecy may occur when Pluto is here and, because of the proximity to the IC, they may arise from the experiences of your earliest years. If there were things left unspoken in the family, then this is the placement to advertise that fact. There may be issues to do with mental illness, or issues with your siblings; everything from disability or crime falls under Pluto's umbrella. However, early experiences may make you empathetic and incisive. You may have the ability to see under surface appearances, secrets, and lies, and you are likely to be highly analytical in any situation.

Pluto here grants you the ability to manipulate and use information - and you may do so to obtain personal advantage. I hesitate to call it the placement of the manipulator or spy, but there's no doubt that you can sift out details that would be lost on others. You're also extremely persuasive. When such plutonic traits fall close to the Nadir, however, it means that you act in this way because - whatever the issues are - they feel existential to you. The ability to manipulate, dissemble or charm is self-protective - and whatever it is that you need protection from it almost certainly happened a long time ago. You may need therapy at some point in your life - and with this placement you would potentially make a good therapist yourself, having the observational and analytical skills to draw out your client's deepest fears and concerns.

Chapter Five

Constructing Reality

First things first. If you're reading this page, I want to thank you for getting so far along in this book. However, there's one more thing that I feel it's important to consider when you're analysing the cardinal points in your birth chart. And it's rulerships. Why, in a book about the natal chart angles - the cardinal points - am I going to include a chapter that discusses rulerships? To answer that, I'm going to remind you of something I said right at the beginning of this book. It's about framing the narrative. Your own story. So, consider this. If the angles represent the major plot lines in your life, then the rulers of your natal chart angles provide some of the twists and turns in your story. They provide the detail and fine tuning. And they function something like this…

Rulerships are the great connectors. They add a rich layer of depth and complexity to natal chart interpretation. However, in the context of this book, I want to look at another aspect of the importance of rulerships, and that is how the ruler of a house cusp enables that energies of the sign on the house cusp to find a 'natural' or easy outlet. If I may put it this way, it's like electricity finding the easiest route to earth. All house cusps fall in a sign and all signs have a ruler - and they are all present in your natal chart in some house or other.

The energies associated with the signs in which any of your cardinal points are located, will manifest most easily in the house where the sign's ruling planet is found. You are probably familiar with the planets that rule the signs - Mars rules Aries, Venus rules Taurus and so on - and I have included at list of the chart rulers at the end of this book if you need a reminder. You will notice that some of the planets - Mercury, Venus - have double the workload of the Sun and Moon as they govern two signs each - Gemini and Virgo (Mercury) and Taurus and Libra (Venus). You will also notice that Mars, Jupiter and Saturn also govern two signs each - Aries and Scorpio (Mars), Sagittarius and Pisces (Jupiter) and Capricorn and Aquarius (Saturn). Those three 'traditional' planets are also paired with an outer 'modern' planet (Saturn/Uranus, Jupiter/Neptune and Mars/Pluto) so that Scorpio, Aquarius and Pisces have two rulers apiece. It's this latter day 'modern rulership' that is the subject of debate in the astrological world - as I am about to explain.

The Rulership Question

Prior to the discovery of Uranus, Neptune and Pluto, there wasn't an issue to debate. All the classical planets - Mercury through Saturn - rule two signs in traditional astrology. The Sun and Moon rule one each - Leo and Cancer - and this is the reason why. In traditional astrology, rulerships reflect the polarity of the signs, the masculine and feminine interplay that keeps the universe in balance or, if you prefer, the 'yin and yang' approach to keeping things in order. Astrology loves balance, and the traditional rulership model certainly emphasises that. If you look at the rulership diagram in Appendix Two, you'll notice that this rulership model emphasises the importance of the Sun and Moon in your natal chart. They sit there - like a King and Queen on their thrones - with the remainder of the classical planets gathered around them like courtiers. It's a neat, tidy and perfectly symmetrical model, but it does more than please a celestial desire for order.

The traditional model enables us to appreciate how our basic human impulses have both an extraverted and introverted form of expression. If you prefer, you can think of this as being energy that is either outwardly expressed or inwardly digested. By connecting the signs in 'pairs' in this way - Cancer & Leo (Sun & Moon); Gemini & Virgo (Mercury); Taurus & Libra, (Venus); Aries & Scorpio (Mars); Sagittarius & Pisces (Jupiter) and Capricorn & Aquarius (Saturn), each planet's energy is given both a masculine (extraverted) and feminine (introverted) form of expression - except the Sun and Moon, of course, as they represent the complementary qualities of masculine and feminine. In the traditional, classical model, we can appreciate how signs ruled by the same planet have similarities and differences. It is polarity - the masculine or feminine forms of expression - that creates those differences. Let's look at some examples.

The planetary ruler of a cardinal point - let's say Mars ruling an Aries Ascendant - will usually be in a different sign to the sign containing the cardinal point. For example, let's suppose Mars, the ruler of that Aries Ascendant, is found in Libra. The ruling planet's own sign shows *how* the ruling planet's energy is expressed. However, because the planet also rules the Ascendant (because of its sign) it also acts as conduit for the energies associated with – in this example – the ascending sign. So, in this example, the expression of Mars in Libra will be affected by an overlay of Aries energy, due to Mars being the ruler of that Aries Ascendant. This Aries energy acts as a modifier to Mars's Libra-style expression. So, in this example, the person with an Aries Ascendant and Mars in Libra may notice an extra boost of Aries impulsiveness or directness that they would not otherwise have.

In some instances, the effect is more marked because of the difference in polarity of the signs involved. Let's look again at Mars as an example of what I mean by this. Mars is the impulse that governs our ability to be assertive - in other words, it enables us to 'go for it'. When Mars rules your Ascendant (because you have the sign of Aries rising), Mars is elevated in your chart because it is your chart ruler. Even if Mars is found in a feminine sign in your natal chart (say Cancer or Virgo) its expression in those signs will be 'punchier' than you would normally expect for Mars in a feminine sign. This is because of the Aries's ascending sign's modifying influence on the way the planet's energies are expressed *and* the importance of the planet as chart ruler.

Of course, polarity goes both ways. In traditional astrology Mars rules both Aries and Scorpio, a feminine sign. So, let's imagine you have Scorpio on an angle, for example, the Midheaven. Mars's expression here, ruling a feminine sign, is more repressed. Mars's traits like assertion, aggression and anger are expressed less directly. If Mars is channeling the Midheaven sign's energies through another 'feminine' sign, then that person's Mars traits will remain 'softened' because of the feminine influences that Mars is channeling. However, what if that Scorpio

Midheaven's ruling Mars is found in a masculine sign? That Mars energy may still not be as 'punchy' as you would expect it to be, particularly (as we are discussing a Midheaven ruler in this example) when it comes to asserting your authority or chasing that career opportunity. I want to stress that Mars will be no less effective; but in this example it would give you a much more internalised and focused drive rather than the fiery, openly combative energy you usually associate with this planet.

That principle applies to all the planets (except the Sun and Moon because they form a masculine/feminine pair on their own) as they all rule two signs in the traditional rulership model. When Mercury-ruled Gemini is found on an angle, the outward, communicative energies associated with 'masculine/air Mercury' are emphasised. When it rules Virgo on an angle, the introspective, practical, inwardly connected 'feminine/earth Mercury' traits dominate. We can make the same observation with Venus, with Taurus on an angle lending this planet a material, or value-driven 'feminine/earth Venus' focus and with Libra, similarly placed, we observe 'masculine/air Venus', with the emphasis on relational and aesthetic concerns. And what of Jupiter and Saturn? The same principle applies. Jupiter as the ruler of Sagittarius is demonstrably 'masculine/fire' Jupiter with a focus on outward expansion, whereas Jupiter ruling Pisces is a 'feminine/water' Jupiter, where expansion is internalised in a spiritual or imaginative manner.

Take a breather for a moment to digest all of that. This is not a book on rulerships (it's a big and complex subject and if you want to go into it more deeply, please see my recommendation below). What I've set out there is the basic principle of how traditional rulerships work. So, what about the modern rulers? If you prefer to use the modern rulers (Uranus/Aquarius, Neptune/Pisces and Pluto/Scorpio) the first thing you notice is that it interrupts that traditional 'yin and yang' model of interpretation. The modern approach to rulerships has a different rationale. There's a thing we talk about in astrology, and it is affinity. It's a word with a simple meaning; 'to have something in common with'. So, the 'new' planets were allocated to the signs that it was felt they had something in common with. For example, has progressive, rebellious Aquarius more in common with the future-oriented energies of Uranus than the serious, structured limitations of Saturn? Similarly, does spaced out Neptune have a natural affinity with dreamy Pisces, and the dark lord Pluto with deep, impenetrable Scorpio? Looked at it this way, the obvious answer may seem to be "yes", but before you dismiss the ancient rulers, I think you need to consider, once more, how they worked in practice.

If we look once more at that Capricorn/Saturn/Aquarius 'love triangle', it seems obvious that Saturn has an affinity with Capricorn. No astrologer is going to argue with you on that one. However, Saturn's relationship with Aquarius is no less valid when you consider how important polarity is to the expression of a planet's energies by sign. Both Capricorn and Aquarius are inflexible; Aquarius is a stubborn fixed sign, and cardinal, earthy Capricorn prefers to be in control. The major difference between how the traditional ruler - Saturn - works with both signs is that, in the case of Capricorn (a feminine sign) energies are directed inwards towards personal ambitions, and with Aquarius (a masculine sign) that same stubborn determination is directed outwards into social, societal or intellectual and idealistic concerns. It's a demonstration of that old 'yin and yang' thing we met earlier.

Many astrologers prefer the elegance of the traditional model, especially when they work with natal charts, and I appreciate why. The traditional planets are the 'visible' planets and, as the chart angles connect you with tangible, material reality, it may seem useful to have planetary rulers that connect to things that can be seen, felt and lived. That's not to say that those of you with signs on your angles that have a 'modern ruler' will not feel a connection to the modern ruling planet. It's likely that most of you will recognise the special place a 'modern ruler' has in your life. It's that affinity thing again. And many astrologers are very comfortable with that too. However, there is one more thing that I think is the astrological 'elephant in the room' as far as modern rulerships are concerned. Why are there only three of them? The solar system contains a great number of small planets and asteroids - more than enough to allocate a ruler to each sign. In fact, there are astrological 'schools of thought' that promote the small planet Ceres as the ruler of Taurus and the dwarf planet Chiron as the ruler of Virgo, given that they too have affinities with those signs. If you're going down the affinities route, the obvious question seems to be, why not go the whole way?

It's an astrological debate that seems set to run, but for now - and for the purpose of this book - my position would be to look at the traditional ruler first and then look at the potential influence of any modern ruler (if applicable). They are not necessarily mutually exclusive positions, as you will see in the examples you'll be reading later in this chapter. Regardless of your preferred approach to rulerships, the key thing to be borne in mind is as follows. As far as the chart angles are concerned, a ruling planet is important in both a very real sense and in a symbolic sense, as it shows how you connect to reality. Things associated with the angular signs and their ruling planets often manifest with great immediacy in your life. So, with that in mind, let's look at the how that works with each angle in turn. You'll note that I've described each cardinal point as a 'complex'. That's not because it's complicated - it simply refers to the network of interconnected energies that combine to create your own personal narrative. They are the threads that weave things together.

The Ascendant Complex

The planet that rules your Ascendant is your chart ruler. Its energies will be of primary importance to you because of its influence on the way that you express yourself - the 'giving out' function of the Ascendant in your natal chart. The qualities of the chart ruler are a vital part of the 'Ascendant Complex', the whole network of connections comprising the ascending sign, its ruler and aspects to and from the ruling planet that influence the ways in which you present yourself physically and materially to the world. It's often said that the 'Ascendant Complex' influences your appearance, however I would qualify that, as I feel it influences *how* you present yourself - your style. I don't believe it influences the genetic inheritance that determines the basics of what you look like.

So, if we look at the Ascendant complex as a determinant of 'presentation', then the ruler of that angle represents the *function* that enables you to best present yourself to the world. For example, the Mercury-ruled (Gemini and Virgo) will present in accordance with the 'Mercury function', i.e., they may 'appear' (a good word to use when you're discussing the Ascendant) everything from scholarly to scattered - or have a marked degree of the mercurial nervous energy that is such a hallmark of both Mercury-ruled signs.

The Ascendant ruler's functions are a visible and defining feature of your outer personality, so it's important to understand *how* and *where* those functions are best expressed. The house position of your chart ruler will often indicate the areas of your life where you are (a) most comfortable in expressing your outer personality or (b) where the activities connected to that house become a defining part of the way in which you present yourself. For example, in a Venus-ruled natal chart, Venus provides the 'outlet' for the qualities of the Ascendant, so Venus-related activities and concerns will have a major role in your approach to life. For example, if that chart-ruling Venus is in the third house, Venus functions (beauty, desire, aesthetics, value) will be best expressed through any of the activities we associate with the third house. You may have a beautiful speaking or singing voice or be notably eloquent in your speech. You may have an expensive car or mobile phone, as the combination of material Venus and the third house works in that way too. You may prefer to keep your expensive mobile phone in a fashionable Venus-inspired protective case. You may even have attractive or wealthy siblings who add value (or otherwise) to your own self-image.

What part does the ruling planet's sign play in all of this? Let's look at a couple of sign placements to see how this affects the third house Venus in our example above. Let's further assume that the Ascendant falls in Taurus with our third house Venus in Leo. Venus in Leo may present as exuberant, flirtatious, and be rather dramatic, playful or amusing in her verbal expression. The Taurus Ascendant's influence may have the effect of adding seductive charm, beauty and artistic expression to her communication abilities. The combination of Taurus and Leo may also give a performer (Leo) with a great singing voice (Taurus) - or at least a notably attractive speaking voice.

If the Ascendant is in Libra, a third house Venus could fall in Capricorn. In that sign, a chart-ruling third house Venus may present as verbally polite and restrained, but Libra would add grace and warmth to what could otherwise be a rather cool location for the goddess of pleasure. Venus in this example may present as smart (in all senses) articulate and business-like - she may be great with finances - but Venus in this example may also have a diplomatic communicating style and highly polished negotiating skills conferred by that Libra Ascendant. Incidentally, in both examples, you may have people who have sisters or siblings (third house) who may be beautiful or artistically accomplished (Venus).

From the above examples, I hope you can see that playing 'follow the ruler' is no more difficult than interpreting your planetary placements in any sign or house. The general principles of the chart ruler's planetary function (what) being expressed in a particular house (where) and a particular sign (how) apply to all the planets and, when that planet is your Ascendant ruler, it will always describe how you create the self-image that you wish to present to the world. It's a lot to unpick, but when you're working through your rulerships, nuance is everything.

The Descendant Complex

The 'Descendant complex' (see above for an explanation) relates to your partner and your approach to relationships. If the Ascendant is what you 'give out' or present to the world, then the

Descendant is what you 'take in' or attract. So, the Descendant ruler has a major role to play in describing not just that process, but the material reality of what - and who - meets the Descendant complex's brief. Unlike the chart ruler, which can have a broad influence on your natal chart, the Descendant ruler really does have a much more specific focus. As you discovered earlier, it's often highly descriptive of both the people you partner up with, as well as describing your own relationship needs. However, it's the description of the partner that tends to be the most immediate manifestation of the 'Descendant complex', both in terms of the Descendant sign itself - and the sign and house where its ruling planet is found.

If I can give you a brief example here, a person who has their Descendant in Aries may have a partner who is (literally) born under that sign, or through their personality, profession, family background, emotional responses or attitudes, they evoke Aries in some way. In astrological terms, they may have strong Aries placements or a heavily tenanted first house. There will always be an Aries-type signature somewhere. In this example the Descendant ruler will be Mars - so what can this planet add to the description?

Let's put Mars (as Descendant ruler) in the fourth house. The partner may be a passionate cook. Or a house builder who uses their physical energies in a constructive way. Or they may be involved with agriculture or horticulture. They may be a passionately involved family person. They may have a military family background. Sadly, they may also be argumentative in the home. With that Mars in the ninth house? The partner may be from another country, or be in military service, or some other occupation that is physical or dangerous and requires the partner to travel overseas in connection with their work. Or the partner could be a passionate traveller. Or you may have met each other overseas, at university or any other type of academic or religious institution.

If we add some signs to those examples, we can add further layers to our interpretations. The fourth house Mars used in our example may be in Capricorn. Mars in Capricorn's ambitious and hard-working energy may be less patient or more overtly ambitious - because of the Aries Descendant rulership connection. Your partner may be extremely goal-oriented and potentially a 'workaholic' - and that energy will be directed towards fourth house matters - the home and family. An example would be a partner whose ambition and drive is devoted to making the best provision for their family - yet they may need to be the person in charge at home too. They may also be practical and spend hours doing 'DIY' projects.

If we turn to that ninth house Mars example, with an Aries Descendant, the ninth house Mars could be in the sign of Gemini. Mars in Gemini is naturally argumentative and, given the influence of the Aries Descendant, an argumentative personality could be something you find repeatedly in your partnerships. However, that's not the sole interpretation. Mars in Gemini is mentally and verbally quick, funny and often clever too. It's a mental energy, so you may see that reflected in your partner's hobbies, interests or career. Any profession or interest that requires passionate debate, the ability for quick thinking, or attacks/defends legal matters, intellectual positions or political ideas would resonate here. As I said earlier, the signature will always be present - and the connections will play out through the ruler's sign and house position.

However, it would be too simplistic to say that the Descendant complex only plays out at this surface level. As you will recall, the Descendant is the place where we project the things that we find difficult to own, so we look to import those things into our lives through our relationships. What the Descendent complex is trying to bring to our attention, is that our partnerships can enable us to integrate those 'things we find hard to own' into our lives in a meaningful way - and that means rather more than simply projecting those qualities onto another human being.

Let's return to our Aries Descendant/Mars in Capricorn and fourth house example. The person with this Descendant complex may find it difficult to own their own assertiveness or their ambition to create a stable and secure home and family base. Through their relationship, that ambition may be realised; rather than simply being projected onto the partner, the ruling planet's energy becomes the driver of the relationship itself, with the best place to express those energies being in the fourth house. A busy, active - and perhaps upwardly mobile - family base may be the focus of the relationship in this example. Together you may even build your own home. It may be just as likely, however, that your partner may be the dominant or driving force in your domestic life together.

It's important to realise that the best way of interpreting the Descendant complex is by recognising it as descriptive of the relationship itself. If we look at the Aries Descendant/Mars in Gemini and ninth house example, both partners may find the relationship mentally stimulating. Together, you may be more actively culturally engaged, or travelling together may be an important part of the relationship. Together you may become more adventurous than you would have been alone. That may enable you both, as individuals, to deepen your understanding of the world - and of your place in the world.

From this example, you can appreciate that there's not so much projection going on. It's the relationship itself that embraces the Descendant complex in a conscious and positive sense to enable integration to occur at a deeper level. When 'me' (the Ascendant) becomes 'we' (the Descendant) it becomes the vehicle for your social integration. It's by meeting others as equals that we realise we can relate in a deep and meaningful way. We incorporate relationships into our lives without losing ourselves in the process - and the Descendant complex is instrumental in showing us how that can be best achieved.

The Midheaven Complex

The Midheaven ruler is important because of its connections with your career and your public image. As you will recall, the Midheaven marks the place we are heading towards, and it's often regarded as being representative of our achievements in a worldly or material sense - our personal summit or apex. As we have also seen, the sign on the Midheaven not only (in some cases) gives a broad indication of the kinds of career you feel drawn towards, but in all cases, it describes your underlying approach and attitudes towards your career. It also describes the qualities that you demand from your career, for you to feel a sense of achievement or personal fulfilment. The Midheaven complex also describes how you approach authority, and that applies to all the meanings we associate with that word - as we discussed earlier.

The Midheaven complex not only adds further layers of meaning to the ways in which you regard your career and personal ambitions, it also speaks volumes about your public image or 'social status'. When I talk about social status, I'm referring to the socially constructed roles we encountered earlier in this book (such as marriage or your occupational title) and the Midheaven complex has an important role to play in defining your public status. Once again, it's probably easier to understand if we look at a brief example. Imagine you - or someone you know - has the Midheaven in the sign of Taurus and Venus, the Midheaven ruler, in the third house. That person's career, public image or social status, find its best outlet in the house of communication, mental process, teaching and learning.

In this example, that third house Venus could be further elevated by being in the other sign of its rulership, Libra. It's a combination that would make a great art or music teacher, or an excellent businessperson who perhaps specialises in marketing, public relations or financial account management, or any occupation where social skills, charm and relationship building are an essential part of the job. If we relocate that natal Venus to the sixth house, that person's career and social status will be best expressed by their organisational capabilities or in the health and wellbeing professions. In the sixth house example, Venus would be situated in Capricorn.

This gives an earthy and ambitious twist to our sixth house Venus, so with this placement of the Midheaven ruler, this person may be a diligent business executive with financial acumen and great administrative skills. Accountancy or book-keeping, perhaps in a corporate environment, would be a great fit here, as would a managerial (especially human resources management) position in a medical or clinical setting. They are simple examples, but they are useful because you can see that the Midheaven complex puts the detail into the picture - and I'm sure you can look at your own natal chart and see your own achievements written in your Midheaven complex.

There is one thing I would like to add to this section on the Midheaven complex. Though I've focused on this as the network of connections that enable you to work through your personal ambitions, and where you act out the plotlines of your public role, there is something else that needs to be considered - particularly in the context of working through Midheaven issues like importance or authority. The assumption is that the Midheaven is the place where we assume authority - that is the objective - however, the Midheaven complex may describe, in detail, those who are influential and important in our lives, and those who may have authority over us. Domineering parents, a boss who has authority over you - all of those may be challenges that you need to face and work through in the context of the 'Axis of Experience'. When we look at the Nadir complex below, you will see how closely both ends of this axis are connected.

The Nadir Complex

This end of the 'Axis of Experience' is one of the most sensitive parts of your natal chart, as it represents your most private and personal life. Though we associate the fourth house in general with things like home and family, your personal history and the past, I like to place a much tighter focus on the Nadir itself - and I'm going to remind you of what the Nadir represents. It is the personal foundation that you build - and your success in doing so has a real influence on what happens at the other end of the 'Axis of Experience'. Without that foundation being properly constructed, it will be hard to achieve the potentials that are available to you. I've written a lot about 'blueprints' in this book, but when we're looking at the Nadir complex, it's a term that's truly applicable.

The Nadir complex is a web of information that shows you the primary influences that underpin your life, the choices that you make and the direction that you take as a result of those choices. The ruler of the IC, by sign and house, shows how and where those things work themselves out in your present. Again, a small example will help you to engage with this. Let's look at a person with the Nadir in Virgo. They may come from a reliable, hard-working family who value education and self-improvement. That sounds like a great start in life. Let's look at the detail. Virgo is ruled by Mercury and this person's Mercury is in Cancer in the second house. With Mercury in Cancer, this person can communicate emotionally - and in the second house, this may be a gift they can use in a professional context. Being able to capitalise on your abilities is a critical part of building your base - but what if we look at this placement in a different light?

What if that ruling Mercury was aspected by a difficult planet, say Saturn? This person may find it difficult to articulate their feelings - and we would be asking questions about whether that Virgo IC was such a beneficial placement after all. In that instance, developing the ability to make contact in that way would be a life challenge to be met in the second house, with the objective of taking possession of confidence and building self-esteem. Such things are an essential part of anyone's foundation. Going back to Melanie Reinhardt's analogy, it's the difference between the seeds falling on fertile - or stony - ground. If we find we have the latter, our challenge is to add some fertiliser.

With this small example, you can appreciate how important the Nadir complex is to your understanding of how the influences of the past affect your place in the present - and your future direction too. The details, like the placements of the ruling planets, aspects to those planets, and the aspects of planets to the cardinal points themselves - all these form part of the complex picture that is your reality. This book does not give you a comprehensive interpretation of planetary aspects - that is for a later volume in this series - however, if you are aware of the basic principles of the planets, the signs and the houses, you will have enough information at your disposal to assess how the influences at work in the Nadir complex - and those of the other cardinal point complexes - are working in your own natal chart.

How The Story Unfolds

Like many things in life, astrology can be as simple or as complicated as you want it to be. To assess how well-integrated a person's life is, we need to ask simple, basic questions. Does what we do in life resonate with our self-image or the way that we relate to people? Does it accord with our fundamental orientation in life? Many would ask whether it accords with our individual soul-purpose - and they would be right to do so. We may want to look at how the 'Axis of Experience' is connected to the 'Axis of Awareness' (if at all) to make those assessments. Square aspects between the cardinal points (or their ruling planets) may imply dynamism and drive, or tension and stress. The rulers of one cardinal point in aspect to another cardinal point may also provide integration and stabilisation to your natal chart and, of course, to your lived experience too. Putting all of that together takes time and understanding; there are rich and multi-layered tales to be told by the angular complexes in your natal chart. I'm going to give you a quick demonstration of how that works by referring to my own 'angle rulers' - and where they find their route to earth in my natal chart. These are my narratives, as told by my cardinal point complexes.

EXAMPLE ONE:

My Gemini Ascendant is ruled by Mercury. Mercury is found in my fifth house, so that indicates that the Mercury function (mental processes, reading, writing, communication) is an important one is my life because, as the ruler of my ascending sign, Mercury is my chart ruler. Those Mercury functions find their most natural outlet in a creative manner (writing this book is a mark of that) and my Mercury sign is Libra, so I hope that gives me the ability to connect with you in a way that you can relate to. I mentioned earlier that the signs on the angles can manifest in a very 'up-front' and literal way - and that's true of their ruling planets too.

My Gemini Ascendant and fifth house Mercury also describe my children. The fifth house is where we create our children, and the Gemini-Mercury synergies here would imply that I have two of them. And I do. The eldest is also a heavily 'Mercury' person - he has a Virgo Sun and is a journalist by profession. Sometimes our natal charts are descriptive of the realities of our lives in the simplest and most obvious ways. Incidentally, Mercury also represents our siblings, so I like to think that my Libra Mercury also represents my Libra sister, who works as an educator.

At the opposite end of that axis, my Descendant falls in Sagittarius and is ruled by Jupiter, that planet being in my tenth house. Jupiter symbolises expansion, belief systems, wisdom, extravagance, understanding adventure and people or things that are 'foreign' to you in some way. In my chart, Jupiter is found in Pisces, late in my tenth house. So how has that affected my relationships? Well, my first husband was a Sagittarius and we met at work (tenth house) as we had the same career path (astrology can be that literal). As for the Pisces part of that? He was financially astute (surprise: that's a little-known Pisces trait) which was just as well as he was also extravagant. Sadly, his poor health and recurrent hospitalisations (Jupiter, Pisces) were also a major part of the relationship.

Incidentally, when Jupiter rules the Descendant it's highly likely you will be married more than once. My second husband also meets the brief set out in my natal chart - but in very different ways. He is extremely well-travelled, and he speaks five languages. Jupiter in Pisces (tenth house) certainly describes his work, which is concerned with a charity (Pisces) that assists refugees (Jupiter). Does the Descendant describe our relationship? We have travelled to some distant shores in a way that I would not have done on my own. And that Jupiter in Pisces has provided a spiritual cast; during one journey we stayed in a Buddhist temple in Japan. The Descendant complex always finds a way of working itself out through your relationships.

There's one more thing. I need to add about my Ascendant and Descendant rulers. They trine each other and that's an important connection. Jupiter is associated with broadcasting and publishing, and, in my tenth house, it helps me to get my mercurial musings out to the public. The Mercury-Jupiter connections work well in my natal chart; when you look at them as the rulers of my AC-DC axis they reveal relationship connections to people who use (or have used) words to make a living - such as linguists, educators, journalists, salespeople and so on.

I'm not going to go into the aspects to your 'angle rulers' in this book (they will be covered in the last book in this series, ***Planets & Aspects***) but I would advise you to look for the connections between the relevant planets in your own chart. Again, any connections you find - especially the easier aspects - signify an easy route to earth for the energies of the signs containing your cardinal points. Hard aspects may also add dynamism to the ways you experience or express the qualities of your cardinal points. If you have a natal chart where none of your 'angle rulers' aspect each other? They will still have that easy 'route to earth' because of their house locations, but you may find that the 'four corners' of your life represent distinct and separate sets of experience for you with little overlap or integration between them.

EXAMPLE TWO:

Turning to the 'Axis of Experience', my IC is found in Leo and that's ruled by my Sun in the sixth house. So, where am I coming from? At a deep level, the Sun represents my 'engine', my driving force, my true nature, ego, 'super-ego' and deep inner sense of who I am. My Sun is in Scorpio, conjunct Neptune, in the sixth house. So, where am I coming from with that placement? My solar function is important to the establishment of a secure base in my life. And what is a secure base? For me, I needed to consciously develop my solar traits of authenticity, authority and a sense of purpose to feel competent enough to follow my own path. With my Sun conjunct Neptune, the great diffuser, that has not always been an easy task. It also makes me untidy – though I have issues seeing that for myself!

That's deep stuff but, at a literal level, the Sun in your natal chart often represents the father or paternal line. My father was a solar Leo who worked as a marine engineer (Sun-Neptune, sixth house) which meant he was qualified to maintain ships engines. He also worked in a ship repair yard (Sun, Neptune Scorpio, sixth house) My paternal line is full of sailors and fisherman - ancestors (Nadir) who literally worked (sixth house) at sea (Neptune). I'll say it again, astrology can be that obvious and up-front. So, if you have a planet in close aspect to the rulers of your cardinal points, look at its associations and you will usually find it adds considerable detail to your personal story - or familial history if the planet in question rules the Nadir.

Finally, where I'm going is defined by my Midheaven in Aquarius, ruled by Uranus - or its traditional ruler, Saturn. If, like me you have a chart angle whose sign has a 'traditional' as well as a 'modern' ruler, you may feel you have a personal dilemma. Which planet rules the sign on the angle? The traditional vs. modern rulership debate is a longstanding one in astrology and it's not one with any clear-cut answers. You'll find as many astrologers who go 'traditional' as go 'modern', and probably just as many who are ambivalent about the whole issue. I probably fall into the latter camp, but with what I hope is a good reason, as I prefer to think of astrology in the modern, psychologically oriented sense, rather than subscribing to the fatalistic notion of the Universe playing games with our fate. Also, with the even-handedness of my Libra Mercury, and the notorious duality of my Gemini Ascendant, I can see both sides of the argument.

However, I also believe astrology should be grounded. There is no doubt that the traditional approach to sign rulership, and traditional astrology *per se*, with its emphasis on external 'literal' realities rather than inner psychological responses, fits that bill. There is a whole book that could be written about rulerships (and I recommend Alan Oken's classic text, ***Rulers of the Horoscope,*** Ibis Press, 2008, if you want to know more on this subject) but the basic premise seems to comes back to whether you prefer a traditional approach to astrology where a sign's energies are 'disposited' through its ruling planet (the 'route to earth' we discussed earlier) or whether you feel more aligned with the affinity/synergy/synchronicity approach of the modern astrologer. Personally, I'm comfortable with both because I get where they're both coming from - and as an astrologer who values both the internalised and externalised manifestations of the movements of the Universe (as you will have seen from the examples above), that suits me just fine.

In the context of your own natal chart angles, you may wish to use the traditional ruler, the modern rulers or check out both. All of this is fine by the way - and you may discover that one, the other or even both rulers align with your life experiences. I'll return to that Midheaven in Aquarius in my natal chart. Aquarius is traditionally ruled by Saturn, and I have Saturn in my tenth house (and it's conjunct the MC) which makes Saturn a big player in my life. There is a raft of associations with this placement from my Capricorn mother ('the influential parent') to my solitary (Saturn) yet independently minded and unusual (Aquarius) career choices - construction (Saturn) was not considered 'usual' (Aquarius) for a woman back in the day and no-one has ever called being an astrologer a mainstream profession - and it's one I came to at a later age and after many decades of interest and study. Saturn's delaying influence strikes again.

But if I use Uranus as my MC ruler, what happens? Uranus is found in my fourth house. Does that independent streak found at the MC have its origins in the past? The fourth house location of Uranus would suggest so - and it's not wrong. I've moved house more than anyone else I know (Uranus is restless) whether I've wanted to - or not. At an inner level, I felt that the only way to get where I wanted to be was to strike out on my own, so I left my family and home base behind (several hundred miles behind) to create a new, independent base of my own. And I have literally built my own home - and I guess not that many women have done that. There's a big inner 'push' that you get with the outer planets and, in my opinion, if you have a cardinal point with both ancient and modern rulers then look at the position of both. The results may surprise you.

This is probably a good time to put down this book, pick up a notepad and pen and note the signs on the angles of your own natal chart, and their rulerships, together with where the planetary rulers of your cardinal points fall by house and sign. The sign will show how the ruling planets energies will be expressed and the house position shows where in your life those energies are likely to be experienced. Note the connections (aspects) made between your cardinal points and their rulers and note any aspects (particularly conjunctions) made to those ruling planets by any other planets in your natal chart - particularly the outer planets. Tracing the story of your life through the angles, their rulerships and their aspects is a fascinating exercise in itself - and it's what this book is about.

Final Words

The Story of Your Life

The story of your life is rich and complex, and it's one that unfolds and re-tells itself continuously. The themes may be set out in your natal chart, but the choices you make concerning which narrative threads you follow are your choice alone. Free will enables us to choose between the options the universe has set out for us - yet every one of those options is written in your natal chart. You cannot choose to be anyone other than the person you are, but you can choose to be the best version of yourself. By understanding how the angles in your natal chart describe the reality that you will have to function within, it becomes easier to accept who you are.

I want to refer to something I mentioned at the beginning of this book. The 'base layers', and underlying orientation of our lives, really do determine the overall thrust of our existence. So much that happens to us is not the random visitation of fate, but the result of our conscious choices or unconscious reactions to the challenges that are set out in our natal charts. We can't escape life's challenges, but we can work with what we have to obtain the best outcome. And that's the key to a good life. You work with what you have available to you - and you don't waste your energies wishing you could have those things that are simply not available to you.

That doesn't mean, by the way, that you should not strive to do as well as you are able; reality - as described by the angles in your birth chart - simply sets out the basic parameters within which your personal narrative will unfold. During my own life, I have been fortunate to study literature at university, and those studies have helped me to draw an analogy between the ways in which we structure the tales that many of us enjoy reading, and the way in which the universe has set out the structure of your life in your natal chart. To my mind, your birth chart sets out the plot lines - but how the story unfolds is something that is yet to be written.

Earlier in this book I referred to the angles as the touchstones of your life, however, don't assume that they represent points of stability. The patterns in your natal charts will mean that some of you experience the realities of life in a stable and productive manner; others will have to work hard to achieve that – and may never do so. And it's important to remember that our cardinal points work with all the other influences in our natal chart. Your solar and lunar traits (and the potentials of all the other planets) work together to create your psyche, but the results of that emerge into the world at the points where the chart angles intersect with your lived experience.

The angles represent the parts of your life where things the things that are experienced matter to you more than anything else; they inform your world. If things are not going well, if you are uncertain about how to present yourself, if you have problematic family or personal relationships, or you find it difficult to achieve in your career, the dynamics that are working to cause problems in those areas will also provide you with the solution to those issues, if you are prepared to engage with those energies in a positive and enlightened manner. If that apples to you, re-frame and re-write your narrative. Finding the right words will be easier than you think.

Appendix One: Rulerships

♈	Aries	First House	Mars
♉	Taurus	Second House	Venus
♊	Gemini	Third House	Mercury
♋	Cancer	Fourth House	Moon
♌	Leo	Fifth House	Sun
♍	Virgo	Sixth House	Mercury
♎	Libra	Seventh House	Venus
♏	Scorpio	Eighth House	Pluto, Mars
♐	Sagittarius	Ninth House	Jupiter
♑	Capricorn	Tenth House	Saturn
♒	Aquarius	Eleventh House	Uranus, Saturn
♓	Pisces	Twelfth House	Neptune, Jupiter

Appendix Two: Traditional Rulerships Diagram

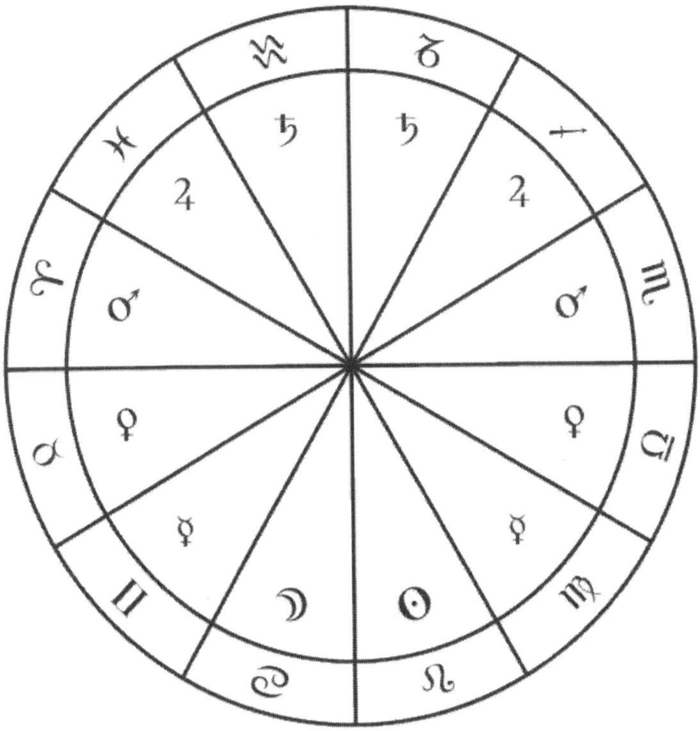

About The Author

Hi, I'm Sara Shipman, astrologer, writer and blogger. I have been a student and astrology practitioner for over forty years and I'm grateful that I now have some time (always precious) to do what I have always wanted to do, and that is write about astrology and share my thoughts with you. My astrological articles can be found on my website - www.starcrazypie.com - where you can also access more astrological resources - including free monthly horoscopes - or contact me for personal astrology reports.

So far, my published full-length books include ***Solar Returns: An Introduction.*** This book is the second of the ***Real Life Astrology*** series of books, and follows ***Planets, Signs & Houses***. The next book in this series will be ***The Planets in Signs.*** I am always delighted and grateful that so many of you take the time to engage with my website and read my books, so I would like to say a huge 'thank you' to those of you who have done so - and 'welcome' to those of you who are new to my work.

I'm based in the UK, have an astro-sceptical partner, between us we have an assorted collection of four children, and I grow herbs, vegetables and flowers to keep myself grounded. Sara Shipman is my professional and pen name.

Other Books by Sara Shipman

Solar Returns: An Introduction

The Lunar Manual

The ***Primal Triad*** series:

Aries

Gemini

Virgo

Scorpio

Printed in Great Britain
by Amazon

53252481R10183